Leaders of Gettysburg: The Lives and Careers of Robert E. Lee, James Longstreet, JEB Stuart, George Meade, Winfield Scott Hancock and Joshua L. Chamberlain

By Charles River Editors

The Monument to Meade at Gettysburg

About Charles River Editors

Charles River Editors was founded by Harvard and MIT alumni to provide superior editing and original writing services, with the expertise to create digital content for publishers across a vast range of subject matter. In addition to providing original digital content for third party publishers, Charles River Editors republishes civilization's greatest literary works, bringing them to a new generation via ebooks.

Visit charlesrivereditors.com for more information.

About Charles River Editors

Charles River Editors was founded by Harvard and MIT alumni to provide superior editing and original writing services, with the expertise to create digital content for publishers across a vast range of subject matter. In addition to providing original digital content for third party publishers, Charles River Editors republishes civilization's greatest literary works, bringing them to a new generation via ebooks.

Visit charlesrivereditors.com for more information.

Leaders of Gettysburg: The Lives and Careers of Robert E. Lee, James Longstreet, JEB Stuart, George Meade, Winfield Scott Hancock and Joshua L. Chamberlain

By Charles River Editors

The Monument to Meade at Gettysburg

Introduction

Robert E. Lee (1807-1870)

Despite the fact that the Civil War began over 150 years ago, it remains one of the most widely discussed topics in America today, with Americans arguing over its causes, reenacting its famous battles, and debating which general was better than others. Americans continue to be fascinated by the Civil War icons who made the difference between victory and defeat in the war's great battles.

With the exception of George Washington, perhaps the most famous general in American history is **Robert E. Lee** (January 19, 1807 – October 12, 1870), despite the fact he led the Confederate Army of Northern Virginia against the Union in the Civil War. As the son of U.S. Revolutionary War hero Henry "Light Horse Harry" Lee III, and a relative of Martha Custis Washington, Lee was imbued with a strong sense of honor and duty from the beginning. And as a top graduate of West Point, Lee had distinguished himself so well before the Civil War that President Lincoln asked him to command the entire Union Army. Lee famously declined, serving his home state of Virginia instead after it seceded.

Lee is remembered today for constantly defeating the Union's Army of the Potomac in the Eastern theater from 1862-1865, considerably frustrating Lincoln and his generals. His leadership of his army led to him being deified after the war by some of his former subordinates, especially Virginians, and he came to personify the Lost Cause's ideal Southern soldier. His reputation was secured in the decades after the war as a general who brilliantly led his men to amazing victories against all odds.

Despite his successes and his legacy, Lee wasn't perfect. And of all the battles Lee fought in, he was most criticized for Gettysburg, particularly his order of Pickett's Charge on the third and final day of the war. Despite the fact his principle subordinate and corps leader, General James Longstreet, advised against the charge, Lee went ahead with it, ending the army's defeat at Gettysburg with a violent climax that left half of the men who charged killed or wounded.

Although the Civil War came to define Lee's legacy, he was involved in some of American history's other turning points, including the Mexican-American War and the capture of John Brown. This ebook closely examines Lee's war records, but it also humanizes the cheerful husband who was raised and strove to be dignified and dutiful.

James Longstreet (1821–1904)

One of the most important, and controversial, Confederate generals during the Civil War was Lieutenant General James Longstreet, the man Robert E. Lee called his "old war horse." Longstreet was Lee's principal subordinate for most of the war, ably managing a corps in the Army of Northern Virginia and being instrumental in Confederate victories at Second Bull Run, Fredericksburg, and Chickamauga. Longstreet was also effective at Antietam and the Battle of the Wilderness, where he was nearly killed by a shot through the neck.

Had Longstreet died on the field in early May 1864, he would almost certainly be considered one of the South's biggest heroes. However, it was his performance at Gettysburg and arguments with other Southern generals after the Civil War that tarnished his image. After the South lost the war and Gettysburg came to be viewed as one of its biggest turning points, former Confederate generals looked to that battle to find scapegoats to blame for losing the war. Longstreet was charged with being slow to attack on the second day of the Battle of Gettysburg, allowing the Union to man Little Round Top. He also resisted Lee's order for Pickett's Charge the next day, making his criticisms clear both that day and after the war through his rightings. The fact that he served in Republican administrations after the Civil War rubbed his former comrades the wrong way, and the Georgian Longstreet's criticism of Lee infuriated the Virginian Lost Cause advocates who idolized Lee.

Near the end of his life, Longstreet authored *From Manassas to Appomattox*, a Civil War memoirs that looked to rebut his critics. Longstreet didn't avoid his critics, facing them head on by fending off criticisms of his record for the most part, usually including letters written by other officers to his defense. Longstreet also didn't pull punches, which he does at times quite poignantly on Lee's mishaps, most notably of course at Gettysburg. In other instances, he defends himself by criticizing others. When Fitz Lee notes that R.E. Lee called Longstreet the hardest man to move in the Army (a comment that can't be confirmed or refuted), he comes to his own defense in part by criticizing Stonewall Jackson during the Seven Days campaign. Hindsight is 20/20, and Longstreet's arguments in the conduct of certain campaigns certainly benefited from the passing of 30 years. At a number of places, Longstreet believes that if his suggestions were followed, the results could have destroyed Union armies or won the War. Nobody will ever be sure if he's right or wrong on these matters, though historians typically consider those kinds of statements bluster.

This ebook looks at the life and career of one of the South's most important and controversial fighters, explaining his biggest accomplishments and discussing the biggest controversies. Along with pictures of Longstreet and other important people, places and events in his life, you will learn about Lee's Old War Horse like you never have before, in no time at all.

James Ewell Brown Stuart (1833–1864)

"Calm, firm, acute, active, and enterprising, I know no one more competent than [Stuart] to estimate the occurrences before him at their true value." – General Joseph E. Johnston, 1861

Alongside Lee, no one epitomized the chivalry and heroism celebrated by the Lost Cause more than JEB Stuart (1833-1864), the most famous cavalry officer of the Civil War. Stuart was equal parts great and grandiose, leading the cavalry for the Confederacy in Lee's Army of Northern Virginia until his death at the Battle of Yellow Tavern in May 1864. Stuart was a throwback to the past, colorfully dressing with capes, sashes, and an ostrich plumed hat, while sporting cologne and a heavy beard. But he was also brilliant in conducting reconnaissance, and he proved capable of leading both cavalry and infantry at battles like Chancellorsville. As the eyes and ears of Robert E. Lee's army, none were better, despite the fact that he was only in his late 20s and early 30s during the Civil War, far younger than most men of senior rank.

Nevertheless, Stuart's tough fighting was and still is eclipsed by his reputation for audacious cavalry movements. He embarrassed the Army of the Potomac by riding around it twice, making him famous and embarrassing Union generals like George McClellan. However, Stuart's role at Gettysburg was far more controversial. Given great discretion in his cavalry operations before the battle, Stuart's cavalry was too far removed from the Army of Northern Virginia to warn Lee of the Army of the Potomac's movements. Lee's army inadvertently stumbled into the Union army at Gettysburg, walking blindly into what became the largest battle of the war. Stuart has been heavily criticized ever since, and it is said Lee took him to task when he arrived on the second day, leading Stuart to offer his resignation. Lee didn't accept it, but he would later note in his after battle report that the cavalry had not updated him as to the Army of the Potomac's movements.

With his record and characteristics, it has proven almost impossible for Americans to hold a neutral view of Stuart, and it has been even harder to ignore him. This ebook addresses the controversies and battles that made Stuart famous, but it also humanizes the man who was courageous and cocky, yet self-conscious enough to hide what he considered to be a weak chin. Along with pictures of Stuart and other important people, places and events in his life, you will learn about the Confederacy's most famous cavalier like you never have before, in no time at all.

George Gordon Meade (1815-1872)

"Meade has more than met my most sanguine expectations. He and Sherman are the fittest officers for large commands I have come in contact with."." – Ulysses S. Grant, 1864

Ironically, one of the generals who often escapes the attention of Civil War fans who compile the lists of best generals is the man who won the war's most famous battle, George G. Meade (1815-1872). In fact, Meade has become a perfect example of how the generals who did not self-promote themselves and write memoirs after the war had their reputations suffer in the ensuing decades. When people think of Appomattox Court House, they think of Ulysses S. Grant and Robert E. Lee. Few remember that the commander of the Army of the Potomac at the end of the Civil War was not Grant but Meade.

Meade exemplified modesty and competence, serving as a career United States Army officer and civil engineer who fought with distinction in the eastern theater of the Civil War. During the first half of the war, Meade rose from command of a brigade to command of a division and finally command of the entire Army of the Potomac just days before the Battle of Gettysburg. Naturally, he is best known for defeating Robert E. Lee's Army of Northern Virginia at Gettysburg in July 1863, although he's not nearly as well remembered as his Confederate counterpart, and he has even been eclipsed in popularity by some of the men he commanded at Gettysburg, like Joshua Chamberlain. Meade continued to lead the Army of the Potomac, but when Grant attached himself to the army in 1864, it was Grant who essentially commanded the army, creating an awkward situation that Meade persevered through until the end of the war, to his credit.

If Meade distinguished himself at places like Antietam and Gettyburg, why is he frequently left out of the historical narrative of the war? Meade had a notoriously short temper that hurt his popularity with the press, his men and contemporaries during the war, despite how well he commanded. Perhaps more importantly, Meade's relatively early death in the decade after the war prevented him from defending his record and his decisions during and after Gettysburg. Lincoln mistakenly thought Meade blundered by not being more aggressive in pursuit of Lee after Gettysburg, when in fact Lee's men constructed strong defenses and invited attack on a number of occasions during their retreat. Just as significantly, Meade came under attack by generals like Daniel Sickles, who sought to shield themselves from scrutiny by blaming Meade for poor decisions. On Day 2 of the Battle of Gettysburg, Sickles disobeyed Meade and moved his III Corps out in front of the rest of the army. Although he would constantly defend his maneuver, the move destroyed his corps and nearly ruined the Army of the Potomac's left flank, creating a salient that led to the near annihilation of the corps. Sickles and Meade would feud over the actions on Day 2 in the years after the war, with Meade explaining his actions, and Sickles taking credit for the victory by disrupting Lee's attack plans. While historians have taken Meade's side since, Sickles outlived Meade and helped tarnish the commanding general's reputation after the war, helping cast a shadow over Meade's record for nearly a century. Today historians credit Meade with doing a solid job at Gettysburg, but no self-effusive praise was forthcoming from the man himself.

Leaders of Gettysburg chronicles the life and career of the commanding general at Gettysburg, but it also humanizes the man who somehow managed to be both modest and short-tempered at the same time. Along with pictures of important people, places, and events in his life, you will learn about General Meade like you never have before, in no time at all.

Winfield Scott Hancock (1824-1886)

"General Hancock is one of the handsomest men in the United States Army. He is tall in stature, robust in figure, with movements of easy dignity…In action…dignity gives way to activity; his features become animated, his voice loud, his eyes are on fire, his blood kindles, and his bearing is that of a man carried away by passion – the character of his bravery" – Regis de Trobriand

Winfield Scott Hancock was an intimidating figure who impressed friends, foes, and fellow generals alike. Known as Hancock the Superb after McClellan described his performance as such during the Battle of Williamsburg in the Peninsula Campaign of 1862, Hancock eventually rose to become the Army of the Potomac's greatest corps commander. Though his reputation and legacy gradually faded over time, Hancock was one of the North's foremost war heroes by the end of the war, and he nearly became president in 1880 when he was just barely defeated by a less decorated Civil War veteran, James Garfield.

Nobody in the Army of the Potomac was in the thick of its biggest battles as often as Hancock and the men he commanded. Hancock superbly led his brigade during the Peninsula Campaign, temporarily commanded a division at Antietam in the center of the lines at the Sunken Lane, and his division was the last to withdraw across the river during the Battle of Chancellorsville.

After the Battle of Chancellorsville, he fortuitously became the new II Corps commander in the Army of the Potomac, just in time to deliver his greatest performance of all. At Gettysburg, Hancock was the commanding general in the field on Day 1, as Meade and the rest of the Union army arrived later that night. On Day 2, Hancock's men assisted Sickles' III Corps when Sickles disobeyed orders and moved it forward, creating a gap in the Union lines. And on Day 3, Hancock's greatest day of the war, he was seriously injured and nearly bled to death while leading his men in their decisive repulse of Pickett's Charge.

Hancock's injury was excruciatingly painful, but he was back in command for the 1864 Overland Campaign, where his men played crucial roles in the Battle of the Wilderness, the Battle of Spotsylvania Court House, and the Battle of Cold Harbor. By the end of the Civil War, Hancock was one of the highest regarded generals in the North.

Like Confederate corps commander James Longstreet, Hancock's reputation was attacked after the war because of politics. His Northern brethren were critical of his opposition to the execution of Mary Surratt for the Lincoln assassination, they were enraged when he was lenient on the Southern military district he governed during Reconstruction, and the final straw came when he ran as a Democrat in 1880.

It would take nearly another century before Hancock's reputation and legacy were revived by Michael Sharaa's *Killer Angels*, a historical fiction about the Battle of Gettysburg that examined the friendship between Hancock and Confederate General Lewis Armistead, who was mortally wounded by Hancock's men during Pickett's Charge. By the time Ken Burns' Civil War documentary had renwed interest in Gettysburg and the Civil War, Hancock was as popular as ever.

Leaders of Gettysburg chronicles the life and career of one of the Union's most indispensable generals, humanizing the courageous and fiery man who was respected and admired by his men and his superiors alike. Along with pictures of important people, places, and events in his life, you will learn about Winfield Scott Hancock like you never have before, in no time at all.

Joshua Lawrence Chamberlain (1828-1914)

For much of the 20th century, Joshua Lawrence Chamberlain's life and career remained mostly obscure, outside of dedicated scholars of the Battle of Gettysburg and alumni and students of Bowdoin College. Colonel Chamberlain had led the 20th Maine regiment at Gettysburg, holding the extreme left of the Union line on Little Round Top, and he continued to rise up the ranks toward the end of the war until he was commanding a brigade and present at the surrender ceremony of the Army of Northern Virginia at Appomattox. After the Civil War, Chamberlain served as Governor of Maine and President of Bowdoin College.

Chamberlain had a respectable Civil War career and life, but he had been largely forgotten in the decades after the Civil War, with the focus on more influential commanding generals and their principal subordinates. Then a remarkable thing happened with the 1974 publication of Michael Sharaa's *The Killer Angels*, a Pulitzer Prize winning historical fiction that focuses on the Battle of Gettysburg and its influential generals and leaders. In one fell swoop, Michael Sharaa breathed life back into the reputations of men like John Buford and Joshua Chamberlain, cast as the Union heroes of Day 1 and Day 2 respectively that made victory at Gettysburg possible. In the novel, Chamberlain's regiment holds the high ground against a series of desperate Confederate charges, and when they ran out of gunpowder, Chamberlain ordered a brave bayonet charge that drove the Confederates in their front from the fight. With that, the Union's left flank was saved.

Thanks to Sharaa, Ken Burns' popular Civil War documentary prominently featured Chamberlain's involvement at Gettysburg, and when Sharaa's novel was turned into the critically acclaimed 1993 movie *Gettysburg*, interest in Chamberlain and the 20th Maine swelled. Chamberlain's reputation and role in the Civil War had been completely revived, and the monument to the 20th Maine on Little Round Top became one of the premier tourist spots on the Gettysburg battlefield.

Naturally, once more attention was focused on Chamberlain's record, historians started to scrutinize his service and post-war writings, leading to ensuing controversies over just what happened on Little Round Top on July 2, 1863. Furthermore, there still remains debate over Chamberlain's participation during the surrender ceremony of the Army of Northern Virginia at Appomattox.

Whether definitive answers are ever reached, there is no doubt that Chamberlain and the 20th Maine will continue to hold a secure and strong reputation in the coming decades. *Leaders of Gettyburg* chronicles the life and career of Joshua Chamberlain, examining his Civil War service and the debates over it, as well as analyzing his legacy. Along with pictures of important people, places, and events, you will learn about Chamberlain like you never have before, in no time at all.

Meade (center), General Andrew A. Humphreys and staff in Culpeper, Virginia outside Meade's headquarters, 1863.

Chapter 1: Robert E. Lee's Early Years

Robert Edward Lee was born on January 19, 1807, at Stratford Hall Plantation in Westmoreland County, Virginia, near Montross, the fifth child to Major General Henry "Light Horse Harry" Lee III (1756–1818) and his second wife, Anne Hill Carter (1773–1829). Though his year of birth has traditionally been recorded as 1807, historian Elizabeth Brown Pryor has noted Lee's writings indicate he may have been born the previous year. Lee's family had Norman-French lineage that could trace itself back to one of Virginia's pioneering families; Robert's great-great grandfather, Henry Lee I, was a prominent Virginian colonist originally arriving in Virginia from England in the early 1600s with Richard Lee I.

Light Horse Harry

Lee's well-regarded family also boasted his father's accomplishments. Lee's father had served with distinction as a cavalry officer under General George Washington in the American Revolution, and after the war Light Horse Harry served as a member of the Virginia legislature and as Governor of Virginia. His mother, daughter of Charles Carter (whose father Robert was one of the first wealthy men in America) and Anne Butler Moore, grew up in an idyllic life at Shirley Plantation, Tyler, one of the most elegant mansions in all Virginia. Both the Lees and Carters were prominent in Virginia's political affairs, with family members regularly sitting in the House of Burgesses, and serving as speakers and governors. Two Lees signed the Declaration of Independence.

The Shirley Plantation at the time of the Civil War

By the time of Robert's birth, Light Horse Harry, 17 years Anne's senior, was in deep financial trouble and scandal loomed over his family. Having retreated to Stratford Hall after failing as both a tobacco farmer and land speculator, Henry was aggressively hounded by creditors and subsequently stripped of property and servants to satisfy his mounting debts. Today "Light Horse Harry" is best remembered as Robert E. Lee's father, but at the time he was so absorbed in his own financial woes that he couldn't even be bothered to name his new son.

In 1809, Henry was arrested twice for debt and imprisoned in Westmoreland County jail, forcing Anne to deliver him food herself for lack of servants. Though offered asylum for herself and her children by her brother-in-law, husband of her late sister, Mildred, Anne refused to abandon her husband, choosing to maintain her home and family despite Henry's imprisonment. Upon his release, however, she insisted they move to Alexandria, Virginia, where she had numerous family members nearby and her children were assured an education at their neighboring plantations, and later, Alexandria Academy.

In 1813, Henry Lee's career and life in America came to a quiet (if not covert) end when he slipped off to Barbados in the West Indies after sustaining serious internal wounds--and by most reports, nearly killed--in a political riot in Baltimore, Maryland. Left to fend for herself, Anne spent her inheritance to provide for her children, writing infrequently to Henry, who was said to have spent little time at home even when things were going well. In 1818, when Robert was just 11, Anne was informed of her husband's death by a letter from her brother-in-law, two weeks after it occurred.

Though little has been written about Robert's boyhood, which was not something he discussed in his personal writings, by all accounts, Robert knew his father only as a shadowy, distant figure who had once been a great soldier and man of social standing. For Robert, it was Light Horse Harry's reputation as a man of apparent dignity, poise, and charm that could serve as a role model. And like any proud Virginian of the period, Light Horse Harry insisted that all his sons learn to swim, ride, shoot, box, dance, and use a sword--but only in self-defense--like every fine Virginia gentleman.

The tragedies of his father's later life, however--and the disgrace it brought his family--invariably drew Robert close to his mother and in many ways shaped the man he became. It would not be unfair to say Robert was his mother's boy.

Young Robert began his formal education in Alexandria, Virginia, at a private school maintained by the wealthy Carter family for their numerous offspring on one of their numerous plantations, then transferred to nearby Alexandria Academy. Today Lee's letters are of great interest to historians and casual readers alike, but amazingly, Robert was only formally instructed in French, not English, resulting in a writing style that consistently utilized uncustomary spelling such as *honour* and *agreable*, with proper names like *french*, *english*, and *yankee* written in lowercase. These linguistic oddities would be well illustrated in countless letters sent to friends and family throughout his life.

Young Robert was also familiar with hard work at a young age. After his eldest brother, William, left for Harvard, brother Sidney Smith joined the U.S. Navy, and sister Anne was away most of the time seeking medical attention for a chronic illness (believed to be tuberculosis), it fell upon Robert as the eldest remaining sibling to assist his mother around the home, forcing him to develop a strong sense of responsibility while still very young.

Chapter 2: Meade's Early Years

Childhood

George Gordon Meade (also Meed) was born in Cádiz, Spain on December 31, 1815, the eighth of eleven children born to Richard Worsam and his wife Margaret Coats (Coates) Butler Meade. Shortly after his birth, George's father, a wealthy Philadelphia, Pennsylvania merchant (and aristocratic, according to some sources) who was serving in Spain as a naval agent for the U. S. government, was financially ruined due to his support of Spain in the Napoleonic Wars (1804-1815). Ultimately forced to return to the United States, the Meade family lived first in Philadelphia, then Baltimore and Washington. George's brother, Richard Worsam Meade II, also later became a naval officer of some notoriety.

Meade's ancestors had been residents of Philadelphia during the colonial era, beginning at least as far back as great-grandfather Robert Meade, who was born in Ireland but living in Philadelphia by 1732. Robert Meade was a shipping and commission merchant, which took him to the West Indies, and he was a prominent member of the Roman Catholics in his community.

Grandfather George Meade was born in Philadelphia in 1741, where he lived for most of his life. He supported the colonists during the Revolution and his firm helped supply food and clothing to Washington's Continental Army. He was well-regarded in society, and his integrity and high sense of honor helped earn him the nickname "Honest George Meade." Meade's father Richard was born in 1778 in Chester County, Pennsylvania, where the family had temporarily taken up residence because the British had occupied Philadelphia.

Since he was born in Cádiz, Spain and subsequently spent his early years in Europe, little is known about George's childhood. Some historians also speculate that the sensitivity of his father's job necessitated that no attention be drawn to family members. In any regard, the accounts that do exist give conflicting reports of the Meade family as either returning to the United States shortly after the close of the Napoleonic Wars (most likely in 1816), or a few months after his father Richard passed away in 1828, at the age of 50.

In either case, the Meade family apparently returned to the U. S. financially devastated, moving first to Philadelphia, then Baltimore and Washington, with the family's financial situation becoming more critical after Richard died.

Education

In that George was born and lived a portion of his childhood in Spain, there is no known record of his earliest education, although it is assumed he attended school prior to retuning to the United States.

At about the age of eight, young George entered a private school in Philadelphia kept by William R. White and Henry Hood. The school had a strong reputation, and George was schooled there for about three years. Accounts indicate that as a child he was amiable and full of life, traits that would have certainly surprised the men who came across him during the Civil War. Meade was also quick to learn his lessons.

George was placed in a boarding-school at Mount Airy, just outside of Philadelphia, in 1826. The principals of the school were M. Constant and A. L. Roumfort, the latter a graduate of the Military Academy at West Point, and the school was modeled upon West Point. Boys at the school were drilled, even performing sentry duty, and the school was strictly disciplined. Meade learned English, French, Latin, Greek, arithmetic, and algebra, showing the greatest proficiency in the mathematical studies.

After his father died, George's mother determined that his mathematical aptitude would make him a good fit for West Point, and apparently his father had wanted him to go there too. Though his mother did not anticipate George would have a military career, and there's no indication he did either, that was the direction the family went in. George's older brother Richard had already become a midshipman in the U.S. Navy in 1826.

During 1829, George was schooled at Mount Hope, near Baltimore, while waiting to find out if he would receive an appointment to West Point. It is said he studied "in Latin, Caesar's Commentaries and six of the orations of Cicero; in French, Telemaque and Charles XII of Sweden; in mathematics, Colburn's Arithmetic and Algebra, Walker's Geometry, Playfair's Euclid, and Trigonometry in Gummies' Surveying; Goodrich's History of the United States, Hart's Geography, and the greater part of Comstock's Chemistry and Natural Philosophy." That he was accomplishing this at the age of 15 was remarkable, and it was noted by his teachers.

Chapter 3: James Longstreet's Early Years

James (K.*) Longstreet was born on January 8, 1821 in Edgefield District, South Carolina (now part of North Augusta, Edgefield County), the fifth child and third son to James Longstreet (1783-1833) and Mary Ann Dent (1793-1855). Originally from New Jersey and Maryland respectively, the senior James owned a cotton plantation near the modern city of Gainesville in northeastern Georgia. James' ancestor, Dirck Stoffels Langestraet, immigrated to the Dutch colony of New Netherlands in 1657, with the "Longstreet" name becoming Anglicized over the generations.

*(All formal documents available list James Longstreet as his full name, while several informal papers included the "K" initial but no clarification of what it stands for.)

According to Longstreet's memoirs, which are still widely considered one of the most important memoirs written about the Civil War: "Grandfather William Longstreet first applied steam as a motive power, in 1787, to a small boat on the Savannah River at Augusta, and spent all of his private means upon that idea, asked aid of his friends in Augusta and elsewhere, had no encouragement, but, on the contrary, ridicule of his proposition to move a boat without a pulling or other external power, and especially did they ridicule the thought of expensive steam-boilers to be made of iron. To obviate costly outlay for this item, he built boilers of heavy oak timbers and strong iron bands, but the Augusta marines were incredulous..."

Of course, history does not credit William Longstreet for the discovery. What happened? According to Longstreet, "He failed to secure the necessary aid, and the discovery passed into the possession of certain New Yorkers, who found the means for practicable application, and now steam is the goddess that enlightens the world."

Though born in Edgefield District, South Carolina, James spent most of his youth in Augusta, Georgia (and later, some time in Somerville, Alabama). It is said that James' father was so impressed by his son's "rocklike" character that he nicknamed him "Peter" (as in "Peter the Rock" of the Bible), leading to him being known as "Pete" or "Old Pete" for much of his life.

Given his son's rocklike character, Longstreet's father charted a course for his son's future. According to Longstreet, "From my early boyhood he conceived that he would send me to West Point for army service." Early on, James' father chose the military life for his son but knew that the local educational system was much too inadequate to provide a good academic background. So in 1830, at the age of nine, James was sent to live with his aunt and uncle in Augusta; his uncle, Augustus Baldwin Longstreet, was a newspaper editor, educator, and Methodist minister. James spent the next eight years on his uncle's plantation, "Westover," while attending the Academy of Richmond County.

In 1833 when James was just twelve, his father died during a cholera epidemic while visiting Augusta. Although James' mother and the remainder of the family then moved to Somerville, Alabama, James remained with Uncle Augustus. While living and working on his Uncle Augustus' plantation in Augusta, Georgia, James spent eight years attending the Academy of Richmond County (and was no doubt greatly influenced by his uncle, who was himself an educator).

In his memoirs, however, Longstreet barely mentions his academic schooling, heading almost straight into a discussion about his West Point years in the first chapter of the memoirs. Some may take that as an indication he wasn't terribly interested in these early years, but it's just as likely that because he was writing the memoirs to rebut and attack his critics, he wanted to spend as little time as possible discussing pre-military life.

Though his father was gone, young James' resolve for a military life was not. In 1837, Augustus attempted to secure an appointment for James to the United States Military Academy at West Point, New York, but the vacancy for his congressional district had already been filled. A year later James got an appointment through another relative, Reuben Chapman, a Representative from the First District of Alabama (where his mother Mary lived).

Chapter 4: Hancock's Early Years, 1824-1840

The Hancock/Hoxworth Family Tree

Winfield Scott Hancock and his identical twin brother Hilary Baker Hancock were born on February 14, 1824, in Montgomery Square, Pennsylvania, a village just northwest of Philadelphia in present-day Montgomery Township, to Benjamin Franklin Hancock and

Elizabeth Hoxworth Hancock. A third son, John, was born around 1830.

The Hancock and Hoxworth families--of English, Scottish, and Welsh descent--had lived in Montgomery County for several generations, where at the time of Winfield's birth, Benjamin was a country schoolteacher, though both the Hancocks and Hoxworths were generations of farmers.

Winfield's grandfather, Richard, was a mariner who fought and was captured during the American Revolutionary War, spending the duration of the War in Great Britain's notorious Dartmoor Prison. During the War of 1812, Richard organized one of the companies that garrisoned at Camp DuPont, Pennsylvania. Both Elizabeth's grandfather and father fought in the American Revolutionary War; her grandfather was killed in battle while serving as a captain under General George Washington.

Though he hoped his son would choose a path of life other than the military, Benjamin Hancock named his son Winfield Scott after the renowned U. S. Army general who came to be his nation's greatest military hero during the 19th century. Winfield Scott was best known for his role in the War of 1812, but over the course of his forty-seven-year military career he also commanded forces in the Mexican-American War (including commanding young Winfield Scott Hancock), the Black Hawk War, and the Second Seminole War. On the strength of his reputation, Winfield Scott was general-in-chief for the Union during 1861.

Winfield Scott, the Hero of 1812

Life in Norristown

In early 1828, Benjamin and Elizabeth Hancock moved with their twin sons Winfield and

Hilary from the countryside to the village of Norristown, Pennsylvania, set on giving their sons a better life than they themselves had. As the county seat, Norristown offered economic and educational opportunities the outlying countryside did not.

Once there, Benjamin continued teaching and began studying law under John Friedley, Esq., while Elizabeth opened a milliner's shop selling women's hats from their home. On August 19, 1828, when Winfield was four years of age, his father Benjamin was admitted to the Montgomery County Bar Association. From that time on, the Hancock home functioned as half law office, half store front.

Becoming a family of some prominence, though far from financially well-off, Benjamin became a deacon in the Norristown Baptist Church, participated in municipal government as Justice of the Peace, helped establish free schooling in Norristown, and later became Collector of Internal Revenue. Prior to this time, the State of Pennsylvania endorsed "subscription" schools, most often, one-room structures run by a hired educator whose wages and board were paid by the community.

Young Winfield Scott Hancock

History describes the young Winfield as tall, thin, and handsome; displaying early in life the heroic leadership qualities that would come to define him in adulthood. Said to have been "sound of body, mind, and morals," he was captain of his school juvenile militia, a leader in sports, and was often chosen by his classmates to arbitrate boyish disputes. These same traits ensured that he was always relied upon to resolve disagreements expediently, using good, common-sense. Rebellions among his mock military ranks were routinely dealt with by dismissing rabble-rousers and sending them home to their mothers.

From a very early age, Winfield is said to have displayed uncommon generosity and always championed the underdog. With no tolerance for bullies, one classmate later said of him, "If a big boy undertook to worry a small boy, he'd find Winfield atop of him in short order."[1] One often-repeated anecdote illustrating his character took place when Winfield was about eleven, when a little orphan boy named John Everman came to live with distant relatives in Norristown. As the youngest, smallest, and poorest boy at Norristown Public School, where he and Winfield attended, the bigger boys immediately set out to bully and tease him. Not only did Winfield fight his battles for him, he forced his classmates to make a place for him in their games and even shared his pocket-money with him. Winfield would form many life-long friendships due to his affable and benevolent nature. As fate would have it, John W. Everman would go on to become a wealthy Philadelphia city council member who would offer his service to Winfield

---

[1]   Goodrich, Frederick Elizur. *Life of Winfield Scott Hancock, Major-General, U. S. A.* Page 30.

when he returned to Philadelphia a famous major general.

Norristown Academy: 183?-1836

Setting out from the start to provide their sons the best education possible, Benjamin and Elizabeth placed their sons at Norristown Academy, a private school where their first teacher was Eliphalet Roberts. After a few years, however, Winfield's father, who played a principle role in establishing the first free school system in the state and was an active member of the Norristown School Board, removed his sons in favor of a public school education. He hoped it would set an example for other parents.

Norristown Public School: 1836--1840

Around 1836, Winfield and his brothers were removed from Norristown Academy in favor of attending the first public school opened in Norristown. Proving to be a studious and bright boy, in 1839 15 year old Winfield was chosen to read aloud the Declaration of Independence during the town's annual July 4th celebration.

Chapter 5: Chamberlain's Early Years

The Chamberlain Family Tree

Joshua Lawrence Chamberlain, known almost exclusively as Lawrence Joshua Chamberlain in his lifetime, was born on September 8, 1828 in Brewer, Maine, the first of five children born to Joshua Chamberlain and Sarah Dupree (also Depuis) Brastow. Lawrence's father, the second in a line of "Joshuas," was a farmer by trade who served as a lieutenant colonel in a militia unit during Maine's Aroostook War with New Brunswick, Canada in 1839. His mother was the fourth daughter to Charles Dupuis, an officer in the Revolutionary War.

The Chamberlain family name is said to date back to the 12th century, when one Richard *de* Tankerville, grandson of a Norman knight, became "chamberlain" to King Stephen of England. In those times, "chamberlain" related to two possible positions: that of an official charged with management of the royal living quarters, or an official who collected rent and revenues-- essentially, a treasurer. Thus the name "Chamberlain" derived from the title or occupation.

Both of Lawrence's great-grandfathers fought in the Revolutionary War, and one of them, Ebenezer Chamberlain, was also a volunteer soldier from New Hampshire during the French and Indian War. Lawrence's grandfather (also named Joshua), a prosperous shipbuilder, was a colonel in the local militia during the War of 1812 who was subsequently court-martialed but later exonerated for his role in the disgraceful Battle of Hampden that led to the sacking of Bangor and Brewer, Maine by British forces (but ultimately ensured that eastern Maine would remain part of the United States). Thus, prior to "Lawrence Joshua," there had been a long tradition of military service in the Chamberlain family dating back generations.

Lawrence's siblings were Horace (1834--1861), Sarah (1836--?), John (who served in the Civil War as a chaplain; 1838--1867), and Thomas Davee (who was an officer under Lawrence and fought at Gettysburg; 1841--1896).

If Chamberlain was named Joshua Lawrence Chamberlain after other family members, why was he known as Lawrence Joshua during his life? Interestingly, while naming his son Joshua in honor of his father, the senior Joshua favored the name Lawrence because his boyhood hero was Captain James Lawrence, known in history as the man who after being mortally wounded while commanding the USS *Chesapeake* in the War of 1812 uttered the famous dying words, "Don't give up the ship!"

Childhood in Maine

From most early 19th century perspectives, Lawrence enjoyed a rather idyllic childhood. As the eldest of five children, he enjoyed the status of first born son, but he had little responsibility for caring for his siblings Horace, Sarah, John, and Thomas. But that's not to say Chamberlain didn't work hard. With hired help around the household for most of his youth, including a man who saw to farmhouse needs and a girl who managed the kitchen, Lawrence's mother tended to the children, leaving Lawrence to help his father work their hundred-acre farm.

Tending the crops (clearing, plowing, planting and harvesting), cutting wood, and caring for the animals became Lawrence's day-to-day life, and it was a lifestyle that taught him responsibility, self-reliance, and how to keep physically fit (though Lawrence was often described as frail and "unhealthy-looking" anyway). When Lawrence got older and his family fell on hard financial times, he took additional work in the nearby brickyards and shipyards-- making fishing lines and ships' cables from hemp. Often slipping across the Penobscot River to Bangor as a boy--the booming "big city" lumber and shipbuilding port--Lawrence became worldly beyond his years, meeting lumberjacks, shipbuilders, land speculators, and sailors from all over the globe.

A very active and inquisitive boy, the young Lawrence learned to sail the family sloop, was known as a strong swimmer, was skillful at a game called "round ball" he learned in Bangor, and often slipped off to the nearby Mohawk village where he'd listen to fascinating stories of more "primitive" times and famous uprisings. And while his father taught him to shoot a gun and use a broadsword, clearly holding aspirations that Lawrence would continue the Chamberlain "military man" tradition, Lawrence preferred to observe and preserve life rather than destroy it. Among his greatest pleasures were singing in the church choir and learning to play the bass viol.

Major Whiting's Military School: 1843?- 184?

At about the age of 15, Lawrence followed his father's encouragement and considered a career in the military, attending Major Whiting's Military Academy in Ellsworth, Maine about 20 miles away. Quickly adapting to military regimentation, Lawrence did well in military drill and organization, and immediately demonstrated a gift for languages; excelling in Latin and French. Family finances, however, made his stay at Major Whiting's a short one, forcing him to try his hand at teaching, or "keeping school" as it was commonly referred to.

Around the year 1843, when Lawrence was about 15 and had spent a year or two at Major Whiting's Military Academy in Ellsworth, Maine, Lawrence tried his hand at teaching--"keeping school" as it was colloquially referred to at that time. And while it required him to immediately inflict a rather severe beating on a student who was larger and had attempted to assert dominance over the single-room classroom, Lawrence grew to appreciate the role of teacher and fostered a strong bond with his students. He even established a winter evening singing school which proved especially popular and allowed him to frequently demonstrate his budding proficiency with the bass viol.

Despite being a popular teacher, and the fact he enjoyed it, Lawrence had still not locked his sights on a specific career, so his mother nudged him towards the ministry, while his father offered to secure for him an appointment to West Point Military Academy in New York.

Bowdoin College: 1848-1852

By the age of 20, as a regular member of the Congregational Church of Brewer, Lawrence developed a serious interest in religion. Resigning himself to becoming a minister, he enrolled in Bowdoin College in Brunswick, Maine after first teaching himself to read ancient Greek (the third language he would master), a requirement of the entrance exam. Lawrence then set his sites on learning the skills needed to become a missionary, his plan to bring the "gospel" to countries where he could teach the social and spiritual message of Christianity to those *less-advantaged* cultures.

Excelling in mathematics and astronomy, Lawrence became a school chemistry assistant, library assistant, and was even honored by being permitted to submit original problems for the Junior- and Senior-year exams. In the spring of 1851, he made a special presentation in German during the school's Scholarly Exhibition.

While at Bowdoin, Lawrence met a number of individuals who would come to have a powerful influence on his life, including Harriet Beecher Stowe, wife of Professor Calvin Stowe, teacher of Natural and Revealed Religion. Lawrence would often go to hear her read passages from what would later become her celebrated--and highly controversial--novel, *Uncle Tom's Cabin*.

While on campus, he joined two literary societies, the Peucinian Society (a group of student poets with Federalist leanings) and Alpha Delta Phi Fraternity, and he also became a member of the Phi Beta Kappa academic honor society.

Proving to be an exemplary student, during his junior and senior years at Bowdoin College, Lawrence taught Sunday school and was leader of the choir at the First Parish Church--just off Bowdoin campus--where the Reverend George E. Adams led the congregation, as well as provided Bowdoin students Baccalaureate services and Commencement exercises. And although pastor Adams drew the interest of young and aspirant minister, it was the minister's adopted daughter Fanny who best held Lawrence's attention. Before long, Lawrence was escorting Fanny to and from prayer meetings and college functions. But though obviously attracted and seemingly suited to one another, two things stood in the way of a future together.

For one, it was widely rumored that Lawrence was attracted to Harriet Beecher Stowe, 17 years his senior. Seeming infatuated with the aspiring novelist and mother of seven, Lawrence often worked in Mrs. Stowe's office during her husband's absence, assisting her with whatever book she was currently writing. Lawrence came to believe that Christ had spoken through her of the death of "Uncle Tom" and for the spiritual and moral need to write the work that would become *Uncle Tom's Cabin*.

1853 portrait of Harriet Beecher Stowe

In August of 1852, Lawrence graduated from Bowdoin with his sights set on completing his

was a prominent politician and attorney who represented Patrick County in both Houses of the Virginia General Assembly and served one term in the U. S. House of Representatives. Jeb's mother, Elizabeth, was known as a stern, religious woman with a great love of nature who ran the family plantation. There can be little doubt that like most boys in this place and time in American history, young Jeb had his share of chores and responsibilities, and received a basic education as time permitted. By surviving accounts, Jeb enjoyed a "happy boyhood," loved his family home at Laurel Hill, displayed an enthusiasm for nature, and often said that one of his fondest dreams for adulthood was to one day own his family home and end his days there in quiet retirement.

The Stuart home has been described as "an unpretentious, comfortable farmhouse" which, tragically, was destroyed by fire in the winter of 1847-48, though no detailed description of the house remains. In a surviving letter, Jeb described the fire as "a sad disaster."

For a few years after the fire, Archibald and son John Dabney lived in the outbuilding that had served as the family kitchen; with Archibald apparently remaining there until his death in 1855. In 1859, Elizabeth Stuart sold the property to two men from Mt. Airy, North Carolina, and the Laurel Hill plantation passed out of the Stuart family's possession.

Although few personal anecdotes regarding the young Jeb survive, one incident that seems to foretell of the bravery and audacity he would later display as a Civil War officer occurred at about the age of ten. As the story is told, while walking through the woods one afternoon with an older brother, a swarm of hornets attacked the two, sending the elder brother running. Young Jeb, however, is said to have "narrowed his eyes defiantly" and knocked the hornets' nest to the ground with a stick, defying the danger the bees posed. As would be seen repeatedly on the battlefield, James seems to have thrived on danger from a very early age.

Formal Education

Jeb received his earliest education at home, lessons presented by his mother and various relatives and neighbors, until 1845, when at the age of 12 he left Laurel Hill to be educated by a series of teachers in Wytheville, Virginia, and at the home of his aunt Anne (Archibald's sister) and her husband Judge James Ewell Brown (Stuart's namesake) at Danville. During the summer of 1848, Jeb became fascinated with military life and attempted to enlist in the U. S. Army, but the 15 year old teenager was rejected due to his age. That fall he entered Emory & Henry College, a private liberal arts school in Emory, Virginia where he studied for the next two years.

Finally, in 1850, Jeb gained entry into the military life he sought, appointed to the United States Military Academy at West Point, New York, by family friend, Representative Thomas Hamlet Averett, a man who had defeated James' father in the 1848 House election.

Chapter 7: West Point Years

Lee's West Point Years, 1825-1829

Following his natural aptitude for mathematics, Robert applied for admission into the United States Military Academy at West Point in early 1825. Today West Point is considered the country's elite military academy, and Lee's fantastic academic record there is still the stuff of legends, but when Lee applied to West Point, it was a highly *unimpressive* school consisting of a few ugly buildings facing a desolate, barren parade ground. Accepted in March of that year, Robert began his formal career as a soldier in July at the age of 18.

Upon Robert's departure for West Point, his mother moved with her two remaining daughters, Elinor and Elizabeth, from Alexandria to Georgetown, Washington D.C. Later, as her health quickly deteriorated, she moved to the home of Henry Lee's grandson, William Henry Fitzhugh, at Ravensworth in Fairfax County, Virginia.

Quickly demonstrating his aptitude for leadership and devotion to duty, Robert ranked high among his West Point classmates from the very beginning of his stint. Never insubordinate, always impeccably dressed, and never receiving even a single demerit; he became the template for his fellow cadets, who referred to him as "The Marble Model." While studying there he made many life-long friends, including fellow Virginian Joseph E. Johnston, as well as Albert Sidney Johnston, Leonidas Polk, Jefferson Davis, John B. Magruder, and William N. Pendleton-- all of whom would come to play critical roles for the Confederacy during the Civil War.

Lee in his 20s

Excelling in both mathematics and military exercises (particularly tactics and strategy), Robert studied engineering, science, and drawing, among other subjects. In his free time, he was known to pore over Alexander Hamilton's autobiography, Napoleon's memoirs, and *Confessions* by the renowned 18th-century Genevan political philosopher and writer, Jean-Jacques Rousseau. Awarded the highest rank in the Corps--cadet adjunct--his senior year, Robert graduated with high honors in 1829, ranked first in his class in artillery and military tactics and second in overall standing. He was immediately commissioned brevet lieutenant in the U.S. Army Corps of Engineers, considered the elite of the army in 1829.

Immediately after graduation, Robert went to visit his mother who was by this time dying of advanced tuberculosis. Tending her to her final day, Anne passed away on June 29, 1829. Robert the boy then became Lee the military man.

Meade's West Point Years, 1831-1835

In 1831, even though he was not yet 16, young George received a commission to West Point Military Academy, New York. At the time, a cadet was usually appointed to West Point by a Congressman. In Meade's case, he was appointed by none other than President Andrew Jackson, who accepted the second application sent in by his mother.

As a cadet, Meade was described as "quite small in stature at this time, slender and delicate in appearance, and there were friends of his family who thought that he would be unequal to the severe training of the academy." But Meade proved more than up to the task, thanks to his strong study habits.

Ironically, it was the military aspects of West Point that he disliked the most, and he had a great disinterest in guard-mounting, drill, and the endless minutiae of routine. The military components nearly drove him to quit going to school there, and he became more withdrawn in his later years, partly a result of the fact that he found his actual studies so easy that he did not need to exert himself to do well. Among the things Meade studied, he seemed to take a greatest interest in topographical engineering, which definitely served him well during the Civil War.

If Meade had been interested in the military, he may very well have graduated near the top of his class. Instead, he finished 19th out of a graduating class of 56 cadets in 1835.

James Longstreet's West Point Years, 1838-1842

In 1838, at the age of seventeen, James was appointed to West Point Military Academy in New York, where he proved to be a very poor student academically, as well as a disciplinary problem.

Longstreet explained why he had academic problems: "As cadet I had more interest in the school of the soldier, horsemanship, sword exercise, and the outside game of foot-ball than in the academic courses. The studies were successfully passed, however, until the third year, when I failed in mechanics. When I came to the problem of the pulleys, it seemed to my mind that a soldier could not find use for such appliances, and the pulleys were passed by. At the January examination I was called to the blackboard and given the problem of the pulleys. The drawing from memory of recitation of classmates was good enough, but the demonstration failed to satisfy the sages of the Academic Board. It was the custom, however, to give those who failed in the general examination a second hearing, after all of the classes were examined. This gave me two days to "cram" mechanics, and particularly on pulleys. But the professors were too wily to introduce them a second time, and took me through a searching examination of the six months course. The bridge was safely passed, however, and mechanics left behind. At the June examination, the end of the academic year, I was called to demonstrate the pulleys. The professor thought that I had forgotten my old friend the enemy, but I smiled, for he had become dear to me,--in waking hours and in dreams,--and the cadet passed easily enough for a maximum mark."

James also found other ways to earn scorn: "The cadets had their small joys and sometimes little troubles. On one occasion a cadet officer reported me for disobedience of orders. As the report was not true, I denied it and sent up witnesses of the occasion. Dick Garnett, who fell in the assault of the 3d, at Gettysburg, was one witness, and Cadet Baker, so handsome and lovable that he was called Betsy, was the other. Upon overlooking the records I found the report still there, and went to ask the superintendent if other evidence was necessary to show that the report was not true. He was satisfied of that, but said that the officer complained that I smiled contemptuously. As that could only be rated as a single demerit, I asked the benefit of the smile; but the report stands to this day, Disobedience of orders and three demerits. The cadet had his revenge, however, for the superintendent was afterwards known as The Punster."

Though popular with the other students (befriended by a number of future prominent Civil War figures, including George Henry Thomas, William S. Rosecrans, John Pope, D. H. Hill, Lafayette McLaws, George Pickett, and Ulysses S. Grant), the nearly 6' 2", 200 lb James racked up too many academic and disciplinary problems to receive high ranks. As a result, when he graduated in 1842, he finished third last in his class.

Upon graduation, James was commissioned brevet Second Lieutenant James Longstreet of the Fourth U.S. Infantry and sent to Jefferson Barracks, Missouri.

In his memoirs, Longstreet notes some of the West Point connections that were made by future Civil War generals, aside from his own. It was Longstreet's friendship with Grant that eventually allowed him to play a role in Grant's Republican administration after the war, which was viewed as almost treasonous by some of his former Confederate comrades.

Longstreet also points out that P.G.T. Beauregard and Irvin McDowell, the two commanding officers at the First Battle of Bull Run, went to West Point together. Beauregard's artillery instructor was Robert Anderson, who was in command of the garrison at Fort Sumter when Beauregard ordered the attack on it April 12, 1861, the first fighting of the Civil War.

Hancock's West Point Years, 1840-1844

In 1840, local Pennsylvania Congressman Joseph Fornance, an influential man who both admired and respected Benjamin Hancock, nominated Winfield for a commission to the United States Military Academy at West Point, New York. Though still not set on making a career of the military, as a young man who by name, family heritage, and natural disposition was undeniably "militarily-minded," it seemed the natural thing to do. And while Winfield's father had by this time become a prominent figure around Norristown, that by no means meant he could afford pricy universities like the University of Pennsylvania in nearby Philadelphia.

While early narratives describe Winfield's attendance at West Point as "esteemed" and his application of himself "brilliant," more recent accounts rate his progress at West Point as merely average, which may be more accurate if his graduation rank is any indication. Winfield ultimately graduated 18th in a class of 25 in 1844, so that June he was commissioned brevet Second Lieutenant and assigned to the Sixth Infantry of the U.S. Army.

JEB Stuart's West Point Years, 1850-1854

In 1850, Jeb entered the U. S. Military Academy at West Point and quickly adapted to military rigors, becoming a popular, happy student. Though not considered handsome during his teen years, and standing just five foot, nine inches tall, James' classmates began calling him "Beauty," which they explained as his "personal comeliness in inverse ratio to the term employed."[2] He is said to have possessed a chin "so short and retiring as positively to disfigure his otherwise fine countenance." The weak chin did not escape his notice, and after graduation he would grow a beard that led a fellow officer to remark, "[He was] the only man I ever saw that [a] beard improved."[3]

Today West Point is the country's elite military academy, but when Stuart entered the school in 1850, its importance in training the Civil War's greatest leaders was not yet known, and the campus hardly befitted a great institution. In 1852, Robert E. Lee, who had a legendary reputation at the Academy for finishing first in his class and not receiving a demerit nearly 20 years earlier, was appointed superintendent of the Academy, and Jeb soon became friends with the Lee family, seeing them socially on numerous occasions. Lee's nephew, Fitzhugh Lee (who would serve under Jeb during the Civil War as a lieutenant colonel of the First Virginia Cavalry beginning in August 1861), also arrived at the academy that year.

---

[2]   Thomas, Emory M. *Bold Dragoon: The Life of J.E.B. Stuart*. Page 18.

[3]   Davis, Burke. *Jeb Stuart: The Last Cavalier*. Page 33.

It was at West Point that Stuart proved to himself and others his cavalry talents. In his final year at West Point, in addition to achieving the cadet rank of second captain of the corps, he was one of only eight cadets designated "honorary cavalry officers" for his exceptional skills in horsemanship. In 1854, at the age of 21, Jeb graduated thirteenth in his class of forty-six, ranked tenth in his class in cavalry tactics. And although he enjoyed the civil engineering curriculum and did well in mathematics as well, his poor drawing skills hampered his engineering studies, so he finished 29th in that discipline. (A Stuart family legend insists that he deliberately slacked-off his academic studies his final year to avoid service in the elite--but dull--Army Corps of Engineers.)

In October of 1854, James was commissioned brevet Second Lieutenant James Ewell Brown Stuart, but he was already most often referred to as "Jeb."

Ultimately, it was not how these men performed at West Point that made their time most memorable, but who they were performing with at the Academy. Aside from Lee's sterling academic record, they would be remembered as one of a handful of West Point men who became the most important generals of the Civil War, and the future generals' years at West Point became a source of colorful stories about the men who became Civil War legends decades down the road.

In 1846, a shy kid named Thomas Jonathan Jackson made few friends and struggled with his studies, finishing 17th in his class 15 years before becoming Stonewall, while George Pickett was more preoccupied with playing hooky at a local bar before finishing last in the same class as Jackson. Future Confederate corps commander A.P. Hill was already in love with the future wife of George McClellan, a young prodigy who finished second in the class of 1846, while a clerical error by West Point administrators ensured that Hiram Ulysses Grant became forever known as Ulysses S. Grant. Years after Lee met Albert Sidney Johnston and Jefferson Davis at West Point, William Tecumseh Sherman roomed with principle subordinate George H. Thomas, and they were friends with Richard S. Ewell, the corps commander who would replace Stonewall Jackson after Chancellorsville. And in the years that followed Thomas and Sherman, important Civil War generals in the West went to school together, including John Bell Hood, Phil Sheridan and James Birdseye McPherson, who would become the only commanding general of a Union army to die in a Civil War battle when he fell in 1864 during Sherman's Atlanta Campaign.

Chapter 8: Early Military Careers and the Mexican-American War

Lee's Early Military Career

Although Lee's position in the U.S. Army Corps of Engineers was a prestigious one, Lee's first military assignment was at a remote army post at Fort Pulaski on Cockspur Island, Georgia (on the Savannah River). Though not yet receiving full lieutenant's pay, he was tasked with full responsibility for seeing to it that the groundwork for the construction of a new fort was laid--a job requiring him to spend much of his time immersed in mud up to his armpits.

Though he was now away from Virginia, Lee's time spent in Georgia also represented perhaps the most social period of his life. Lee managed to find sufficient distraction from his less-than-pleasant duties in the home of West Point friend, Jack Mackay, whose family home was located in Savanna and where Lee often spent time with Jack's two sisters Margaret and Eliza. Said to have enjoyed dancing, gossip, and parties, Lee, the Southern gentleman, was in his element, conversing and cavorting with Georgia's social elites. Still, even though Lee was often the charming "life of the party" and was sharing the company of many eligible women, he seems to have fancied few.

After serving 17 months at Fort Pulaski, Robert was transferred to Fort Monroe, Virginia, where he was made assistant to the chief of engineers. While stationed there, Lee met his second cousin, Mary Anna Randolph Custis. Mary was the pampered and frail daughter of Mary Lee Fitzhugh and famously wealthy but slovenly agriculturalist George Washington Parke Custis (grandson of Martha Washington). Although they outwardly had very little in common--he was elegant, admired stoicism, and relished social gatherings, while she was dull, complained incessantly, and loathed parties--Lee proposed marriage. Some historians believe the attraction was at least in part based on Mary's profession to having a religious epiphany the year before, damning the keeping of slaves. On July 5, 1831, the two were wed. The 3rd U.S. Artillery served as honor guard.

1862 map of Fort Monroe

In that Lee could scarcely support Mary in the style she'd been accustomed, he agreed to move into her family home, which still stands on a hill overlooking Washington, D.C. Even so, beginning in August of 1831, the couple shared Lee's cramped junior officer's quarters at the fort for a period of two years, during which Mary brought along one of her slaves, Cassy, to tend to her personal needs. A little more than a year later, Mary gave birth to their first child, George Washington Custis--who Lee nicknamed "Boo." In the years that followed, the Lees would produce six more children: Mary, William H. Fitzhugh, Eleanor Agnes, Annie, Robert Edward Jr., and Mildred. All three sons would serve in the Confederate Army under their father during the Civil War.

1854 engraving of Mary

From 1834 to 1837, Robert served as assistant engineer in Washington, but spent the summer of 1835 helping survey the boundary line between the states of Ohio and Michigan. In 1836 he was given his first solo project, that of finding a way to control the course of the "Mighty" Mississippi River, which was constantly threatening to destroy the burgeoning commerce of the city of St. Louis. Through the ingenious accomplishment of this daunting project involving the moving of 2,000 tons of rock to build strategically-placed dikes, an engineering feat in itself, Lee established once and for all his professional standing. Recognition for this monumental accomplishment came in the form of promotion to first lieutenant of engineers, assigned to supervise the engineering work for the St. Louis harbor, thus becoming a member of the board of engineers for U.S. Atlantic coast defenses. But while his professional life excelled during these years, his family life began to falter.

Shortly after giving birth to their second child, Mary Curtis, in 1835 (whom Lee would refer to simply as "Daughter"), his wife's health began a downward spiral that would plague her throughout her life. Chronic pelvic infection, abscesses of the groin, and rheumatism would come to define her day-to-day existence, and her physical limitations and mental state weighed heavily on Lee. In May 1837, Lee's third child, William Henry Fitzhugh was born, followed by Anne Carter in 1839, and Eleanor Agnes in 1841--with whom Lee kept in constant contact through letters while away performing his duties. That same year, he was promoted to captain and transferred to Fort Hamilton in New York Harbor, where he was put in charge of building fortifications. A short time later his family came to join him, and for the first time he was able to spend more than a few days at a time with them.

Ironically, as his family grew in size, despite his preference for spending his time close to home, Lee began hoping hostilities would erupt somewhere in the U.S. territories. Even on a captain's salary, soon the basic upkeep and education of his children would reach a critical point, and military men were seldom promoted above the rank of captain in peace time.

Lee with his son William, circa 1845

Meade after West Point

For a year following graduation from West Point Military Academy, brevet Second Lieutenant George Gordon Meade served with the Third U. S. Artillery in Florida, fighting the Seminole Native Americans. Meade had never had a desire to serve in the Army, and on top of it, it was feared that he could not physically handle military duty in the Florida climate where he was stationed. Sure enough, he contracted a debilitating fever, after which he was assigned to ordnance duty at the Watertown (Massachusetts) Arsenal.

After serving in the U. S. Army for a year, with no desire to pursue a military career, in 1836 George resigned his commission to work in civilian surveying, which entailed the official surveying of the Texas and Maine borders.

In 1840, George met Margaretta Sergeant, daughter of prominent Philadelphian John Sergeant, the running mate of Henry Clay in the 1832 Presidential election. Though Meade's civilian life was clearly unsettled, Sergeant thought he saw great things ahead for the young man and predicted he would have a brilliant career, which certainly would have come as a surprise to George himself. The couple subsequently married at St. Peter's Church, in Philadelphia, Pennsylvania on December 31, 1840, George's 25th birthday.

The couple would have seven children together--four sons and three daughters: John Sergeant, George (who would serve as a colonel under his father in the Civil War), Margaret Butler, Spencer, Sarah Wise, Henrietta, and William.

After marrying and finding steady civilian employment difficult to secure, in 1842 Meade reentered the U. S. Army as a second lieutenant in the Corps of Topographical Engineers. It was certainly a much better fit for a man who had proven so apt with engineering studies.

Meade continued with his work in the Army until he was assigned to Texas in 1845, where Second Lieutenant George Gordon Meade served as a staff officer in Major General Zachary Taylor's army. Now 30, Meade was visibly more robust than he had been as a young adult, but he still was not of a mind for military service, and when he had to say goodbye to his family, he was doing so at a time when one of his young sons was so ill that Meade never expected to see his child again. Meade would write his wife in August 1845, "I trust you have not placed any fond hopes on seeing me come back from this place. I found on my arrival here this morning that there was nothing to be done but to proceed to the destination assigned me. Since leaving Philadelphia the news is more belligerent from Mexico, and though I have not the slightest fear of any hostilities on the part of the Mexicans, yet the existence of such reports renders it a point of honor for me to go."

Meade did report some more light-hearted moments during his time in Mexico before hostilities truly commenced. On New Year's Day 1846, he relayed one anecdote to his wife. "I have had rather a stupid day of it for the First of the year. In the morning I was engaged making official complimentary visits to the 'big-bugs' of the camp, all of whom had egg-nogg and cake for their visitors; then we had a race, gotten up by the officers for their amusement; and then I dined with a party who endeavored to be as merry as they could be under the circumstances; and, in the evening, I accompanied them to the theatre; for you must know that since our arrival here they have built a theatre and imported a company of strolling actors, who murder tragedy, burlesque comedy, and render farce into buffoonery, in the most approved style. And now late at night I am jotting down a few thoughts to you."

Hancock after West Point

Soon after leaving West Point, it became apparent to those around him that brevet Second Lieutenant Winfield Scott Hancock carried significant ambition and personally hoped to bring honor to his parents and the country he was now sworn to serve. Earnest, industrious, conscientious, and vocally patriotic, by all accounts Hancock had the makings of a successful soldier.

On July 1, 1844, brevet Second Lieutenant Hancock was ordered to report to his Sixth Infantry regiment at "Red River" on the Western frontier, in the Red River Valley of present day North Dakota and Minnesota. As the only policing authority in the region, it was the duty of the U. S. Army at that time to protect settlers as they slowly pushed their way across the frontier. Stationed first at Fort Towson and then Fort Washita, Hancock's time there was largely uneventful, aside from the occasional "Indian incident", with little opportunity for glory and little expected. After nearly two years of undistinguished duty, on June 18, 1864, Hancock received his commission as full second lieutenant.

When war broke out with Mexico in 1846, Second Lieutenant Hancock hoped he'd be sent to the front but made no formal request to join the action. Transferred instead from Fort Washita to Newport Barracks, Kentucky, he was assigned to recruiting duties, proving so proficient at signing up soldiers that his superiors were reluctant to ever release him from his post.

In July 1847, Hancock was finally sent to join the Sixth Infantry in Puebla, Mexico, where his unit became part of the army under the command of Winfield's namesake, General Winfield Scott.

Longstreet's Early Military Career

Brevet Second Lieutenant James Longstreet spent his first two years of military service at Jefferson Barracks, Missouri, where he was soon joined by his West Point friend, Lieutenant Ulysses S. Grant. Longstreet pointed out in his memoirs that he loved his assignment, but not for military reasons. "I was fortunate in the assignment to Jefferson Barracks, for in those days the young officers were usually sent off among the Indians or as near the borders as they could find habitable places. In the autumn of 1842 I reported to the company commander, Captain Bradford R. Alden, a most exemplary man, who proved a lasting, valued friend. Eight companies of the Third Infantry were added to the garrison during the spring of 1843, which made garrison life and society gay for the young people and interesting for the older classes. All of the troops were recently from service in the swamps and Everglades of Florida, well prepared to enjoy the change from the war-dance of the braves to the hospitable city of St. Louis; and the graceful step of its charming belles became a joy forever."

Longstreet even recalls being with Grant when he met his wife Julia, writing, "Of the class of 1843, Ulysses S. Grant joined the Fourth Regiment as brevet lieutenant, and I had the pleasure to ride with him on our first visit to Mr. Frederick Dent's home, a few miles from the garrison, where we first met Miss Julia Dent, the charming woman who, five years later, became Mrs. Grant. Miss Dent was a frequent visitor at the garrison balls and hops, where Lieutenant Hoskins, who was something of a tease, would inquire of her if she could tell where he might find "the small lieutenant with the large epaulettes."

Grant

In 1847, while serving in the Mexican-American War, Major Longstreet met Maria Louisa Garland (called "Louise" by her family), the daughter of Longstreet's regimental commander, Lt. Colonel John Garland.

Married in March of 1848 (one month after the conclusion of the war), the couple had ten children together (only five of whom lived to adulthood): John G. (1848-1918), Augustus Baldwin (1850-1862), William Dent (1853-1854), James (1857-1862), Mary Anne (1860-1862), Robert Lee (1863-1940), James (1865-1922), Fitz Randolph (1869-1951), Louise Longstreet Whelchel (1872-1957), and an unnamed child presumed to have died at birth.

Although their marriage would last over 40 years, Longstreet never mentioned Louise in his memoirs, and most of what is known today about their relationship came from the writings of his second wife, Helen Dortch Longstreet.

At about the same time that Longstreet began courting Maria Louisa Garland, Longstreet's West Point friend and fellow Jefferson Barracks comrade Ulysses S. Grant met and began a relationship with Longstreet's fourth cousin, Julia Dent, with the couple marrying on August 22, 1848 in St. Louis, Missouri. While historians agree that Longstreet attended the Grant-Dent wedding, his specific role during the ceremony remains unclear. Grant biographer Jean Edward Smith asserts that Longstreet served as Grant's Best Man, while John Y. Simon, editor of Julia

Grant's memoirs, states that Longstreet "may have been a groomsman."[4] But as Longstreet biographer Donald Brigman Sanger points out, neither Grant nor Longstreet mentioned the role of "Best Man" in either of their memoirs or other personal writings.

The Mexican-American War

When the United States declared war on Mexico on May 13, 1846, Lee thought the opportunity to prove himself as a field officer had finally arrived. But the growing sentiment in the North was that the annexation of Texas was just a slaveholders' ploy to seize more territory for the further expansion of slavery. Ulysses S. Grant, one of the first American soldiers to cross the disputed border, believed the Army was being sent there just to provoke a fight, and a young Congressman from Illinois named Abraham Lincoln first gained national attention for sponsoring legislation demanding that President Polk show the spot where Mexicans had fired on American troops, believing that "President Polk's War" was full of deception.

Regardless, in September of 1846, Lee was sent to San Antonio de Bexar, Texas, with orders to report to Brigadier General John E. Wool. Considering that he might not return from this mission, Lee made out his will, leaving everything to his wife Mary, before setting off. There he was tasked with selecting travel routes for the troops and supervision of the construction of bridges for Wool's march toward Saltillo, the capital city of the northeastern Mexican state of Coahuila, just south of Texas.

Daguerreotype of General John E. Wool

On January 16, 1847, Lee was then attached to General Winfield Scott's command at Brazos,

---

[4]   Sanger, Donald B., and Thomas Robson Hay. *James Longstreet, I: Soldier*. Page 13.

Texas. Scott was planning to take the war deeper into Mexico, to Veracruz (in east-central Mexico) and then Mexico City. Immediately acknowledged for his excellent intuition as a scout, Lee became a member of Scott's staff and experienced his first active combat while taking part in the capture of Veracruz.

During the march to Mexico City, Lee was promoted to brevet major, receiving high praise for his insightful reconnaissance and choice of artillery placement that ultimately made the capture of Mexico's capital possible. It was also Lee's engineering skills that enabled American troops to cross the treacherous mountain passes leading to the capital. General Scott's official reports raved about Lee's war-time efforts, declaring that his "success in Mexico was largely due to the skill, valor, and undaunted courage of Robert E. Lee," calling him "the greatest military genius in America."[5] Diaries of many of his fellow officers showed how impressed they all were with the brave "Virginian."

Winfield Scott was a military hero in the War of 1812 and the Mexican-American War

Sent into the action sometime in 1846, Second Lieutenant Longstreet served with distinction in the Mexican-American War with the Eighth U. S. Infantry, receiving brevet promotions to captain for the battles at Contreras and Churubusco, and major for the action at Molino del Rey-- having been cited for gallant and meritorious conduct numerous times. In the Battle of Chapultepec, September 12-13, 1847, Major Longstreet was severely wounded in the thigh with a musket ball while charging up the hill carrying his regimental colors. Naturally, the color bearer who holds the flag marches front and center and is unarmed, making it the most dangerous position in 19th century warfare, and one that requires incredible bravery. As the incident is recorded, upon falling, Longstreet handed the flag to his friend, a young Lieutenant

---

5   Thomas, Emory M. *Robert E. Lee: A Biography.* Page 128.

who finished last in his West Point class of 1846, George E. Pickett. Pickett earned distinction for reaching the summit during the battle, and both men earned reputations at Mexico that would allow them to command brigades early in the Civil War.

Longstreet and General Winfield Scott Hancock (whose performance at Gettysburg during Pickett's Charge on Day 3 was crucial for the Union's success) fought together in the Battle of Churubusco. Second Lieutenant Hancock also displayed "exceptional bravery" at the Battles of Contreras and Churubusco on August 20, 1847, after which he was appointed a brevet first lieutenant. Wounded in the knee at Churubusco, Hancock developed a fever, and though well enough to lead his regiment at Molino del Rey on September 8, high fever kept him from participating in the final breakthrough to Mexico City, something he is said to have regretted for the remainder of his life.

There is no question that Longstreet made a name for himself in Mexico, and it was a reputation that would help earn him command over a brigade right at the outset of the Civil War. Yet Longstreet barely mentions his actual service during the Mexican-American war in his memoirs, instead recalling the politics behind the war and two heroic vignettes about other men he fought with in battle. Again, readers can quickly get the sense that he considered Mexico cursory to his life and legacy.

After the outbreak of the Mexican-American War the following year, Meade became part of Taylor's staff in Mexico, and ultimately assigned to carry messages between Generals Taylor, Winfield Scott, William J. Worth, and Robert A. Patterson. Meade also served under General Winfield Scott as an engineer with the adversary he would be forever linked with, Robert E. Lee.

Although Meade was in a staff position, he revealed his very astute military observations to his wife, demonstrating how clear of mind he was when it came to both tactics and strategy. In one letter to his wife, correctly predicted the Mexicans' military strategy. "My own opinion is that the Mexicans will never disturb us on the river, our present position, but that they will make a stand at Monterey, should we advance into the interior. They will without doubt fortify that place, and it is understood to be capable of strong defense. Then they have a distance of eighty miles to Saltillo, which is a pass through the mountains, capable of being made impregnable if defended by brave and intrepid men, and which it will be difficult for us to force if they defend it properly. But I do not believe it is in the people to resist us as brave men would do, although every effort will be made to arouse their national prejudices and religious feelings against us. If we only had fifteen thousand regular troops, I believe sincerely we could march to the City of Mexico, but I doubt the practicability of so doing with a force of volunteers."

Present at the Battles of Palo Alto and Resaca de la Palma (May 8 and 9, 1846), Meade was brevetted to first lieutenant for gallantry at the Battle of Monterrey (September 21–24, 1846).

In addition to Lee, Meade served with several other junior officers during the Mexican-American War who would become prominent figures of the Civil War, including Ulysses S, Grant, Thomas J. "Stonewall" Jackson, Albert S. Johnston, Joseph E. Johnston, George B. McClellan, P. G. T. Beauregard, James Longstreet, Braxton Bragg, Joseph Hooker, George H. Thomas, and Jefferson Davis.

JEB Stuart's Early Military Career

Among Lee and his principle subordinates in the Army of Northern Virginia, JEB Stuart was the only one who didn't fight in the Mexican-American War.

On January 28, 1855, brevet Second Lieutenant James "Jeb" Stuart was assigned to the U. S. Mounted Rifles Cavalry at Fort Davis, Texas (in what is today Jeff Davis County), becoming a leader on scouting missions over the San Antonio to El Paso Road, where for the next three months he fought the Apaches. He was then transferred to the newly formed First Cavalry Regiment at Fort Leavenworth, Kansas Territory, where he became regimental quartermaster and commissary officer under the command of Colonel Edwin V. Sumner. His organizational and logistical talents quickly becoming apparent, he was promoted to first lieutenant later that same year.

Edwin "Bull" Sumner would lead a corps for the Army of the Potomac in the major campaigns of 1862

Chapter 9: Life before the Civil War

Chamberlain the Teacher

Immediately after graduation from Bangor Theological Seminary in 1855, the 27 year old

Lawrence married 29 year old Fanny Adams, adopted daughter of Dr. George E. Adams. Fanny was a highly complex and spoiled "princess", orphaned from virtual European royalty and prone to puerile emotional outbursts. Dr. Adams, who was actually a cousin rather than adoptive father, thought it unwise that Fanny should pledge herself to a man two years her junior with at least three more years of serious study to complete before considering marriage. Even so, Lawrence told Fanny resolutely, "Your father has not such faith in our relation . . . he does not expect that much will ever come of it or that it will last long. As to this I simply say he has 'mistaken his man.' I am not so easily managed."[6] Setting his sites on a wedding date after the completion of his ministerial training, in the fall of 1852, Lawrence entered Bangor Theological Seminary. And although Reverend Adams did not initially approve of the union--believing it doomed from the start--over time, George and Lawrence developed a mutual respect.

With their first child coming just one year later, Grace "Daise" Dupree (born October 16, 1856), Lawrence and Fanny would have four more children together: a boy who died a year after birth (in 1857), a second son, Harold Wyllys (born October 10, 1858), a child born in the early 1860s born too premature to survive, and another who died in infancy.

In 1855, after completing a three-year curriculum at Bangor Theological Seminary in Bangor, Maine, Lawrence was invited to return to Bowdoin College to fill the spot left by Professor Calvin Stowe. Highly impressed with a paper Lawrence had presented at Bowdoin entitled, "Law and Liberty" (presented partially in hopes of acquiring a Masters of Arts degree from his old college), in which Lawrence successfully agued that law without liberty is tyranny, and liberty without law is irresponsible and chaotic--and thus an easy prey to would-be despots--they offered him the position of Professor of Natural and Revealed Religion. Lawrence eventually went on to teach every subject in the curriculum with the exception of science and mathematics.

Adopting a rather unusual approach to teaching, Professor Chamberlain introduced a number of methods previously unknown at Bowdoin. For one, he believed that every student should be required to pass a course in voice culture (a singing class), stating that "those who most need the benefit of it are not always those who voluntarily attend."[7] For another, he also believed that students should learn how to express themselves effectively in writing. In 1856 alone, he received over 1100 writing assignments which he had made his students rewrite until they had reached an "acceptable standard of proficiency." Now fluent in nine languages other than English, in 1861 he was appointed Professor of Modern Languages (a position originally established by world-renowned poet and educator Henry Wadsworth Longfellow), a position he held, at least on paper, until 1865.

---

[6]   Wallace, Willard M. *Soul of the Lion: A Biography of General Joshua L. Chamberlain.* Page 27.
[7]   Wallace, Willard M. *Soul of the Lion: A Biography of General Joshua L. Chamberlain.* Page 29.

In 1861, with the commencement of the Civil War, Bowdoin College offered to further finance Professor Chamberlain's education by sending him to Europe for two years to study additional languages, rather than lose him to the War, an offer he ultimately declined. Unbeknownst to his superiors and colleagues, Chamberlain had already sent a letter to the governor of Maine offering his services to the Union Army.

Meade the Engineer

After the Mexican-American War, Second Lieutenant Meade was primarily involved in lighthouse and breakwater construction, and coastal surveying, in Florida and New Jersey. He designed Barnegat Light on Long Beach Island, Absecon Light in Atlantic City, and Cape May Light in Cape May (in New Jersey), as well as Jupiter Inlet Light in Jupiter (Florida), and Sombrero Key Light in the Florida Keys. Furthermore, as a credit to his inventive skills, he also designed an hydraulic lamp that was adopted by the Lighthouse Board for use in all American lighthouses.

In 1856, Second Lieutenant Meade was promoted to captain. The following year he relieved Lt. Colonel James Kearney on the Great Lakes Survey mission--completing the survey of Lake Huron, with surveys of Lake Michigan down to Grand and Little Traverse Bays also completed under his command.

Also to his credit, prior to Meade's command, the Great Lakes' water level readings were taken locally with temporary gauges, with no uniform plane of reference established. In 1858, based on Meade's recommendation, instrumentation was set in place for the standardized tabulation of records across the basin. As a result, in 1860 the first detailed report on the Great Lakes was published--due to Meade's contribution. Meade stayed with the Great Lakes Survey until the outbreak of the Civil War in 1861.

In 1852, both Mr. and Mrs. Meade suffered personal tragedy. On March 22 of that year, Meade's mother died, and with her died one of George's best friends and closest confidants. In November of that year, Meade's father-in-law, John Sergeant, died, a blow to the entire family. It was not lost on Meade that the two people with the most confidence in him died within months of each other.

Hancock the Quartermaster

After returning from Mexico in February of 1848, Hancock reverted back to second lieutenant and served at a number of posts as an army quartermaster and adjutant, based primarily at Fort Snelling, Minnesota, and St. Louis, Missouri. It was at St. Louis that he was finally promoted to full first lieutenant.

While serving as army quartermaster and adjunct of his unit in St. Louis, Missouri, First Lieutenant Winfield Scott Hancock met Almira ("Allie") Russell, daughter of a prominent St. Louis, Missouri merchant, in 1849. After a quick courtship, the couple was married on January 24, 1850, eventually having two children together: Russell in 1850 and Ada in 1857. Unfortunately, neither child would outlive their parents; Ada died in 1875, and Russell died in 1884.

Almira Russell Hancock

After serving as quartermaster at a number of posts, Hancock was promoted to captain and assigned to Fort Myers, Florida in 1855, where his new family accompanied him. In fact, his wife was the only woman on the post. Despite the promotion, his assignment was largely coinciding with the end of the Third Seminole War, and he primarily retained his duties as a quartermaster, keeping him from seeing action in that campaign.

Lee Tries to Find His Place

When the Mexican-American War ended in 1848, Lee returned to service with the U.S. Army Corps of Engineers. After spending three years at Fort Carroll in Baltimore harbor, Lee was made superintendent of West Point in 1852, a tribute to both his exemplary military record and his natural ability to lead. Although he voiced his preference for field duty rather than a desk job, he assumed his new position with zeal. Lee made numerous improvements to the buildings, revamped the curriculum, and was known to spend a great deal of time with the cadets, gaining him a reputation as a fair and kind superintendent.

Lee had proven himself at West Point a second time, but his destiny was not to remain there. With dissension mounting between the North and South, exacerbated by the Mexican-American War, it wasn't long before Lee would find himself in the middle of an insurgence.

In early 1855, Lee was promoted to lieutenant colonel of the newly organized 2nd Cavalry and stationed at Jefferson Barracks in St. Louis, Missouri. Much of his time spent during the next few years at his new post were spent in court-martial service or with the 2nd Cavalry on the Texas frontier, where local Native American tribes posed an ongoing threat to settlers.

During this time, Lee continued to demonstrate his talent as both soldier and organizer, but as would later be revealed in his letters, these were not happy years for Lee. He disliked being separated from his family and felt guilty for not being available to his wife, who by now had become a chronically-ill invalid. Indeed, for nearly two decades, Lee found himself constantly being pulled in opposite directions by his wife's needful requests and his sense of duty to the job he was assigned. In one famous letter in 1834, Lee responded to one of Mary's requests to return by writing to her, "But why do you urge my immediate return, & tempt one in the strongest manner... I rather require to be strengthened & encouraged to the full performance of what I am called on to execute."

Lee in 1850

Although Lee returned to Washington at every opportunity, it was the death of his father-in-law in October of 1857 that would ultimately lead him to request an extended leave from the Army. Having to deal with the settlement of her father's estate exacerbated Mary's already frail condition, prompting Lee to find a way to remain at her side. And as it would happen, Lee was home in 1859 tending to family matters when he received orders from Washington to hurry to Harpers Ferry, West Virginia.

Longstreet on the Frontier

After the Mexican-American War and his recovery from the wound sustained at Chapultepec, Longstreet served on routine frontier duty in Texas, primarily at Forts Martin Scott (near Fredericksburg) and Bliss (in El Paso). During this time, Longstreet advanced to the rank of major, mostly performing scouting missions.

Beginning in July of 1858, he began serving as paymaster for the Eighth Infantry. Author Kevin Phillips of *The Cousins' Wars* claims that during this period, Longstreet was involved in a plot to draw the Mexican state of Chihuahua into the Union as a slave state.

As Longstreet put it, "I was stationed at Albuquerque, New Mexico, as paymaster in the United States army when the war-cloud appeared in the East. Officers of the Northern and Southern States were anxious to see the portending storm pass by or disperse, and on many occasions we, too, were assured, by those who claimed to look into the future, that the statesman would yet show himself equal to the occasion, and restore confidence among the people." Clearly Longstreet at the time was hoping for some sort of grand compromise that would avert war.

JEB Stuart's Family Life

In July of 1855 while stationed at Fort Leavenworth, Kansas Territory, Stuart met Flora Cooke, daughter of Lieutenant Colonel Philip St. George Cooke, commander of the Second U. S. Dragoon Regiment. (Cooke is noted for his authorship of the standard Army Cavalry Manual and is sometimes called the "Father of the U. S. Cavalry.") Biographer and historian Burke Davis described Flora as "an accomplished horsewoman, and though not pretty, an effective charmer," to whom "Stuart succumbed with hardly a struggle."[8]

In September of that year, less than two months after meeting, Stuart proposed marriage. In a clever play off another famous general's words, Stuart wrote of his whirlwind courtship, "*Veni, Vidi, Victus sum,*" Latin for "I came, I saw, I was conquered".[9] Although the couple had planned a gala wedding at Fort Riley, Kansas, the death of Stuart's father on September 20, 1855, brought

---

[8]   Davis, Burke. *Jeb Stuart: The Last Cavalier*. Page 36.

[9]   Wert, Jeffry D. *Cavalryman of the Lost Cause: A Biography of J.E.B. Stuart*. Pages 30--31.

a change of plans, with the wedding subsequently held on November 14, attended only by family members.

In 1856 the couple's first child, a girl, was born, but died the same day. Then on November 14, 1857, Flora gave birth to a second daughter whom they named Flora. In early 1858 the Stuart's relocated to Fort Riley, Kansas with their two slaves--one inherited from his father's estate, one purchased to help around the Stuart household--where they remained until 1859.

In October of 1859, while still in service to the U. S. Army, Stuart developed a new saber hook, "an improved method of attaching sabers to belts"--for which the U. S. government paid him $5,000 for a "right to use" license. It was while he was in Washington discussing the contract (and applying for an appointment to the quartermaster department) that Stuart heard about John Brown's raid on the U. S. Arsenal at Harpers Ferry and volunteered to be Colonel Lee's *aide-de-camp*.

On June 26, 1860, wife Flora gave birth to a son who would at first be named Philip St. George Cooke Stuart, after Jeb's well known father in law.

Chapter 10: 1850s Politics and the Election of 1860

Bleeding Kansas

Throughout the 1850s, American politicians tried to sort out the nation's intractable issues. In an attempt to organize the center of North America – Kansas and Nebraska – without offsetting the slave-free balance, Senator Stephen Douglas of Illinois proposed the Kansas-Nebraska Act. The Kansas-Nebraska Act eliminated the Missouri Compromise line of 1820, which the Compromise of 1850 had maintained. The Missouri Compromise had stipulated that states north of the boundary line determined in that bill would be free, and that states south of it *could* have slavery. This was essential to maintaining the balance of slave and free states in the Union. The Kansas-Nebraska Act, however, ignored the line completely and proposed that all new territories be organized by popular sovereignty. Settlers could vote whether they wanted their state to be slave or free.

Stephen Douglas, "The Little Giant"

When popular sovereignty became the standard in Kansas and Nebraska, the primary result was that thousands of zealous pro-slavery and anti-slavery advocates both moved to Kansas to influence the vote, creating a dangerous (and ultimately deadly) mix. Numerous attacks took place between the two sides, and many pro-slavery Missourians organized attacks on Kansas towns just across the border.

The best known abolitionist in Bleeding Kansas was a middle aged man named John Brown. A radical abolitionist, Brown organized a small band of like-minded followers and fought with the armed groups of pro-slavery men in Kansas for several months, including a notorious incident known as the Pottawatomie Massacre, in which Brown's supporters murdered five men. Over 50 people died before John Brown left the territory, which ultimately entered the Union as a free state in 1859.

John Brown

Now a veteran of the Native American frontier conflicts, from 1855 to 1861 First Lieutenant Stuart was given a leadership position in defusing "Bleeding Kansas" (or the "Border War"), the violent political confrontations between anti-slavery "Free-Staters" (like John Brown) and pro-slavery "Border Ruffians" that took place in the Kansas Territory and neighboring towns of Missouri, and ended with the "Pottawatomie Massacre."

On July 29, 1857, Stuart demonstrated his knack for initiative and bravery during the Cheyenne uprising known as the Battle of Solomon's River in present day Kansas. According to reports, after his commander, Colonel Sumner, ordered a "drawn sabers" charge against a band of Cheyenne who were firing a barrage of arrows, Stuart and three other lieutenants chased one Cheyenne down, who Stuart then shot in the thigh. The Native American, however, turned and fired at Stuart with a flintlock, striking him directly in the chest, but doing little actual damage. By the time Stuart returned to Fort Leavenworth that September to reunite with his family, word of his courage and exceptional leadership abilities preceded him.

At the same time, Captain Hancock had been reassigned to Fort Leavenworth, Kansas, where he served with his Sixth Infantry in the anti-slavery "Bleeding Kansas" border war during the mid-1850s. Eventually, Hancock was stationed in the Utah Territory, where he was present for the conclusion of the Utah War/Mormon Rebellion in July of 1858. After a peaceful resolution to the Utah War/Mormon Rebellion was negotiated, in November of 1858, Hancock was transferred to Los Angeles in southern California, where he remained until the outbreak of the Civil War in 1861. Again he was joined by wife "Allie" and their children, and he continued serving as a captain and assistant quartermaster under Albert Sidney Johnston, who was just a few years away from being the Confederacy's most prominent general.

Albert Sidney Johnston

While stationed in Los Angeles, Captain Hancock befriended a number of men who would later become Confederate officers, famously becoming particularly close with Virginian Lewis A. Armistead, who would rise to the rank of Brig. General of the Confederate Army and oppose Hancock at Gettysburg. At the outbreak of the Civil War, Armistead and the other "Southerners" left to join the Confederate States Army, while Hancock remained in the service of the Federal, "Union" forces.

Armistead

Harpers Ferry

After his activities in Kansas, John Brown spent the next few years raising money in New England, which would bring him into direct contact with important abolitionist leaders, including Frederick Douglass. Brown had previously organized a small raiding party that succeeded in raiding a Missouri farm and freeing 11 slaves, but he set his sights on far larger objectives. In 1859, Brown began to set a new plan in motion that he hoped would create a full scale slave uprising in the South. Brown's plan relied on raiding Harpers Ferry, a strategically located armory in western Virginia that had been the main federal arms depot after the Revolution. Given its proximity to the South, Brown hoped to seize thousands of rifles and move them south, gathering slaves and swelling his numbers as he went. The slaves would then be armed and ready to help free more slaves, inevitably fighting Southern militias along the way.

In recognition of how important escaped slave Frederick Douglass had become among abolitionists, Brown attempted to enlist the support of Douglass by informing him of the plans. While Douglass didn't blow the whistle on Brown, he told Brown that violence would only further enrage the South, and slaveholders might only retaliate further against slaves with devastating consequences. Instead of helping Brown, Douglass dissuaded freed blacks from joining Brown's group because he believed it was doomed to fail.

Despite that, in July 1859, Brown traveled to Harper's Ferry under an assumed name and waited for his recruits, but he struggled to get even 20 people to join him. Rather than call off the plan, however, Brown went ahead with it. That fall, Brown and his men used hundreds of rifles to seize the armory at Harper's Ferry, but the plan went haywire from the start, and word of his attack quickly spread. Local pro-slavery men formed a militia and pinned Brown and his men down while they were still at the armory.

After being called to Harpers Ferry, Robert E. Lee took decisive command of a troop of marines stationed there, surrounded the arsenal, and gave Brown the opportunity to surrender peaceably. When Brown refused, Lee ordered the doors be broken down and Brown taken captive, an affair that reportedly lasted just three minutes. A few of Brown's men were killed, but Brown was taken alive. Lee earned acclaim for accomplishing this task so quickly and efficiently.

Young JEB Stuart played an active role in opposing the raid at Harpers Ferry. In October of 1859, while conducting business in Washington, D.C., Stuart volunteered to carry secret instructions to Lieutenant Colonel Robert E. Lee and then accompany him and a squad of U. S. Military Militia to Harpers Ferry, where Brown had staged a raid on the armory. While delivering Lee's written ultimatum to the leader of the raid, who was going by the pseudonym Isaac Smith, Stuart remembered "Old Ossawatomie Brown" from the events at Bleeding Kansas, and ultimately assisted in his arrest.

The fallout from John Brown's raid on Harpers Ferry was intense. Southerners had long suspected that abolitionists hoped to arm the slaves and use violence to abolish slavery, and Brown's raid seemed to confirm that. Meanwhile, much of the northern press praised Brown for his actions. In the South, conspiracy theories ran wild about who had supported the raid, and many believed prominent abolitionist Republicans had been behind the raid as well. On the day of his execution, Brown wrote, "I, John Brown, am now quite *certain* that the crimes of this *guilty land* will never be purged away but with *blood.* I had, as I now think vainly, flattered myself that without very much bloodshed it might be done."

The man in command of the troops present at Brown's hanging was none other than Thomas Jonathan Jackson, who was ordered to Charlestown in November 1859. After Brown's hanging, the future Stonewall Jackson began to believe war was inevitable, but he wrote his aunt, "I think we have great reason for alarm, but my trust is in God; and I cannot think that He will permit the madness of men to interfere so materially with the Christian labors of this country at home and abroad."[10]

For his own part, Meade kept track of the political events, despite being far away from the "front lines" of the strife. While he was no doubt a Union man, Meade believed that the best course would be a conservative one, in the hopes of allowing partisans on both sides to step

---

[10]   Davis, Burke. *They Called Him Stonewall: A Life of Lieutenant General T. J. Jackson, C. S. A.* Page 131.

back, catch their breath, and reflect on the direction they were headed. In a sense, Meade's Civil War generalship would follow the same tack, often described as conservative. And like during the Civil War, it would not be conservative leadership that would capture headlines.

The Election of 1860

In his memoirs, General James Longstreet summed up the national mood in the 1850s, likening it to a "war-cloud". "Officers of the Northern and Southern States were anxious to see the portending storm pass by or disperse, and on many occasions we, too, were assured, by those who claimed to look into the future, that the statesman would yet show himself equal to the occasion, and restore confidence among the people."

Longstreet

Clearly men like Longstreet and Meade were hoping at the time for some sort of grand compromise that would avert war, but by the Fall of 1860, everyone could see the "war-cloud" on the horizon. With the election of Republican candidate Abraham Lincoln as president on November 6, 1860, many Southerners considered it the final straw. Someone they knew as a "Black Republican", leader of a party whose central platform was to stop the spread of slavery to new states, was now set to be inaugurated as President in March. Meade was so concerned about the Southern reaction to the potential election of Lincoln that he actually voted against him in 1860, instead voting for John Bell and his running mate, Edward Everett. Coincidentally, it was Everett who would give the keynote address at Gettysburg in 1863, speaking just before Lincoln delivered his immortal Gettysburg Address.

Throughout the fall and winter of 1860, Southern calls for secession became increasingly serious. In a last-ditched effort to save the Union, Kentucky's Senator John Crittenden tried to assume the stateliness of his predecessor Henry Clay. Crittenden, however, proved to be no Henry Clay: his proposal that a Constitutional Amendment reinstate the Missouri Compromise line and extend it to the Pacific failed. President Buchanan supported the measure, but President-Elect Lincoln said he refused to allow the further expansion of slavery under any conditions.

The Crittenden Compromise failed on December 18. Two days later, South Carolina seceded from the Union. President Buchanan sat on his hands, believing the Southern states had no right to secede, but that the Federal government had no effective power to prevent secession. In January, Mississippi, Florida, Alabama, Georgia, Louisiana and Kansas followed South Carolina's lead. The Confederacy was formed on February 4th, in Montgomery, Alabama, with former Secretary of War Jefferson Davis as its President. On February 23rd, Texas joined the Confederacy.

Meade never had any doubt where his loyalties lay. It was noted that Meade "denounced the Southern leaders who were goading their people into civil war. He expressed himself as deploring the necessity of using force, but as believing, if the necessity should come, in the employment promptly and energetically of the whole power of the government to prevent a disruption of the Union. But that necessity had not yet arisen, and so, trying to hope for the best, but fearing the worst, he awaited the event, before which he had no national active course to take, but which, if it should arrive, was to place him face to face with his duty as a patriot, to contribute the full measure of his knowledge as a military man to the salvation of his country."

Chapter 11: The Start of the Civil War

Fort Sumter

Lincoln's predecessor was among those who could see the potential conflict coming from a mile away. As the Confederacy continued to grow during his last months in office, President James Buchanan instructed the federal army to permit the Confederacy to take control of forts in its territory, hoping to avoid a war. Conveniently, this also allowed Southern forces to take control of important forts and land ahead of a potential war, which would make secession and/or a victory in a military conflict easier. Many Southern partisans within the federal government at the end of 1860 took advantage of these opportunities to help Southern states ahead of time.

One of the forts in the South was Fort Sumter, an important but undermanned and undersupplied fort in the harbor of Charleston, South Carolina. Buchanan attempted to resupply Fort Sumter in the first few months of 1860, but the attempt failed when Southern sympathizers in the harbor fired on the resupply ship.

In his Inauguration Speech, President Lincoln struck a moderate tone. Unlike most

Inauguration Addresses, which are typically followed by balls and a "honeymoon" period, Lincoln's came amid a major political crisis. To reassure the South, he reiterated his belief in the legal status of slavery in the South, but that its expansion into the Western territories was to be restricted. He outlined the illegality of secession and refused to acknowledge the South's secession, and promised to continue to deliver U.S. mail in the seceded states. Most importantly, he pledged to not use force unless his obligation to protect Federal property was restricted: "In doing this there needs to be no bloodshed or violence, and there shall be none unless it be forced upon the national authority. The power confided to me will be used to hold, occupy, and posess the property and places belonging to the Government and to collect the duties and imposts; but beyond what may be necessary for these objects, there will be no invasion, no using of force against or among the people anywhere."[11]

Lincoln had promised that it would not be the North that started a potential war, but he was also aware of the possibility of the South initiating conflict. Although he vowed not to fire the first shot, Lincoln was likely aware that his attempt to resupply Fort Sumter in Charleston Harbor would draw Southern fire; it had already happened under Buchanan's watch. After his inauguration, President Lincoln informed South Carolina governor Francis Pickens that he was sending supplies to the undermanned garrison at Fort Sumter. When Lincoln made clear that he would attempt to resupply the fort, Davis ordered Beauregard to demand its surrender and prevent the resupplying of the garrison.

In early April, the ship Lincoln sent to resupply the fort was fired upon and turned around. On April 9, Confederate President Davis sent word to General Beauregard to demand the fort's evacuation. At the time, the federal garrison consisted of Major Robert Anderson, Beauregard's artillery instructor from West Point, and 76 troops. Even before the bombardment, upon learning that he was opposed by Beauregard, Anderson remarked that the Southern forces in Charleston harbor would be exercised with "skill and sound judgment". Beauregard also remembered his former superior, and before the bombardment, he sent brandy, whiskey and cigars to Anderson and his garrison, gifts the Major refused.

At 4:30 a.m. on the morning of April 12, 1861, Beauregard ordered the first shots to be fired at Fort Sumter, effectively igniting the Civil War. After nearly 34 hours and thousands of rounds fired from 47 artillery guns and mortars ringing the harbor, on April 14, 1861, Major Anderson surrendered Fort Sumter, marking the first Confederate victory. No casualties were suffered on either side during the dueling bombardments across Charleston harbor, but, ironically, two Union soldiers were killed by an accidental explosion during the surrender ceremonies.

---

11 "Abraham Lincoln, First Inaugural Address." *Presidents: Every Question Answered.* Page 322.

Beauregard

After the attack on Fort Sumter, support for both the northern and southern cause rose. Two days later, Lincoln issued a *call-to-arms* asking for 75,000 volunteers. That led to the secession of Virginia, Tennessee, North Carolina, and Arkansas, with the loyalty of border states like Kentucky, Maryland, and Missouri still somewhat up in the air. The large number of southern sympathizers in these states buoyed the Confederates' hopes that those too would soon join the South. Moreover, the loss of these border states, especially Virginia, all deeply depressed Lincoln. Just weeks before, prominent Virginians had reassured Lincoln that the state's historic place in American history made its citizens eager to save the Union. But as soon as Lincoln made any assertive moves to save the Union, Virginia seceded. This greatly concerned Lincoln, who worried Virginia's secession made it more likely other border states and/or Maryland would secede as well.

Despite the loss of Fort Sumter, the North expected a relatively quick victory. Their expectations weren't unrealistic, due to the Union's overwhelming economic advantages over the South. At the start of the war, the Union had a population of over 22 million. The South had a population of 9 million, nearly 4 million of whom were slaves. Union states contained 90% of the manufacturing capacity of the country and 97% of the weapon manufacturing capacity. Union states also possessed over 70% of the total railroads in the pre-war United States at the start of the war, and the Union also controlled 80% of the shipbuilding capacity of the pre-war United States.

However, like William Tecumseh Sherman, Longstreet was among the few who thought the

Civil War would last a long time. "Speaking of the impending struggle, I was asked as to the length of the war, and said, 'At least three years, and if it holds for five you may begin to look for a dictator,' at which Lieutenant Ryan, of the Seventh Infantry, said, 'If we are to have a dictator, I hope that you may be the man.'"

Although the North blockaded the South throughout the Civil War and eventually controlled the entire Mississippi River by 1863, the war could not be won without land battles, which doomed hundreds of thousands of soldiers on each side. This is because the Civil War generals began the war employing tactics from the Napoleonic Era, which saw Napoleon dominate the European continent and win crushing victories against large armies. However, the weapons available in 1861 were far more accurate than they had been 50 years earlier. In particular, new rifled barrels created common infantry weapons with deadly accuracy of up to 100 yards, at a time when generals were still leading massed infantry charges with fixed bayonets and attempting to march their men close enough to engage in hand-to-hand combat.

Lee Chooses Sides

By the Fall of 1860, however, everyone could see the "war-cloud" on the horizon. Despite having virtually zero support in the slave states, Abraham Lincoln ascended to the presidency at the head of a party that was not yet 10 years old, and one whose stated goal was to end the expansion of slavery. Although Lincoln did not vow to abolish slavery altogether, southerners believed Lincoln's presidency constituted a direct threat to the South's economy and political power, both of which were fueled by the slave system. Southerners also perceived the end of the expansion of slavery as a threat to their constitutional rights, and the rights of their states, frequently invoking northern states' refusals to abide by the Fugitive Slave Act. With the election of Republican candidate Abraham Lincoln as president on November 6, 1860, many Southerners considered it the final straw. Someone they knew as a "Black Republican" was now set to be inaugurated as President in March.

Throughout the fall and winter of 1860, Southern calls for secession became increasingly serious. In a last-ditched effort to save the Union, Kentucky's Senator John Crittenden tried to assume the stateliness of his predecessor Henry Clay. Crittenden, however, proved to be no Henry Clay: his proposal that a Constitutional Amendment reinstate the Missouri Compromise line and extend it to the Pacific failed. President Buchanan supported the measure, but President-Elect Lincoln said he refused to allow the further expansion of slavery under any conditions.

The Crittenden Compromise failed on December 18. Two days later, South Carolina seceded from the Union. President Buchanan sat on his hands, believing the Southern states had no right to secede, but that the Federal government had no effective power to prevent secession. In January, Mississippi, Florida, Alabama, Georgia, Louisiana and Kansas followed South Carolina's lead. The Confederacy was formed on February 4th, in Montgomery, Alabama, with former Secretary of War Jefferson Davis as its President. On February 23rd, Texas joined the Confederacy.

Jefferson Davis

When Texas seceded from the Union in 1861, Lee was recalled to Washington to await orders while an appropriate response was formulated. A devout admirer of George Washington and the monumental self-sacrifice he'd made to establish the Union, Lee hated the idea of a divided nation. Thus, he began to see his destiny as protecting the freedom, liberty, and legal principles for which Washington had so gallantly risked his life. Even so, he suffered great trepidation in choosing between standing with his native Virginia and the Northern Union, should it come down to a civil war, especially when President Lincoln would offer Lee command of the United States Army.

In a letter to his sister Lee wrote, " …in my own person I had to meet the question whether I should take part against my native state…with all my devotion to the Union, and the feeling of loyalty and duty of an American citizen, I have not been able to make up my mind to raise my hand against my relatives, my children, my home. I have therefore resigned my commission in the army, and, save in defense of my native state--with the sincere hope I may never be called upon to draw my sword."[12]

---

[12]   Dowdey, Clifford (editor). *The Wartime Papers of R. E. Lee.* Page 9.

Lee grieved his choice to break with his men, and particularly General Scott, whom he considered a close, personal friend. Ultimately, however, just as Washington had chosen to separate himself from the British Empire, Lee chose to separate from the Union to fight what the South regarded a second war of independence. And once he chose sides, Lee never looked back.

Longstreet Chooses Sides

Although Major James Longstreet was not enthusiastic about the idea of states' secession from the Union, he had learned from his uncle Augustus about the doctrine of states' rights early in his life and seen his uncle's passion for it.

Historically-speaking, there are two quite divergent accounts of Longstreet's entry into the Confederate Army at the start of the War. One states that although born in South Carolina and reared in Georgia, Longstreet offered his services to the state of Alabama (which had appointed him to West Point and where his mother had lived). Thus, as the senior West Point graduate from that state, he was automatically commissioned a rank commensurate with that state's policy. Other accounts, however, assert that Longstreet deliberately traveled to Richmond, Virginia - not Alabama - and offered his services as a paymaster of the new Confederate army. Perhaps, both scenarios are somehow true.

Here's how Longstreet remembered the early days of the Civil War in his memoirs: "When mail-day came the officers usually assembled on the flat roof of the quartermaster's office to look for the dust that in that arid climate announced the coming mail-wagon when five or ten miles away; but affairs continued to grow gloomy, and eventually came information of the attack upon and capture of Fort Sumter by the Confederate forces, which put down speculation and drew the long-dreaded line. A number of officers of the post called to persuade me to remain in the Union service. Captain Gibbs, of the Mounted Rifles, was the principal talker, and after a long but pleasant discussion, I asked him what course he would pursue if his State should pass ordinances of secession and call him to its defence. He confessed that he would obey the call. It was a sad day when we took leave of lifetime comrades and gave up a service of twenty years. Neither Union officers nor their families made efforts to conceal feelings of deepest regret. When we drove out from the post, a number of officers rode with us, which only made the last farewell more trying."

In any regard, on June 17 1861, Major Longstreet resigned from the U. S. Army and on June 22 he met with Confederate President Jefferson Davis at the executive mansion, where he was informed that he had been appointed a brigadier general, a commission he accepted on June 25.

Stuart Chooses Sides

On April 22, 1861, First Lieutenant Stuart received a commission as captain in the U. S. Army, but this came 10 days after the assault on Fort Sumter, recognized as the beginning of the Civil War. After Abraham Lincoln's election in 1860, a handful of Southern states had already seceded, and Virginia would join them after Sumter. By the time Stuart received the promotion, he was already determined to fight with Virginia, and thus the Confederacy, in the civil conflict. A little over a week later, in early May, he tendered his resignation from the Federal army.

Moving his family to Virginia, on May 10, 1861, "Jeb" was commissioned a lieutenant colonel of the Virginia Infantry. Meanwhile, his father-in-law, Philip St. George Cooke, chose not to resign his Army commission, prompting Stuart to write his wife that it would "do irreparable injury to our only son" to have him named after Cooke. "Jeb" wrote to his brother-in-law (future Confederate Brig. General John Rogers Cooke) saying, "[Philip] will regret it but once, and that will be continuously."[13] After consideration, "Jeb" and Flora renamed the boy, James Ewell Brown Stuart, Jr., an obvious indicator of his disgust with his father-in-law's political views.

Colonel Cooke

Once Jeb left for Richmond to join the fighting, Flora settled in at Wytheville, Virginia, arranging to sometimes stay at or near her husband's camp where they could share meals, music, and conversation. Even so, their frequent separations strained their relationship, and it didn't help that in addition to writing frequently to his wife, "Jeb" also carried on correspondences with other women attracted to his fame. Although the couple acknowledged these exchanges as "insubstantial flirtations," Flora detested the photographs and gifts the women sent, and wrote of feeling laughed at for her husband's fondness for society and the ladies. But by all other accounts, "Jeb" was a thoughtful and romantic husband who always carried his wife's photograph in a silver frame near his heart.

---

[13]   Wright, C. M. "Flora Cooke Stuart (1836–1923)."

On November 3, 1862, while "Jeb" was with the Army of Northern Virginia during the early stages of what would become the Fredericksburg campaign, their daughter Flora died of typhoid fever. In the following weeks, Stuart wrote that his wife was "not herself since the loss of her little companion." The following October, their daughter Virginia Pelham was born--both easing the pain and intensifying the loss. Flora wrote, "She is said to be like Little Flora. I hope she is."[14]

Meade and Hancock Seek Active Duty

In the wake of Fort Sumter, Captain Meade repeatedly asked the government to assign him to active duty, but he received no official response. Thus, during the opening months of the Civil War, Captain George Gordon Meade continued to serve in his capacity as a captain of engineers, until his frustration finally boiled over. In June, 1861, Meade headed to Washington of his own accord and protested against being kept in charge of the Great Lakes survey. Meade hoped to join one of the many new regiments being raised and mustered, but his repeated requests continued to be denied, forcing him to eventually return to Detroit.

As it turned out, it would be his wife's connections that got Meade an opening. Trading on his wife's considerable political connections, he was taken under consideration for command of a brigade of Pennsylvania volunteers. On August 31, 1861, Meade was promoted from captain to brigadier general of volunteers, based primarily on the recommendation of Pennsylvania Governor Andrew Curtin, not merit or experience. Meade was assigned to the division commanded by Major-General George A. McCall, known as the Pennsylvania Reserves.

In command of the Second Brigade of the Pennsylvania Reserves, from late 1861 until mid-1862, Meade led the construction of defenses around Washington, D. C. and near Tenallytown, Maryland. While there, he developed a friendship with John F. Reynolds of Lancaster, Pennsylvania, who would play an integral role in the fighting on the first day of the Battle of Gettysburg. It also didn't take long for Meade to earn the nickname "The Old Snapping Turtle" by his men, both for his personality and physical appearance. Already, Brigadier General Meade was quickly gaining a well-deserved reputation for being testy, short-tempered, and obstinate with both junior officers and his superiors.

---

[14]   Thomas, Emory M. *Bold Dragoon: The Life of J.E.B. Stuart.* Page 95.

Reynolds

At the outbreak of the Civil War, Captain Winfield Scott Hancock was the chief quartermaster of the military depot in Los Angeles, in southern California. Hancock hosted a farewell dinner for the comrades who were departing California to join the Confederate Army, but he was an ardent Union man, and he went about helping secure Los Angeles from the Californians who favored and planned to support the South.

When Captain Hancock traveled east to get involved in the war effort in September 1861, he expected to assume quartermaster duties for the rapidly growing Union Army. Upon arrival in Washington, D. C. on September 23, 1861, however, General McClellan appointed him a brigadier general of infantry volunteers in Brig. General William F. "Baldy" Smith's division in the newly organized Army of the Potomac.

Chamberlain's Opinion on the Subject of Civil War

When talk of civil war reached the world of academia--which by this time had virtually enveloped the young Professor Chamberlain--Lawrence felt no ambiguity whatsoever about the Union needing support by all those willing and able to resist the Confederate "uprising." And while the events of 1861--the bombardment of Fort Sumter and President Lincoln's call for volunteers--had very little direct effect on the college, word of the Union's many defeats brought increasing concern for Lawrence.

While Lawrence strongly disapproved of slavery on moral and religious grounds, his bigger consternation was the secession (the *betrayal*) of the Southern states which had first pledged themselves to a unified government but now threatened to break that concord in favor of individual rights--which he saw as a threat to not just the laws of man, but the laws of "God."

On several occasions, Professor Chamberlain spoke openly of his beliefs concerning the War, urging students to follow their hearts regarding the conflict, but unwavering in his own proclamation that he believed the cause was just. (Of Bowdoin's approximately twelve hundred member student body, two hundred ninety would ultimately serve in the Union Army.)

Expressing his obligation to serve the Union in the War, Chamberlain wrote to Maine's Governor Israel Washburn, Jr., saying, "I fear, this war, so costly of blood and treasure, will not cease until men of the North are willing to leave good positions, and sacrifice the dearest personal interests, to rescue our country from desolation, and defend the national existence against treachery."[15] Though Bowdoin faculty tried to convince him that his true duty and obligation lay in the education of the young men who represented the American future, and that he should help preserve life instead of destroy it, Lawrence's conviction to the Union struggle only continued to increase.

Chapter 12: The First Battle of Bull Run (First Manassas)

Although Lee, Stuart, and Longstreet were destined to become 3 of the most famous soldiers of the Confederates' most famous army, they all took different paths to get there. And of the 3, it was Robert E. Lee who wasn't part of the first major battle of the war, the First Battle of Bull Run or Manassas.

On May 10, 1861, Stuart was commissioned a lieutenant colonel of the Virginia Infantry and ordered by Maj. General Robert E. Lee to report to Colonel Thomas J. Jackson at Harpers Ferry. Stuart's reputation had clearly made the rounds, because when he reported to the man who would months later become Stonewall Jackson, Jackson ignored Stuart's infantry designation and instead assigned him command of all the cavalry companies of the Army of the Shenandoah, organized as the First Virginia Cavalry Regiment. Thus, on July 4, 1861, Jeb Stuart began his service in the Confederate cavalry, less than 3 weeks before the First Battle of Bull Run.

Although Stuart would soon appear in his trademark flamboyant line attire--a scarlet-lined gray cape, yellow sash, hat cocked to the side displaying a peacock plume, jack boots, gauntlets, red flower in his lapel, and full red beard doused with cologne (reminiscent of commanders of the Napoleonic era)--when he accepted his Confederate commission, he was still wearing his Federal uniform and would do so even as he fought at Falling Waters, Virginia, on July 2, 1861. And

---

[15]   Desjardin, Thomas A. "Why People Admire Joshua Lawrence Chamberlain."

while most Confederate officers were somehow distinguishable on the battlefield, Stuart--whose horse "Highfly" soon became as famous as his extraordinary rider--became one of the most visually stunning.

Quickly becoming one of the most dominant commanders in the field, on July 16, Stuart was promoted to Full Colonel of the First Virginia Cavalry.

Ordered to report to Brig. General P.G.T. Beauregard at Manassas, Brig. General Longstreet was given command of a brigade of three regiments—the First, Eleventh, and Seventeenth Virginia Infantry. Immediately assembling his staff, Longstreet trained his brigade incessantly and within just a few weeks had trained his "green" recruits in close-order drill and battlefield maneuvers. Though considered a dogged combat trainer and able defensive commander, ultimately, his field tactics would make him the object of great controversy before the War's end.

After Fort Sumter, the Lincoln Administration pushed for a quick invasion of Virginia, with the intent of defeating Confederate forces and marching toward the Confederate capitol of Richmond. Lincoln pressed Irvin McDowell to push forward. Despite the fact that McDowell knew his troops were inexperienced and unready, pressure from the Washington politicians forced him to launch a premature offensive against Confederate forces in Northern Virginia. His strategy during the First Battle of Bull Run was grand, but it proved far too difficult for his inexperienced troops to carry out effectively.

McDowell

In late Spring 1861, Davis ordered Beauregard to northern Virginia as second-in-command to

General Joseph E. Johnston, where he was to oppose the federal forces building up under McDowell. Though Johnston was the superior in rank, he ceded authority to Beauregard near Manassas Junction, leaving Beauregard in command there. At Manassas, Beauregard took charge of the Confederate forces assembling near the rail junction at Manassas and had his men construct defenses along a 14 mile front along Bull Run Creek. Meanwhile, Johnston was gathering and training additional troops in the Shenandoah Valley.

Joseph E. Johnston

McDowell's strategy during the First Battle of Bull Run was grand, and in many ways it was the forerunner of a tactic Lee and Stonewall Jackson executed brilliantly on nearly the same field during the Second Battle of Bull Run or Manassas in August 1862. McDowell's plan called for parts of his army to pin down Beauregard's Confederate soldiers in front while marching another wing of his army around the flank and into the enemy's rear, rolling up the line. McDowell assumed the Confederates would be forced to abandon Manassas Junction and fall back to the next defensible line, the Rappahannock River. In July 1861, however, this proved far too difficult for his inexperienced troops to carry out effectively.

On July 18, Union General Irwin McDowell set out with two divisions on a twelve-mile circuitous march west from Centreville, Virginia to cross Bull Run at Sudley Springs Ford, intending to strike Beauregard's troops at Manassas-Sudley Road in an effort to turn the Southern left flank. Meanwhile, another division was set to drive directly west along the turnpike and across Stone Bridge, while back at Centreville, another division stayed in reserve. The remaining division, scattered along the lines of communication all the way back to

Washington but would ultimately take no part in the ensuing battle, made a total of 32,000 men at McDowell's disposal.

Longstreet's new recruits achieved one of the first Confederate victories, seeing action at Blackburn's Ford on July 18 and successfully stopping the lead Union division in its march towards Manassas. And unbeknownst to McDowell, several days earlier, General Beauregard had received advance warning of troop movement from a civilian and had forwarded a coded message to Jefferson Davis along with a request to move General Joseph E. Johnston and his 12,000 men from the Shenandoah Valley to Manassas, via rail. Beauregard's intelligence placed the Union Army within attack position by July 17.

The First Battle of Bull Run made history in several ways. McDowell's army met Fort Sumter hero P.G.T. Beauregard's Confederate army near the railroad junction at Manassas on July 21, 1861. Located just 25 miles away from Washington D.C., many civilians from Washington came to watch what they expected to be a rout of Confederate forces. And for awhile, it appeared as though that might be the case.

McDowell's strategy fell apart though, thanks to railroads. Confederate reinforcements under General Joseph E. Johnston's Army, including JEB Stuart's cavalrymen and a brigade led by Thomas Jonathan Jackson, arrived by train in the middle of the day, a first in the history of American warfare. With Johnston's army arriving midday on July 21, it evened up the numbers between Union and Confederate. Shoring up the Confederates' left flank, some of Johnston's troops, led by Jackson's brigade, helped reverse the Union's momentum and ultimately turn the tide. As the battle's momentum switched, the inexperienced Union troops were routed and retreated in disorder back toward Washington in an unorganized mass. With over 350 killed on each side, it was the deadliest battle in American history to date, and both the Confederacy and the Union were quickly served notice that the war would be much more costly than either side had believed.

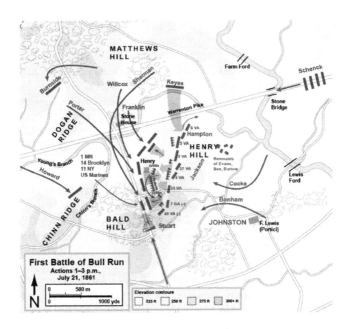

First Battle of Bull Run
Actions 1–3 p.m.,
July 21, 1861

N

0   500 m
0   1000 yds

Elevation contours
225 ft   250 ft   275 ft   300+ ft

Ironically, McDowell commanded the Army of Northeastern Virginia and Joseph E. Johnston commanded the Army of the Potomac at First Bull Run. A little over a year later it would be Lee's Army of Northern Virginia fighting elements of the Union Army of the Potomac at Second Bull Run, on nearly the same ground.

It was also during First Manassas or Bull Run that Jackson earned the famous nickname "Stonewall", but there is an enduring mystery over the origin of his nickname. What is known is that during the battle, Jackson's brigade arrived as reinforcements at a crucial part of the battlefield on the Confederate left. Confederate Brigadier General Barnard Bee, commanding a nearby brigade, commanded his men to reestablish their battle line next to Jackson's brigade, shouting, "There is Jackson standing like a stone wall. Rally behind the Virginians." General Bee was mortally wounded shortly after that command and died the following day. Thus, it remains unclear whether Bee was complimenting Jackson's brigade for standing firm or whether he was criticizing Jackson's brigade for inaction. Without Bee around to explain his command, nobody will ever know for certain. However, that has not stopped people from debating Bee's comment. Regardless, the nickname Stonewall stuck, and Jackson was henceforth known as Stonewall Jackson. His brigade also inherited the title, known throughout the war as the Stonewall brigade.

Longstreet's brigade played almost no role in the fighting on July 21, other than having to sustain artillery fire for several hours. But when the Union army was routed and began fleeing in a disorganized panic, Longstreet was incensed that his commanders did not attempt to pursue the disorganized federal troops running back toward Washington. Longstreet's staff officer, Moxley Sorrel, later wrote that Longstreet "dashed his hat furiously to the ground, stamped, and bitter words escaped him."

Jackson eventually emerged as the man who gained the most fame during the battle, but others at the time thought the man of the hour was Jeb Stuart. When Jackson's brigade turned the tide, Stuart then executed a highly-aggressive charge during which, "[the] Confederate cavalry-men were armed with costly English shot guns, which they held at the breast and fired (both barrels at once) as they approached . . . ."[16] In a panic, many of McDowell's men ran frantically toward Washington, with Stuart's cavalry among the units pursuing them some 12 miles, and subsequently taking the Union headquarters on Munson's hill (within sight of Washington). Of this remarkable Confederate victory, General Jubal Early, who served under Stonewall Jackson, wrote: "Stuart did as much toward saving the Battle of First Manassas as any subordinate who participated in it."[17]

From this point on, Stuart's celebrity grew, and he became known as Stuart "the brash," Stuart "the fearless," Stuart the "*beau sabreur*" of mounted infantry."

Chapter 13: Lee vs. McClellan, Part 1

Today Lee is remembered as the Civil War's greatest general, and George B. McClellan is often derided as one of the Union's most ineffective generals. And most associate Lee with the Army of Northern Virginia, which he came to command in the summer of 1862 and defeat McClellan in the Seven Days Battles. However, in 1861, it was McClellan that got the best of Lee.

Though Lee took no direct part in the first battle at Manassas (Bull Run) in July of 1861, he was tasked with saving western Virginia from Union forces under General George B. McClellan who'd defeated Confederate troops in Kanawha Valley. Bad weather, poorly trained men, and lack of cooperation among his officers, however, ultimately led to a dismal defeat for Lee. With the Union taking control of western Virginia, Lee considered the campaign a miserable, personal failure, and western Virginia would formally become the new state of West Virginia and part of the Union in 1863.

Given such a crushing defeat at the beginning of the war, that might have been the end of Lee's

---

[16]   Stepp, John W. & Hill, William I. (editors), *Mirror of War, the Washington Star Reports the Civil War*. Page 145.
[17]   Sifakis, Stewart, "Who Was Who In The Civil War."

Civil War career. However, Jefferson Davis's faith in Lee's abilities ensured it was just the beginning. It's quite possible that Lee was saved by his past association with Davis at West Point. History has accorded Abraham Lincoln a spot in the pantheon of American politics for the manner in which he steered the Union to victory and into the Reconstruction period after the war. In turn, Davis has been heavily criticized. While Jefferson Davis had personal favorites like Lee and Albert Sidney Johnston, Davis constantly clashed with other Confederate generals like Joseph Johnston, which led to often discombobulated war strategy. At the same time, part of the Confederacy's raison d'etre was that the federal government was too centralized, so the decentralized nature of the Southern states hampered Davis's ability to manage and coordinate the war effort.

Though only a few months into the war, by August 1861, things were already going badly for the South. Although eyes remained intently focused on the Eastern theater, with the two capitals (Washington D.C. and Richmond) located within 100 miles of each other, several forts to the west had fallen to General Ulysses S. Grant, most of Kentucky and a large portion of Tennessee were all but abandoned, and Confederate general Joseph E. Johnson was planning a draw back from Manassas after the battle there. Equally disheartening, European recognition didn't come as expected, and supplies were already running dangerously low.

At this point, Jefferson Davis put Lee in command of the southeastern coast of the Confederacy, an area under imminent threat from a Union unit out of Hampton Roads near Norfolk. Mustering what was becoming Lee's trademark determination, he took decisive action by enlisting more troops, establishing blockades at all access points, and establishing an inner line of defense beyond the reach of Union naval guns. Lee quickly and decisively brought an abrupt halt to the advance of Union forces.

Chapter 14: The End of 1861

On October 7, 1861, Longstreet was promoted to major general and assumed command of a division in the newly reorganized Confederate Army of Northern Virginia. He was now in command of 4 infantry brigades and Hampton's Legion.

Though he had attained personal success thus far, he suffered personal tragedy in January 1862 due to a scarlet fever epidemic in Richmond that killed his one-year-old daughter Mary Anne, his four-year-old son James, and six-year-old son Augustus ("Gus"), all in the span of a week. Understandably depressed, Longstreet became personally withdrawn and melancholy, turning to religion. Those close to him and who served under him noted the change in camp around him after January 1862. What had once been a boisterous headquarters that tolerated partying and poker games had become a solemn, somber and more devout one.

Brigadier General Stuart

After commanding the Confederate Army's outposts along the upper Potomac River at Fairfax Court House and Munson's Hill, Stuart was then given command of the cavalry of the ironically named Army of the Potomac, which eventually became the Army of Northern Virginia. On September 24, 1861, Stuart was promoted to Brigadier General. Among those advocating his promotion was General Joseph E. Johnston who in August wrote to Confederate President Jefferson Davis saying: "[Stuart] is a rare man, wonderfully endowed by nature with the qualities necessary for an officer of light cavalry. Calm, firm, acute, active, and enterprising, I know no one more competent than he to estimate the occurrences before him at their true value. If you add to this army a real brigade of cavalry, you can find no better brigadier-general to command it."[18]

Chapter 15: The Beginning of the Peninsula Campaign

Planning the Peninsula Campaign

Historians who are critical of George B. McClellan's generalship in the field are unanimous in their praise of McClellan's organizational skills. Displaying outstanding organizational and logistical skills, General McClellan quickly whipped the disheartened Union Army into a tight-knit fighting unit with high morale, a highly efficient staff, and optimal supporting services. Just as much, the nearly 175,000 man army loved "Little Mac". With the work of engineers like Meade, McClellan also turned Washington D.C. into the most fortified spot on the continent, ringing it with forts that would make the city all but invulnerable to attack if manned.

---

[18]   Wert, Jeffry D. *Cavalryman of the Lost Cause: A Biography of J.E.B. Stuart.* Page 62.

McClellan

All that now lay ahead was for McClellan to take the offensive Lincoln had entrusted in him; to march his men into the Southern states and capture Richmond--and demolish Confederate forces in the process. But even by the fall of 1861, Little Mac, as he was now commonly called, still refused to follow President Lincoln's mandate, claiming that his army was still unprepared. Displaying both arrogance and reluctance to fight, McClellan demanded more men, supplies, and time to better prepare, refusing to even meet with the President to share his plan of attack on the Confederate capital. As Lincoln's frustrations began to grow, McClellan's stated opposition to emancipation of slaves angered the Radical Republicans who comprised an important bloc in Congress. Meade understood how the game worked, even if he would never bother playing it, confiding in a letter to his wife in 1862, "War is a game of chance, and besides the chances of service, the accidents and luck of the field, in our army, an officer has to run the chances of having his political friends in power, or able to work for him."

Finally, in March of 1862, after nine months in command, General McClellan began his invasion of Virginia, initiating what would become known as the "Peninsula Campaign." Showing his proclivity for turning movement and grand strategy, McClellan completely shifted the theater of operations. Rather than march directly into Richmond and use his superior numbers to assert domination, he opted to exploit the Union sea dominance and move his army via an immense naval flotilla down the Potomac into Chesapeake Bay and land at Fort Monroe in Hampton, Virginia—at the southern tip of the Virginia Peninsula. In addition to his 130,000 thousand men, he moved 15,000 thousand horses and mules by this means as well. There he planned for an additional 80,000 men to join him, at which time he would advance westward to Richmond. One of the European observers likened the launch of the campaign to the "stride of a giant."

McClellan's Peninsula Campaign has been analyzed meticulously and is considered one of the grandest failures of the Union war effort, with McClellan made the scapegoat. In actuality, there was plenty of blame to go around, including Lincoln and his Administration, which was so concerned about Stonewall Jackson's army in the Shenandoah Valley that several Union armies were left in the Valley to defend Washington D.C., and even more were held back from McClellan for fear of the capital's safety. The Administration also micromanaged the deployment of certain divisions, and with Stanton's decision to shut down recruiting stations in early 1862, combined with the Confederacy concentrating all their troops in the area, the Army of the Potomac was eventually outnumbered in front of Richmond.

At the beginning of the campaign, however, McClellen had vastly superior numbers at his disposal, with only about 70,000 Confederate troops on the entirety of the peninsula and fewer than 17,000 between him and the Capital). McClellan was unaware of this decisive advantage, however, because of the intelligence reports he kept receiving from Allen Pinkerton, which vastly overstated the number of available Confederate soldiers.

Meanwhile, Lee was called to Richmond in March 1862 and became part of Jefferson Davis's inner circle. At this time, his primary job was to mediate between feuding generals. While some Southern generals, including Lee, believed troops should be shifted as needed to meet new threats, General Johnston insisted that all troops should be concentrated around Richmond as preparation for a final showdown.

Yorktown

From the beginning, McClellan's caution and the narrow width of the Peninsula worked against his army. At Yorktown, which had been the site of a decisive siege during the Revolution, McClellan's initial hopes of surrounding and enveloping the Confederate lines through the use of the Navy was scuttled when the Navy couldn't promise that it'd be able to operate in the area. That allowed General John Magruder, whose Confederate forces were outmanned nearly 4-1, to hold Yorktown for the entire month of April. Magruder accomplished it by completely deceiving the federals, at times marching his men in circles to make McClellan think his army was many times larger. Other times, he spread his artillery batteries across the line and fired liberally and sporadically at the Union lines, just to give the impression that the Confederates had huge numbers. The ruse worked, leaving the Union command thinking there were 100,000 Confederates.

As a result of the misimpressions, McClellan chose not to attack Yorktown in force, instead opting to lay siege to it. In part, this was due to the decisive advantage the Union had in siege equipment, including massive mortars and artillery. The siege successfully captured Yorktown in early May with only about 500 casualties, but Magruder bought enough time for General Joseph E. Johnston to march south and confront McClellan on the Peninsula.

During the Civil War, one of the tales that was often told among Confederate soldiers was that Joseph E. Johnston was a crack shot who was a better bird hunter than just about everyone else in the South. However, as the story went, Johnston would never take the shot when asked to, complaining that something was wrong with the situation that prevented him from being able to shoot the bird when it was time. The story is almost certainly apocryphal, used to demonstrate the Confederates' frustration with a man who everyone regarded as a capable general. Johnston began the Civil War as one of the senior commanders, leading (ironically) the Army of the Potomac to victory in the Battle of First Bull Run over Irvin McDowell's Union Army. But Johnston would become known more for losing by not winning. Johnston was never badly beaten in battle, but he had a habit of "strategically withdrawing" until he had nowhere else to go.

Williamsburg

As chance would have it, the first Union general to distinguish himself during the Peninsula Campaign was none other than Winfield Scott Hancock, who experienced his first major action of the Civil War on May 5, 1862 at the Battle of Williamsburg, Virginia.

After withdrawing from Yorktown, McClellan sent Stoneman's cavalry in pursuit and attempted to move swiftly enough to cut off Johnston's retreat by use of Navy ships. At the battle of Williamsburg, which the Confederates fought as a delaying action to retreat, Hancock led his brigade in a successful flanking attack against General Longstreet's Confederates and quickly occupied two abandoned Confederate strongholds. Hancock's brigade then sharply repulsed a Confederate assault by the 24th Virginia regiment.

At this point, Hancock had been ordered by General Edwin "Bull" Sumner to pull back his men to Cub Creek, but he instead decided to hold his ground, and his men repulsed an assault by the 5th North Carolina regiment in short order. As Confederate General D.H. Hill scrambled to stop that regiment's assault, Hancock's men counterattacked and drove them off the field, inflicting nearly 1,000 casualties on the two regiments that had attacked his brigade and losing just 100.

The Battle of Williamsburg was ultimately inconclusive, with the Confederates suffering 1600 casualties and the Army of the Potomac suffering 2200, but McClellan labeled it a "brilliant victory" over superior forces. While that was inaccurate, the press accounts of Hancock's performance fairly earned him national renown, and McClellan telegraphed Washington to report, "Hancock was superb today." Hancock had just forever won the nickname "Hancock the Superb".

The Battle of Fair Oaks or Seven Pines

After Williamsburg, the Union army still had a nearly 2-1 advantage in manpower, so Johnston continued to gradually pull his troops back to a line of defense nearer Richmond as McClellan advanced. In conjunction, the U.S. Navy began moving its operations further up the James River, until it could get within 7 miles of the Confederate capital before being opposed by a Southern fort. McClellan continued to attempt to turn Johnston's flank, until the two armies were facing each other along the Chickahominy River. McClellan's Army of the Potomac got close enough to Richmond that they could see the city's church steeples.

By the end of May, Stonewall Jackson had startlingly defeated three separate Northern armies in the Valley, inducing Lincoln to hold back the I Corps from McClellan. When McClellan was forced to extend his line north to link up with troops that he expected to be sent overland to him, Johnston learned that McClellan was moving along the Chickahominy River. It was at this point that Johnston got uncharacteristically aggressive. Johnston had run out of breathing space for his army, and he believed McCellan was seeking to link up with McDowell's forces. Moreover, about a third of McClellan's army was south of the river, including Hancock's brigade in the IV Corps, while the other parts of the army were still north of it, offering Johnston an enticing target. Therefore he drew up a very complex plan of attack for different wings of his army, and struck at the Army of the Potomac at the Battle of Seven Pines on May 31, 1862.

Like McDowell's plan for First Bull Run, the plan proved too complicated for Johnston's army to execute, and after a day of bloody fighting little was accomplished from a technical standpoint. At one point during the Battle of Seven Pines, Confederates under General James Longstreet marched in the wrong direction down the wrong road, causing congestion and confusion among other Confederate units and ultimately weakening the effectiveness of the massive Confederate counterattack launched against McClellan. In his official report, Longstreet blamed fellow Maj. General Benjamin Huger for the logistical confusion, an indication of the contention that would follow his personal and military life from that time on.

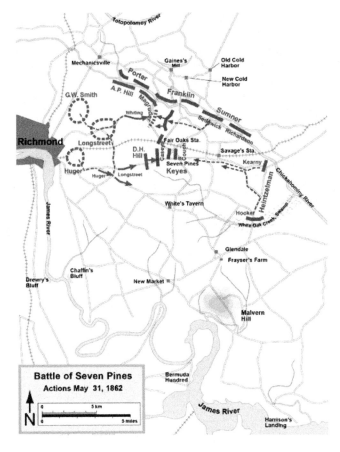

Battle of Seven Pines
Actions May 31, 1862

N

By the time the fighting was finished, nearly 40,000 had been engaged on both sides, and it was the biggest battle in the Eastern theater to date (second only to Shiloh at the time). However, McClellan was rattled by the attack, and Johnston was seriously wounded during the fighting, resulting in military advisor Robert E. Lee being sent to assume command of the Army of Northern Virginia. McClellan confided to his wife, "I am tired of the sickening sight of the battlefield, with its mangled corpses & poor suffering wounded! Victory has no charms for me when purchased at such cost."

Meade had not been part of the fighting at Fair Oaks, and the confusion of the battle and its aftermath were apparent in the letter he wrote to his wife after the battle. "The news of the attempt to break through McClellan's line is looked upon as favorable, inasmuch as the attacking party, having the selection of time and place, could and should have concentrated superior numbers; their failure to succeed proves either their weakness or our superior prowess."

Although the Battle of Seven Pines was tactically inconclusive, McClellan's resolve to keep pushing forward vanished. He maneuvered his army so that it was all south of the Chickahominy, but as he settled in for an expected siege, Lee went about preparing Richmond's defenses and devising his own aggressive attacks.

Stuart's Ride around McClellan

From his first day in command, Lee faced a daunting, seemingly impossible challenge. McClellan had maneuvered nearly 100,000 troops to within seven miles of Richmond, three Union units were closing in on General Jackson's Confederates in Virginia's Shenandoah Valley, and a fourth Union army was camped on the Rappahannock River ostensibly ready to come to McClellan's aid. On June 12, as McClellan sat on Richmond's eastern outskirts waiting for reinforcements, Lee began to ring the city with troop entrenchments. Realizing that McClellan's flank appeared to be exposed, Lee tasked Stuart with assessing whether the Union army had any real protection north and west of the exposed flank. Stuart suggested that his men circumnavigate McClellan's army, to which Lee responded with deference that would become his trademark and a symbol of his trust in his subordinates. Lee gave Stuart unspecifically vague orders:

> "You will return as soon as the object of your expedition is accomplished, and you must bear constantly in mind, while endeavoring to execute the general purpose of your mission, not to hazard unnecessarily your command or to attempt what your judgment may not approve; but be content to accomplish all the good you can without feeling it necessary to obtain all that might be desired. I recommend that you take only such men as can stand the expedition, and that you take every means in your power to save and cherish those you take. You must leave sufficient cavalry here for the service of this army, and remember that one of the chief objects of your expedition is to gain intelligence for the guidance of future operations."

With that, Stuart embarked with 1200 troopers on a spectacular three-day, 150 mile ride in the rear of and around the entire Army of the Potomac, a mission that would require him to keep just ahead of pursuing horsemen led by Union Brig. General Philip St. George Cooke, Stuart's father-in-law. Though daunting and dangerous, Stuart and his men successfully completed the historic ride, with Stuart returning to Richmond to report to Lee on June 14 and most of his cavalry returning the following day. Stuart was able not only to report that McClellan's flank was indeed completely unguarded, he delivered 165 captured Union soldiers, 260 horses and mules, and a collection of quartermaster and ordinance supplies as well. The "ride around

McClellan" proved to be a public relations sensation for Stuart, resulting in dramatic newspaper accounts, hordes of women cheering and strewing flower petals in his path when he rode through the streets of Richmond, and his face appearing on the front pages of most newspapers in both the North and South. The flamboyant officer relished every second of his ride, later writing, "There was something of the sublime in the implicit confidence and unquestioning trust of the rank and file in a leader guiding them straight, apparently, into the very jaws of the enemy, every step appearing to them to diminish the faintest hope of extrication."

Stuart also knew how to cultivate his newfound glory. When Stuart reported to General Lee, he also gave a verbal report to Virginia's governor, who rewarded him with a sword. During one visit to the governor, Stuart gave an impromptu address on the steps of the executive mansion to an assembling crowd, playfully telling them he "had been to the Chickahominy to visit some of his old friends of the United States Army, but they, very uncivilly, turned their backs upon him." The man who wrote the account of that speech also noted Stuart very conspicuously galloped off as the crowd cheered.

Although it was this kind of bombast that would come to color Stuart's legacy and in some ways eclipse his solid work, his men realized just how capable he was. In his 1887 memoirs, Colonel John Singleton Mosby (assigned as a first lieutenant to Stuart's cavalry scouts) wrote: "In his work on the outposts Stuart soon showed that he possessed the qualities of a great leader of cavalry. He never had an equal in such service. He discarded the old maxims and soon discovered that in the conditions of modern war the chief functions of cavalry are to learn the designs and to watch and report the movements of the enemy."[19] And for his own part, Stuart always reported which of his subordinates had distinguished themselves in post-battle reports.

The Seven Days Battles

With more Confederate troops swelling the ranks, Lee's army was McClellan's equal by late June, and on June 25, Lee commenced an all-out attempt to destroy McClellan's army in a series of fierce battles known as the Seven Days Battles. After a stalemate in the first fighting at Oak Grove, Lee's army kept pushing ahead, using Stonewall Jackson to attack McClellan's right. Although Stonewall Jackson was unusually lethargic during the week's fighting, the appearance of his "foot cavalry" spooked McClellan even more, and McClellan was now certain he was opposed by 200,000 men, more than double the actual size of Lee's army. It also made McClellan think that the Confederates were threatening his supply line, forcing him to shift his army toward the James River to draw supplies.

On June 26, the Union defenders sharply repulsed the Confederate attacks at Mechanicsville, in part due to the fact that Stonewall Jackson had his troops bivouac for the night despite the fact

---

[19]   Mosby, John Singleton. *The Memoirs of Colonel John S. Mosby.*

heavy gunfire indicating a large battle was popping off within earshot. When the Confederates had more success the next day at Gaines' Mills, McClellan continued his strategic retreat, maneuvering his army toward a defensive position on the James River and all but abandoning the siege.

McClellan managed to keep his forces in tact (mostly through the efforts of his field generals), ultimately retreating to Harrison's Landing on the James River and establishing a new base of operation. Feeling increasingly at odds with his superiors, in a letter sent from Gaines' Mills, Virginia dated June 28, 1862, a frustrated McClellan wrote to Secretary of War Stanton, "If I save the army now, I tell you plainly that I owe no thanks to any other person in the Washington. You have done your best to sacrifice this army."[20] McClellan's argument, however, flies in the face of common knowledge that he had become so obsessed with having sufficient supplies that he'd actually moved to Gaines' Mill to accommodate the massive amount of provisions he'd accumulated. Ultimately unable to move his cache of supplies as quickly as his men were needed, McClellan eventually ran railroad cars full of food and supplies into the Pamunkey River rather than leave them behind for the Confederates.

Meade's brigade saw its first major action during the Seven Days Battles on June 30, 1862 at the Battle of Glendale (Frazier's Farm). Meade's men were part of a resistance against a Confederate attack that eventually devolved into bitter hand-to-hand combat involving bayonets and using rifles as clubs. During the fighting Meade was badly wounded in the arm, back, and side. Though the battle was inconclusive, it served to establish Meade as fearless and aggressive.

Despite the fact all of Lee's battle plans had been poorly executed by his generals, particularly Stonewall Jackson, he ordered one final assault against McClellan's army at Malvern Hill. Incredibly, McClellan was not even on the field for that battle, having left via steamboat back to Harrison's Landing. Biographer Ethan Rafuse notes McClellan's absence from the battlefield was inexcusable, literally leaving the Army of the Potomac leaderless during pitched battle, but McClellan often behaved cooly under fire, so it is likely not a question of McClellan's personal courage.

Ironically, Malvern Hill was one of the Union army's biggest successes during the Peninsula Campaign. Union artillery had silenced its Confederate counterparts, but Lee still ordered an infantry attack by D.H. Hill's division, which never got within 100 yards of the Union line. After the war, Hill famously referred to Malvern Hill, "It wasn't war. It was murder." Later that evening, as General Isaac Trimble (who is best known for leading a division during Pickett's Charge at Gettysburg) began moving his troops forward as if to attack, he was stopped by Stonewall Jackson, who asked "What are you going to do?" When Trimble replied that he was going to charge, Jackson countered, "General Hill has just tried with his entire division and been

---

[20]   Lanning, Michael Lee. *The Civil War 100*. Page 189.

repulsed. I guess you'd better not try it."

After Malvern Hill, McClellan withdrew his army to Harrison's Landing, where it was protected by the U.S. Navy along the James River and had its flanks secured by the river itself. At this point, the bureaucratic bickering between McClellan and Washington D.C. started flaring up again, as McClellan refused to recommence an advance without reinforcements. After weeks of indecision, the Army of the Potomac was finally ordered to evacuate the Peninsula and link up with John Pope's army in northern Virginia, as the Administration was more comfortable having their forces fighting on one line instead of exterior lines. Upon his arrival in Washington, McClellan told reporters that his failure to defeat Lee in Virginia was due to Lincoln not sending sufficient reinforcements.

During the Seven Days Battles, Longstreet was more effective. In command of an entire wing of Lee's army, Longstreet aggressively attacked at Gaines' Mill and Glendale. Historians have credited Longstreet for those battles and criticized Stonewall Jackson for being unusually lethargic during the Seven Days Battles, ultimately contributing to Lee's inability to do more damage or capture McClellan's Army of the Potomac. Jackson's performance was not lost on Longstreet, who pointed out that he performed poorly at the Seven Days Battles to defend charges that he was slow at Gettysburg. By the end of the campaign, Longstreet was one of the most popular and praised men in the army. Like Longstreet's father, Sorrel considered him a "rock in steadiness when sometimes in battle the world seemed flying to pieces." General Lee himself called Old Pete "the staff in my right hand." Though it is often forgotten, Longstreet was now Lee's principle subordinate, not Stonewall Jackson.

At Richmond, Lee reorganized the Army of Northern Virginia into the structure it is best remembered by. Jackson now took command of a force consisting of his own division (now commanded by Brig. General Charles S. Winder) and those of Maj. General Richard S. Ewell, Brig. General William H. C. Whiting, and Maj. General D. H. Hill. The other wing of Lee's army was commanded by Longstreet. On July 25, 1862, after the conclusion of the Seven Days Battles had brought the Peninsula Campaign to an end, Stuart was promoted to Major General, his command upgraded to Cavalry Division.

Chapter 16: Second Bull Run (Second Manassas)

Sending Jackson to Cedar Creek

Even before McClellan had completely withdrawn his troops, Lee sent Jackson northward to intercept the new army Abraham Lincoln had placed under Maj. General John Pope, formed out of the scattered troops in the Virginia area. Pope had found success in the Western theater, and he was uncommonly brash, instructing the previously defeated men now under his command that his soldiers in the West were accustomed to seeing the backs of the enemy. Pope's arrogance turned off his own men, and it also caught the notice of Lee.

On June 26, General Pope deployed his forces in an arc across Northern Virginia; its right flank under Maj. General Franz Sigel positioned at Sperryville on the Blue Ridge Mountains, its center columns under Maj. General Nathaniel P. Banks at Little Washington, and its left flank under Maj. General Irvin McDowell at Falmouth on the Rappahannock River. On July 13, Lee responded by sending Jackson with 14,000 men to Gordonsville, with Maj. General A. P. Hill's division of 10,000 men set to join him by July 27. This would set off one of the most significant battles of Jackson's military career.

On August 6, Pope marched his forces south into Culpeper County intending to capture the rail junction at Gordonsville in an attempt to draw Confederate attention away from General McClellan's withdrawal from the Virginia Peninsula. In response, Jackson went on the offensive, attacking Banks' center division, which proved precisely the right move. Jackson's larger intention was to then move on to Culpeper Court House, 26 miles north of Gordonsville-- the focal point of the Union arc--and then take on each of the Union armies separately. It was an ambitious plan to say the least.

Setting out on August 7, Jackson's march was immediately hampered by a severe heat wave, worsened by his now characteristic secrecy about his strategy. His field officers were so confused as to the exact route they were to follow that his column only progressed 8 miles over the next twenty-four hours. This slow progress allowed the Union cavalry to alert Pope of Confederate movement, and he countered by sending General Sigel to meet up with General Banks at Culpeper Court House and maintain a defensive line on a ridge above Cedar Run, seven miles to the south.

On the morning of August 9, Jackson's army crossed the Rapidan River into Culpeper County, led by Maj. General Richard S. Ewell's division, followed by Brig. General Charles S. Winder's division, with Maj. General A. P. Hill's troops picking up the rear. Just before noon, Brig. General Jubal Early's brigade, the front line of Ewell's division, came upon Union cavalry and artillery occupying the ridge above Cedar Run. Winder's division quickly formed to Early's left (on the west side of the Turnpike), with Brig. General William Taliaferro's brigade positioned closest to Early, and Col. Thomas S. Garnett's units forming on the far Confederate left. Then, Winder's artillery filled the gap on the road between the two divisions, the "Stonewall" Brigade, led by Col. Charles R. Ronald were brought up as support behind the cannons, while A. P Hill's division stood in reserve on the Confederate left. Meanwhile, the Union formed a line joining the armies of Brig. Generals Crawford, Auger, Geary, and Prince, while Brig. General George S. Greene's brigade was kept in reserve in the rear.

A little before 5:00 p.m., Confederate General Winder was mortally wounded while standing in the open attempting to direct his troops. As a result, command of his division fell to General Taliaferro, who was completely ignorant of Jackson's battle plan. Meanwhile, the "Stonewall Brigade," which was supposed to come up to support Garnett's brigade should they become separated from the main Confederate line, remained a half mile behind instead. Then before leadership could be reestablished, Union forces attacked again. When Jackson's brigade finally advanced, they were quickly dispended of by Crawford's troops--with Jackson ordering the batteries withdrawn before they could be captured. At this point, Taliaferro and Early's left were hit hard by the Union advance and were nearly broken.

As the story is told, determined to inspire his men to take the offensive, Jackson suddenly rode into the battlefield and attempted to brandish his sword, but the man who had once warned his VMI cadets to be ready to throw the scabbards of their swords away found that due to the infrequency with which he had drawn it, it had rusted in its scabbard. Undaunted, he unbuckled the sword from his belt--scabbard and all--and waved it over his head. Then he grabbed a battle flag from a retreating standard bearer and called for his men to rally around him. Heartened by their commander's zeal, the Stonewall Brigade set fiercely into the Union troops, quickly driving them back. And although Union forces were subsequently able to regroup and attack, the Stonewall Brigade had given the Confederate front line time to reform and A. P Hill's troops time to come up and fill in the gaps.

Almost immediately, the Union forces collapsed and went in full retreat. Confederate infantry and General William E. Jones' 7th Virginia Cavalry chased in hot pursuit, nearly capturing Banks and Pope at their headquarters a mile behind the Union line). But with darkness setting in, Jackson decided to give up the pursuit because he was unsure of where the rest of Pope's army was positioned. For the next two days, Jackson maintained his position south of Cedar Run, waiting for a Union attack that never came. Finally, after receiving news that Pope's entire army had arrived at Culpeper Court House, on August 12, Jackson fell back to a more defensive position behind the Rapidan River.

Though steeped in difficulties and a series of errors, the Battle at Cedar Mountain was deemed an unqualified victory for the Confederacy and for Stonewall Jackson himself. He'd wreaked such havoc against the Northern forces (Union casualties numbered at over 2300) that Union General-in-Chief Henry W. Halleck called off Pope's planned advance on Gordonsville, thereby giving Lee the initiative in the Northern Virginia Campaign and effectively shifting the fighting in Virginia from the Virginia Peninsula into northern Virginia--essentially a Union retreat.

The Second Battle of Bull Run or Manassas

Once certain McClellan was in full retreat, Lee joined Jackson, planning to strike Pope before McClellan's troops could arrive as reinforcements. In August 1862, Stuart completed yet another ride around the Union army, though this one was not as historic or memorable. On

August 21, while conducting a series of highly-effective raids against Union forces, Stuart was nearly captured (and did lose his signature peacock plumed hat and cloak), but the following day managed to overrun Union commander Maj. General John Pope's headquarters during a raid on Catlett's Station, Virginia, not only capturing Pope's full uniform, but several staff officers and secret orders that provided Lee invaluable intelligence concerning troop reinforcements for Pope's army.

In late August 1862, in a "daring and unorthodox" move, Lee divided his forces and sent Jackson northward to flank them, ultimately bringing Jackson directly behind Pope's army and supply base. This forced Pope to fall back to Manassas to protect his flank and maintain his lines of communication. Recognizing Lee's genius for military strategy, General Jackson quickly became Lee's most trusted commander, and he would later say that he so trusted Lee's military instincts that he would even follow him into battle blindfolded.

In a letter dated August 24, Meade made extremely accurate predictions about what Lee would attempt over the next few weeks. "I presume the enemy will not let us be quiet here. They have a large force in front of us, and are evidently determined to break through Pope and drive us out of Virginia, when they will follow into Maryland and perhaps Pennsylvania. I am sorry to say, from the manner in which matters have been mismanaged, that their chances of success are quite good. Whether I shall get back with the army to Washington, or go to Richmond, to live on bread and water, or go to my long and final account, are questions that the future only can solve. I am well, which, considering the night and hot sun marches we have just accomplished, is saying a good deal. I am also in good spirits, which is saying a good deal more."

When Pope's army fell back to Manassas to confront Jackson, his wing of Lee's army dug in along a railroad trench and took a defensive stance. The Second Battle of Manassas or Bull Run was fought August 28-30, beginning with the Union army throwing itself at Jackson the first two days. But the concentration on Stonewall's men opened up the Union army's left flank for Longstreet's wing, which marched 30 miles in 24 hours to reach the battlefield by the late afternoon of August 29. When Longstreet's men finally arrived around noon on August 29, Lee informed Longstreet of his plan to attack the Union flank--which was at that time concentrating its efforts on General Jackson. Longstreet initially rejected Lee's suggestion to attack, recommending instead that a reconnaissance be conducted to survey the field. And although Longstreet's artillery was ultimately a major factor in helping Jackson resist the Union attack on August 29, his performance that day was described by some Lost Cause advocates as slow, and they considered his disobedience of General Lee insubordination. Lee's most famous biographer, Douglas Southall Freeman, later wrote: "The seeds of much of the disaster on July 2, 1863, at the Battle of Gettysburg were sown in that instant—when Lee yielded to Longstreet and Longstreet discovered that he would."[21]

---

[21]   Tagg, Larry. *The Generals of Gettysburg*. Page 205.

Nevertheless, the Second Battle of Bull Run or Manassas is considered one of Longstreet's most successful. While Jackson's men defended themselves the first two days, Lee used Longstreet's wing on August 30 to deliver a devastating flank attack before reinforcements from the retreating Army of the Potomac could reach the field. With over 25,000 men, Longstreet's attack lasted several hours, while he and Lee were in the thick of things directing brigades and artillery batteries while coming under fire themselves. Eventually, Longstreet's attack swept Pope's army off the field. Fought on the same ground as the First Battle of Manassas nearly a year earlier, the result was the same: a decisive Confederate victory that sent Union soldiers scrambling back to the safety of Washington. Longstreet called Lee's campaign "clever and brilliant", and it helped reinforce the belief that using offensive marching and defensive battle tactics (like having Jackson's wing flank Pope's army and forcing Pope to attack it) was the key to success.

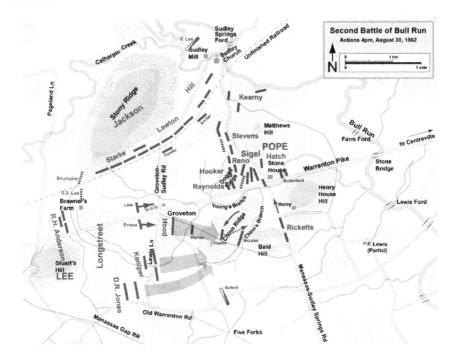

After the battle, General Lafayette McLaws (who had joined Longstreet's First Corps as First Division Commander and subsequently stayed with Longstreet for most of the War) assessed Longstreet unapologetically, saying, "James Longstreet is a humbug--a man of small capacity who is very obstinate, not at all chivalrous, exceedingly conceited, and entirely selfish!"[22] Thus it seems that Longstreet's propensity for friction was apparent long before that fateful day at Gettysburg.

Very few of the men who were with the Army of the Potomac on the Peninsula participated at all during the battle, but Meade was one of them. Partially recovered from wounds sustained at the Battle of Glendale, Meade and his brigade was attached to Irvin McDowell's corps in Pope's army. Meade's brigade covered the retreat of the Union Army along the Henry House Hill that allowed General Pope to safely evacuate his army to Centreville.

Meade wrote his wife after the battle a very frank letter that expressed both his military acumen and his private desire for the credit he felt was due to him. "The Pennsylvania Reserves were engaged throughout the whole time, and particularly distinguished themselves on the afternoon of the 30th, when our attack on the enemy's right flank having failed, they attacked us very vigorously on our left flank; when the Reserves came into action, and held them in check and drove them back, so that when other troops came up, we were enabled to save our left flank, which if we had not done, the enemy would have destroyed the whole army. That night we retreated to Centreville. In a few words, we have been, as usual, out-manoeuvred and out-numbered, and though not actually defeated, yet compelled to fall back on Washington for its defense and our own safety. On these recent battle-fields I claim, as before, to have done my duty. My services, then, should, I think, add to those previously performed, and that I may now fairly claim the command of a division. I suppose, now that McClellan is up again, all his old friends will be as affectionate as ever. I expect the enemy will follow us up, and though I hardly think they will adventure to attack Washington, yet I believe they will try to get into Maryland, and that will necessitate our moving to meet them."

Chapter 17: Forming the 20th Maine

When Confederate forces attacked Fort Sumter in South Carolina on April 12, 1861, Professor Lawrence Joshua Chamberlain was a highly successful and popular teacher at Bowdoin College. And having had no formal military training to speak of and a promising future in academics ahead of him, it seems unlikely that his first impulse would be to abandon his family and career to join a fight upon which he could *logically* have no great impact. Yet that is precisely what he chose to do.

During the spring academic term of 1862, Professor Chamberlain sent off a letter to the governor of Maine, offering his services to the Union Army. Upon discovering his plan, several of his professional colleagues forwarded notes to the governor in an effort to derail his intentions, asserting that the frail Professor Chamberlain would "never amount to much of a

---

[22]   Garrison, Webb. *Civil War Curiosities*. Page 236.

leader," and was, quite frankly, "unfit to command."[23]

In August of 1862, Professor Chamberlain tentatively accepted a two-year leave of absence from teaching, ostensibly to study languages in Europe at Bowdoin's expense. Instead, to the dismay of his family and colleagues, Chamberlain traveled to Augusta, Maine to see Governor Washburn. With Washburn's Adjutant General John L. Hodsdon under constant pressure from President Lincoln to raise troops, Washburn immediately offered Chamberlain the rank of colonel of the 20th Maine Regiment under the command of Colonel Adelbert Ames. Stating that he preferred to start at a subordinate position, "but one in which he could master the art of command in war," on August 8, 1862, the Governor commissioned him Lieutenant Colonel of the new 20th Regiment Infantry, Maine Volunteers. Lawrence's younger brother Thomas was also an officer of the 20th Maine, and with that, Lieutenant Colonel Lawrence Joshua Chamberlain was sent to Camp Mason at Portland, Maine.

As the 20th regiment to form (Civil War regiments received their numerical designations in the order in which they were formed), Chamberlain's 20th Maine was not exactly expected to be a crack unit. Civil War regiments typically consisted of 1,000 volunteers when they were mustered into service, meaning nearly 20,000 men from Maine had already enlisted. Thus, the 20th Maine was formed from the less motivated, less experienced men of the state. Unlike the early regiments, which were comprised of those most eager to serve and those who had served in active militia or in previous conflicts like the Mexican-American War, later regiments typically contained far less militarily-oriented men. Instead, these volunteers typically had ulterior motives for joining the ranks more than a year into the war; some men were evading legal authorities, and others had clearly proven in their societies that they could not get along with authority figures. Thus, as a commander with utterly no leadership experience outside the classroom leading men who were not exactly fit for military service, expectations were low for Lieutenant Colonel Chamberlain and the 20th Maine among senior officers of the Army of the Potomac. And that was before a partial company of suspected deserters was added to his motley brigade.

Chapter 18: The Maryland Campaign

Lee Invades Maryland

After two days' fighting, Lee had achieved another major victory, and he now stood unopposed 12 miles away from Washington D.C. While Johnston and Beauregard had stayed in this position in the months after the first battle, Lee determined upon a more aggressive course: taking the fighting to the North.

In early September, convinced that the best way to defend Richmond was to divert attention to

---

[23]   Sell, Bill. *Civil War Chronicles: Leaders of the North and South.* Page 46.

Washington, Lee had decided to invade Maryland after obtaining Jefferson Davis's permission. Today the decision is remembered through the prism of Lee hoping to win a major battle in the North that would bring about European recognition of the Confederacy, potential intervention, and possible capitulation by the North, whose anti-war Democrats were picking up political momentum. However, Lee also hoped that the fighting in Maryland would relieve Virginia's resources, especially the Shenandoah Valley, which served as the state's "breadbasket". And though largely forgotten today, Lee's move was controversial among his own men. Confederate soldiers, including Lee, took up arms to defend their homes, but now they were being asked to invade a Northern state. An untold number of Confederate soldiers refused to cross the Potomac River into Maryland.

Despite that, Longstreet also held the same view as Lee, believing an invasion of Maryland had plenty of advantages. He wrote in his memoirs, "The Army of Northern Virginia was afield without a foe. Its once grand adversary, discomfited under two commanders, had crept into cover of the bulwarks about the national capital. The commercial, social, and blood ties of Maryland inclined her people to the Southern cause. A little way north of the Potomac were inviting fields of food and supplies more plentiful than on the southern side; and the fields for march and manoeuvre, strategy and tactics, were even more inviting than the broad fields of grain and comfortable pasture-lands. Propitious also was the prospect of swelling our ranks by Maryland recruits."

In the summer of 1862, the Union suffered more than 20,000 casualties, and Northern Democrats, who had been split into pro-war and anti-war factions from the beginning, increasingly began to question the war. As of September 1862, no progress had been made on Richmond; in fact, a Confederate army was now in Maryland. And with the election of 1862 was approaching, Lincoln feared the Republicans might suffer losses in the congressional midterms that would harm the war effort. Thus, he restored General McClellan and removed General Pope after the second disaster at Bull Run. McClellan was still immensely popular among the Army of the Potomac, and with a mixture of men from his Army of the Potomac and Pope's Army of Virginia, he began a cautious pursuit of Lee into Maryland.

Although McClellan had largely stayed out of the political fray through 1862, McClellan's most ardent supporters could not deny that he actively worked to delay reinforcing Pope during the Second Manassas campaign once the Army of the Potomac was evacuated from the Peninsula. Nevertheless, McClellan ultimately got what he wanted out of Pope's misfortune. Though there is some debate on the order of events that led to McClellan taking command, Lincoln ultimately restored McClellan to command, likely because McClellan was the only administrator who could reform the army quickly and efficiently. McClellan didn't have much time to reorganize the mob, with Lee's army crossing the Potomac in early September, but one of the changes made was that Brigadier General Meade was placed in command of the Third Division, First Corps, Army of the Potomac.

The Lost Order

Naturally, McClellan's ascension to command of the armies around Washington outraged the Republican segment of the Administration, making it even more ironic that McClellan's campaign into Maryland during the next few weeks would bring about the release of the Emancipation Proclamation.

Once again, McClellan correctly predicted Lee's movements, and now realized that Lee was not the timid, indecisive general McClellan initially thought. Though it was clear Lee had crossed the Potomac, the Army of Northern Virginia decided to use ridges and cavalry to screen their movements. McClellan believed the most realistic goal was to drive the Confederates out of Maryland.

The Army of the Potomac understandably moved conservatively into Maryland during the early portion of the campaign while still dealing with logistics. Meanwhile, a Pleasanton report reaching McClellan estimated the Rebel force at 100,000, and other reports couldn't ascertain the nature of the that army's movements or motives. McClellan told the Administration on September 10 that the estimates of the Rebel force put it somewhere between 80,000-150,000, which would obviously have a huge effect on the campaign.

Historians believe that Lee's entire Army of Northern Virginia had perhaps 50,000 men at most and possibly closer to 30,000 during the Maryland campaign. However, Lee sized up George McClellan, figured he was a cautious general, and decided once again to divide his forces throughout Maryland. In early September, he ordered Jackson to capture Harpers Ferry while he and Longstreet maneuvered his troops toward Frederick. With McClellan now assuming command of the Northern forces, Lee expected to have plenty of time to assemble his troops and bring his battle plan to fruition.

However, the North was about to have one of the greatest strokes of luck during the Civil War. For reasons that are still unclear, Union troops in camp at Frederick came across a copy of Special Order 191, wrapped up among three cigars. The order contained Lee's entire marching plans for Maryland, making it clear that the Army of Northern Virginia had been divided into multiple parts, which, if faced by overpowering strength, could be entirely defeated and bagged. The "Lost Order" quickly made its way to General McClellan, who took several hours to debate whether or not it was intentional misinformation or actually real. McClellan is usually faulted for not acting quickly enough on these orders, but much of the instructions are vague and seemingly contradicted recent Rebel movements. Of course, there was also a concern that the orders could be false. Regardless, by noon of that day, McClellan was confident of success and told Lincoln that he would "send...trophies." Once he decided it was accurate, McClellan is said to have famously boasted, "Here is a paper with which if I cannot whip *Bobby Lee*, I will be willing to go home." Ironically, the Orders may have reinforced McClellan's belief that Lee's army had a significant advantage in manpower through its vague wording of "commands."

The North's luck was helped by Stuart, who had no clue orders had been lost and was busy handling public relations instead of reconnaissance. Now officially designated the "Eyes of the Army," in September of 1862, Stuart committed what many military historians deem his first tactical error when, for a five-day period at the beginning of the Maryland Campaign, he rested his men and entertained local civilians at a gala ball at Urbana, Maryland rather than keep the Union enemy under surveillance. With no incoming intelligence, Lee was unaware of McClellan's location and the speed at which his forces approached.

Harpers Ferry

The Confederates were completely unaware of the North's luck as they began to carry out Lee's plans. To Jackson's advantage, Col. Dixon S. Miles, Union commander at Harpers Ferry, had insisted on keeping most of his troops near the town instead of taking up commanding positions on the most important position, Maryland Heights. On September 12, Confederate forces engaged the Union's marginal defenses on the heights, but only a brief skirmish ensued. Then on September 13, two Confederate brigades arrived and easily drove the Union troops from the heights--but the critical positions to the west and south of town remained heavily defended.

By September 14, Jackson had methodically positioned his artillery around Harpers Ferry and ordered Maj. Gen. A. P. Hill to move down the west bank of the Shenandoah River in preparation for a flank attack on the Union left the next morning. By the following morning, Jackson had positioned nearly fifty guns on Maryland Heights and at the base of Loudoun Heights. Then he began a fierce artillery barrage from all sides, followed by a full-out infantry assault. Realizing the hopelessness of the situation, Col. Miles raised the white flag of surrender.

Stonewall Jackson

Battle of South Mountain

Eventually, the Confederates figured out where McClellan was, and to Lee's great surprise, McClellan's army began moving at an uncharacteristically quick pace, pushing in on his Confederate forces at several mountain passes at South Mountain, including at Turner's Gap and Crampton's Gap.

During the Battle of South Mountain, Meade distinguished himself and his men by ordering his brigade to storm the heights despite overwhelming odds, prompting corps commander Maj. General Joseph Hooker to exclaim, "Look at Meade! Why, with troops like those, led in that way, I can win anything!"[24] A clear Confederate defeat, Meade helped secure an important morale boost for the Army of the Potomac while further making a name for himself.

By the time the Maryland Campaign had started, the 20th Maine was one of six regiments assigned to the Third Brigade, First Division, V Corps. On September 12, 1862, Chamberlain's 20th Maine set out on a 40 mile march that would bring it to Sharpsburg, Maryland, at Antietam Creek. Arriving at nightfall on September 16, Lieutenant Colonel Chamberlain and his men, due to their inexperience, were held in reserve on the east bank of the Antietam.

The Battle of Antietam

While Jackson's wing was forcing the Harpers Ferry garrison to surrender, Lee regathered his other scattered units around Sharpsburg near Antietam Creek. McClellan's army, which may have outnumbered Lee's forces by about 50,000 men, confronted the Confederates around the night of September 16.

Longstreet described the scene before the battle commenced: "The blue uniforms of the federals appeared among the trees that crowned the heights on the eastern bank of the Antietam. The number increased, and larger and larger grew the field of blue until is seemed to stretch as far as the eye could see, and from the tops of the mountains down to the edge of the stream gathered the great army of McClellan."[25]

As fate would have it, the bloodiest day in the history of the United States took place on the 75th anniversary of the signing of the Constitution. On September 17, 1862, Lee's Army of Northern Virginia fought McClellan's Army of the Potomac outside Sharpsburg along Antietam

---

24   Eicher, John H., and David J. Eicher. *Civil War High Commands.* Page 385.
25   Gaffney, P., and D. Gaffney. *The Civil War: Exploring History One Week at a Time.* Page 179.

Creek. That day, nearly 25,000 would become casualties, and Lee's army barely survived fighting the much bigger Northern army.

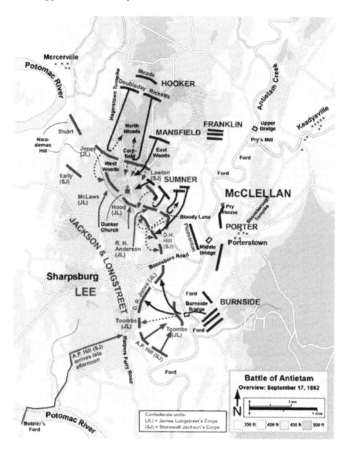

The fighting that morning started with savage fighting on the Confederate left flank near Dunker church, in a corn field and forests. The Confederates barely held the field in the north sector and might not have but for the injury of I Corps Commander Joe Hooker, which helped cause the Union's attack to fizzle. With that injury, Meade temporarily assumed command of the corps. He explained the fighting in that area to his wife in a latter written the day after the battle, "Yesterday and the day before my division commenced the battle, and was in the thickest of it. I was hit by a spent grape-shot, giving me a severe contusion on the right thigh, but not breaking the skin. Baldy [Meade's horse] was shot through the neck, but will get over it. A cavalry horse I mounted afterwards was shot in the flank. When General Hooker was wounded, General McClellan placed me in command of the army corps, over General Ricketts's head, who ranked me. This selection is a great compliment, and answers all my wishes in regard to my desire to have my services appreciated. I cannot ask for more, and am truly grateful for the merciful manner I have been protected, and for the good fortune that has attended me. I go into the action to-day as the commander of an army corps. If I survive, my two stars are secure, and if I fall, you will have my reputation to live on. God bless you all! I cannot write more. I am well and in fine spirits. Your brother Willie is up here, but was not in action yesterday."

During the late morning and early afternoon, Hancock's men were engaged in the center of the line near a sunken road that would become forever known as "Bloody Lane". Following the mortal wounding of Union Maj. General Israel B. Richardson at about 1:00 p.m. as the fighting flared across Bloody Lane, Brigadier General Hancock was ordered to assume temporary command of the First Division of the II Corps.

Making "a grand and dramatic entrance onto the battlefield," Hancock galloped between his troops and the enemy along Bloody Lane, obviously prepared for battle. Knowing how aggressive their general was, Hancock's men braced themselves to mount a counterattack against the exhausted Confederates.   To their surprise, however, commanding officer General McClellan instead ordered Hancock and his men to maintain their position.

Lee's army may have been saved by the Northern army's inability to cross the creek near "Burnside's Bridge". Ambrose Burnside had been given command of the "Right Wing" of the Army of the Potomac (the I Corps and IX Corps) at the start of the Maryland Campaign for the Battle of South Mountain, but McClellan separated the two corps at the Battle of Antietam, placing them on opposite ends of the Union battle line. However, Burnside continued to act as though he was a wing commander instead of a corps commander, so instead of ordering the IX corps, he funneled orders through General Jacob D. Cox. This poor organization contributed to the corps's hours-long delay in attacking and crossing what is now called "Burnside's Bridge" on the right flank of the Confederate line.

Making matters worse, Burnside did not perform adequate reconnaissance of the area, which afforded several easy fording sites of the creek out of range of the Army of Northern Virginia. Instead of unopposed crossings, his troops were forced into repeated assaults across the narrow bridge which was dominated by Confederate sharpshooters on high ground across the bridge. The delay allowed General A.P. Hill's Confederate division to reach the battlefield from Harpers Ferry in time to save Lee's right flank that afternoon.

By the end of the afternoon, Union attacks on the flanks and the center of the line had been violent but eventually unsuccessful. Fearing that his army was badly bloodied and figuring Lee had many more men than he did, McClellan refused to commit his reserves to continue the attacks, unnerved by Fitz John Porter telling him, "Remember, General, I command the last reserve of the last Army of the Republic." Thus, the day ended in a tactical stalemate.

After the battle, McClellan wrote to his wife, "Those in whose judgment I rely tell me that I fought the battle splendidly and that it was a masterpiece of art. ... I feel I have done all that can be asked in twice saving the country. ... I feel some little pride in having, with a beaten & demoralized army, defeated Lee so utterly. ... Well, one of these days history will I trust do me justice." Historians have generally been far less kind with their praise, criticizing McClellan for not sharing his battle plans with his corps commanders, which prevented them from using initiative outside of their sectors. McClellan also failed to use cavalry in the battle; had cavalry been used for reconnaissance, other fording options might have prevented the debacle at Burnside's Bridge. Meade was also far more conservative in his appraisal of the battle, reporting, "We hurt them a little more than they hurt us."[26]

On the morning of September 18, Lee's army prepared to defend against a Union assault that ultimately never came. Finally, an improvised truce was declared to allow both sides to exchange their wounded. That evening, Lee's forces began withdrawing across the Potomac to return to Virginia.

Battle of Shepherdstown

Chamberlain and his men hadn't fought during the battle of Antietam, but that would change days later. Following the Battle of Antietam, Confederate General Robert E. Lee began withdrawing his men across the Potomac River, to return to Virginia. Shortly before dusk on September 19, Union Brig. General Charles Griffin sent 2,000 infantry and sharpshooters from Maj. General Fitz-John Porter's V Corps across the Potomac River at Boteler's Ford (also known as Shepardstown Ford) in pursuit, only to pull them back the following day when Confederate commander General "Stonewall" Jackson entered the fray. However, Chamberlain's immediate commander, Union General Adelbert Ames, had mistakenly received orders to advance across the Potomac into Virginia, so he sent the 20th wading into the water -- actually encountering the retreating Union troops as they did – and they were promptly fired upon by a barrage of Confederate artillery.

Just as soon as Chamberlain's 20th had crossed, their bugles sounded retreat. Remaining calm atop his horse, Chamberlain redirected his men back across the river, "steadying his men through a deep place in the river where several of the Fifth New York were drowned in his presence."[27] And although Lieutenant Colonel Chamberlain had his horse shot out from under him, he succeeded in returning his regiment safely back to shore with only three casualties suffering

---

[26]   Catton, Bruce. *This Hallowed Ground.* Page 169.
[27]   Wallace, Willard M. *Soul of the Lion: A Biography of General Joshua L. Chamberlain.* Page 42.

minor wounds, his ability to remain calm under pressure now apparent.

Though McClellan did try to strike at Lee, most notably at Shepherdstown, Lee's rear guard was formidable enough that officers throughout the Army of the Potomac concurred with McClellan's actions. Lee's army then moved toward the Shenandoah Valley while the Army of the Potomac hovered around Sharpsburg.

Nevertheless, Antietam is now widely considered a turning point in the war. Although the battle was tactically a draw, it resulted in forcing Lee's army out of Maryland and back into Virginia, making it a strategic victory for the North and an opportune time for President Abraham Lincoln to issue the Emancipation Proclamation.

Although Lee and Jackson would ultimately receive the lion's share of credit for stopping McClellan's advance, it had been Longstreet's men who had held Lee's position long enough on the left and middle for Jackson to arrive and administer damage. One account describes Longstreet as coming upon an abandoned piece of artillery during one of the assaults, jumping off his horse, and then manning the gun himself for a half hour as his men kept reloading.

The same day as the Battle of Antietam, the *Washington Star* erroneously reported, "At the latest advices everything was favorable. Gen. Longstreet was reported killed and [General] Daniel Harvey Hill taken prisoner."[28] Later that same day, the *Star* dispatched, "Gen. Longstreet was wounded and is a prisoner." All of that was incorrect.

Chapter 19: The Fredericksburg Campaign

Once the Army of Northern Virginia was safely back in Virginia, Stuart executed another of his daring circumnavigations of the Army of the Potomac, this time traveling 120 miles in under 60 hours. Once again he had embarrassed his Union opponents while seizing horses and supplies. Afterwards, Stuart gifted "Stonewall" Jackson a fine, new officer's tunic, trimmed with gold lace, commissioned from a Richmond tailor, which he thought would give Jackson more of a "proper" general appearance--a gift to which Jackson was famously indifferent and almost always refuse to wore (with the exception of his last official portrait, which was taken less than two weeks before Chancellorsville). And while these exploits proved only marginally significant (resulting in little military advantage), when word reached the newspapers, they did much to boost Southern morale.

Even then, it did not escape the notice of observers that Stuart and Jackson were an odd couple, and Jackson biographer James Robertson Jr. later wrote, "Stuart and Jackson were an unlikely pair: one outgoing, the other introverted; one flashily uniformed, the other plainly dressed; one

---

28   Stepp, John, W. and Hill, William I. (editors). *Mirror of War, The Washington Star Reports the Civil War.* Page 151.

Prince Rupert and the other Cromwell. Yet Stuart's self-confidence, penchant for action, deep love of Virginia, and total abstinence from such vices as alcohol, tobacco, and pessimism endeared him to Jackson... Stuart was the only man in the Confederacy who could make Jackson laugh—and who dared to do so."

Despite heavily outnumbering the Southern army and badly damaging it during the battle of Antietam, McClellan decided not to pursue Lee across the Potomac, citing shortages of equipment and the fear of overextending his forces. General-in-Chief Henry W. Halleck wrote in his official report, "The long inactivity of so large an army in the face of a defeated foe, and during the most favorable season for rapid movements and a vigorous campaign, was a matter of great disappointment and regret." Lincoln had also had enough of McClellan's constant excuses for not taking forward action, and he relieved McClellan of his command of the Army of the Potomac on November 7, effectively ending the general's military career.

For his part, Meade agreed with McClellan's decision not to aggressively pursue Lee, telling his wife, "Whether the country will be satisfied with this or not I cannot say, but it ought to be, as I am free to confess I feared at one time the movement from Washington was a dangerous one, for if we were defeated and this army broken up, the country was gone. Now, if there is any common sense in the country, it ought to let us have time to reorganize and get into shape our new lines, and then advance with such overwhelming numbers that resistance on the part of the enemy would be useless."

As for his own personal reputation, Meade became more pessimistic in the days after Antietam, complaining to his wife, "I am afraid I shall not get the credit for these last battles that I did for those near Richmond, for two reasons: First, I was not wounded; second, old Sam Ringwalt was not there to write letters about me. I find the papers barely mention the Pennsylvania Reserves, call them McCall's troops, never mentioning my name; whereas I was not only in command, but at South Mountain, on the 14th, I was on the extreme right flank, had the conduct of the whole operations, and never saw General Hooker, commanding the corps, after getting his instructions, till the whole affair was over. I must, however, do Hooker the justice to say that he promptly gave me credit for what I did, and have reason to believe it was his urgent appeal to McClellan, that I was the right man to take his place when he was wounded, which secured my being assigned to the command of the corps."

In place of McClellan, Lincoln appointed Burnside, who had just failed at Antietam. Burnside didn't believe he was competent to command the entire army, a very honest (and accurate) judgment. However, Burnside also didn't want the command to fall upon Joe Hooker, who had been injured while aggressively fighting with his I Corps at Antietam in the morning. Thus, he accepted.

Under pressure from Lincoln to be aggressive, Burnside laid out a difficult plan to cross the

Rappahannock and attack the Confederates near Fredericksburg. The plan was doomed from the very beginning. On December 12, Burnside's army struggled to cross the river under fire from Confederate sharpshooters in the town. During the day, Lieutenant Colonel Chamberlain's 20th Maine was called into action, and Chamberlain later described the scene: "The enemy's cannoneers knew the ranges perfectly. The air was thick with the flying, bursting shells; whooping [sic] solid shot swept lengthwise our narrow bridge, fortunately not yet plowing a furrow through the midst of us, but driving the compressed air so close to our heads that there was an unconquerable instinct to shrink beneath it, although knowing it was then too late. The crowding, swerving column set the pontoons swaying, so that the horses reeled and men could scarcely keep their balance."[29]

On December 13, the day that saw most of the fighting of the battle, the first fighting took place on the Confederates' right flank, as the Army of the Potomac tried to dislodge Stonewall Jackson. Meade and Stuart found themselves in the thick of the fighting. Maj General Stuart and his cavalry—more specifically, his horse artillery under Major John Pelham—protected Stonewall Jackson's flank when it came under attack from General William B. Franklin. Franklin's "grand division" was able to penetrate General Jackson's defensive line to the south, but it was ultimately driven back.   After the battle, General Lee commended Stuart's cavalry which, in his words, "effectually guarded our right, annoying the enemy and embarrassing his movements by hanging on his flank and attacking when the opportunity occurred."[30]   Stuart informed his wife Flora that he had been shot through his fur collar during the encounter, but was otherwise unhurt.

Meade's division was part of Franklin's grand division, and was Meade's division that made the only significant breakthrough of the Confederate lines. Meade described the fighting to his wife, "On the 13th it was determined to make an attack from both positions, and the honor of leading this attack was assigned to my division. I cannot give you all the details of the fight, but will simply say my men went in beautifully, carried everything before them, and drove the enemy for nearly half a mile, but finding themselves unsupported on either right or left, and encountering an overwhelming force of the enemy, they were checked and finally driven back. As an evidence of the work they had to do, it is only necessary to state that out of four thousand five hundred men taken into action, we know the names of eighteen hundred killed and wounded. There are besides some four hundred missing, many of whom are wounded."

Although the Union was nearly successful on the Confederate left, the battle is mostly remembered for the piecemeal attacks the Union army made on heavily fortified positions Longstreet's men took up on Marye's Heights. With the massacre at Antietam still fresh in his

[29]   Wallace, Willard M. *Soul of the Lion: A Biography of General Joshua L. Chamberlain.* Pages 52--53.
[30]   Wert, Jeffry D. *Cavalryman of the Lost Cause: A Biography of J.E.B. Stuart.* Page 193.

mind (partially caused by the Confederates having not constructed defensive works), Longstreet ordered trenches, abatis (obstacles formed by felled trees with sharpened branches), and fieldworks to be constructed - which to Longstreet's credit, set a precedent for all future defensive battles in the Eastern theater. In addition to the artillery positions, 2,500 Confederates lined up four-deep behind a quarter-mile long four-foot stone wall would deter even the most foolhardy. Thus when it was learned that General Burnside was planning a direct assault on "the Heights," even the other Union generals couldn't believe it.

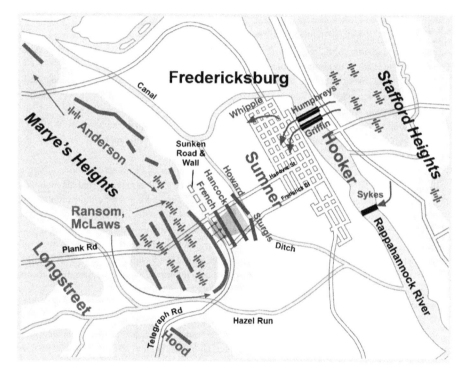

Unfortunately for Hancock and his men, Hancock's division was one of the ones ordered to make the desperate attack in support of General French's division. Making matters worse, Hancock had to send his brigades in individually, instead of in one concerted attack as a division. Hancock first sent Zook's brigade, which was almost immediately repulsed as it followed on the heels of one of the brigades of French's division. Hancock then sent in the famed Irish Brigade, which by chance was attacking positions held by fellow Irishmen in the 24th Georgia Infantry. One Confederate who spotted the Irish Brigade's green regimental flags coming on yelled, "Oh God, what a pity! Here comes Meagher's fellows."

Hancock's final brigade was led by Brig. Gen. John C. Caldwell. Like the others, that brigade marched in formation, got within firing range, fired, stopped to reload, and then continued the assault. In other words, they were sitting ducks. At one point during the carnage, when Lee saw yet another assault massing, he expressed concern to Longstreet, to which Longstreet replied, "General, if you put every man on the other side of the Potomac on that field to approach me over the same line, and give me plenty of ammunition, I will kill them all before they reach my line."

The brigade including Chamberlain's regiment joined two other brigades of the First Division, and the Second and Third Divisions, in one of the assaults. Directed to move forward to the left -- where bodies were mounting as man after man was being cut down -- officers on horseback were forced to abandon their mounts as they approached fences where the dead and wounded lied in heaps. Wounded men lying on the ground reached out to grab their legs to keep them from proceeding. In the midst of the chaos, Union General Adelbert Ames called to Chamberlain, "God help us now! Colonel, take the right wing, I must lead here!"[31] With no choice and little hope, Chamberlain led his men deeper into the deadly mêlée.

Once they neared the Confederate stronghold, a stone wall with Confederate soldiers three-man deep, Chamberlain and his men exchanged gunfire until dark. That night, he and his men were forced to bivouac in the killing field among the dead and dying; when temperatures plummeted, they huddled close to the corpses for warmth or stripped their bodies of their clothing. At dawn, 200-300 Confederates came from behind the wall to fire directly on the 20th Maine, whose members were forced to use the bodies of their comrades to build a barrier, unable to even raise themselves off the ground to load their weapons for fear of being shot. That night they finally received orders to withdraw, and as they retreated, they attempted to scoop out shallow graves with their hands and bayonets into which to push their fallen comrades.

Of this horrendous scene, Chamberlain wrote, "We had to pick our way over the field strewn with incongruous ruin; men torn and broken and cut to pieces in every indescribable way, cannon dismounted, gun carriages smashed or overturned, ammunition chests flung wildly about, horses dead and half-dead still held in harness, accouterments of every sort scattered as by whirlwinds. It was not good for the nerves, that ghastly march, in the lowering night!"[32]

As they threw themselves at Longstreet's heavily fortified position along the high ground, the Northern soldiers were mowed down again and again. General Longstreet compared the near

---

[31]   Wallace, Willard M. *Soul of the Lion: A Biography of General Joshua L. Chamberlain.* Page 53.
[32]   Wallace, Willard M. *Soul of the Lion: A Biography of General Joshua L. Chamberlain.* Pages 55--56.

continuous fall of soldiers on the battlefield to "the stead dripping of rain from the eaves of a house."[33] Still, Burnside sent wave after wave up the hill, with the Union injured (or those just cowering in the field) trying to stop the advancing men by grabbing at their legs and feet-- begging them to turn back. In the end, a recorded 14 assaults were made on Marye's Heights, all of which failed, with over 12,650 Union soldiers killed, wounded, or missing during the battle. Hancock himself suffered a wound in the abdomen.

Despite all their efforts, not one Union soldier got within 100 feet of the wall at Marye's Heights before being shot or forced to withdraw. As men lay dying on the field that night, the Northern Lights made a rare appearance. Southern soldiers took it as a divine omen and wrote about it frequently in their diaries. The Union soldiers saw less divine inspiration in the Northern Lights and mentioned it less in their own. The Battle of Fredericksburg also spawned one of Lee's most memorable quotes. During the battle, Lee turned to Longstreet and commented, "It is well that war is so terrible, otherwise we would grow too fond of it."[34]

After the virtual slaughter (with the dead said to have been stacked up in rows), the Union army retreated across the river in defeat. Although Lee had accomplished a decisive victory over Burnside's forces, the Union general had positioned his reserves and supply line so strategically that he could easily fall back without breaking lines of communication--while Lee had no such reserves or supplies. And since Lee didn't have the men to pursue and completely wipe out Burnside's army (and simply holding them would ultimately prove too costly), Lee chose not to give chase. Some military strategists contend this was a military blunder, but either way, the fighting in 1862 was done.

Though Fredericksburg was clearly a Union disaster, Hancock was noted for his valor. In turn, Hancock noted the valor of his own men, writing in his official report after the battle:

"Colonel Zook's brigade was the first in order. As soon as it had formed line, it advanced to the attack with spirit, passing the point at which the preceding troops had arrived, and being joined as it passed by the brave regiments of Kimball's brigade and some other regiments of French's division. It failed, however, to take the stone wall, behind which the enemy was posted, although our dead were left within 25 paces of it. These troops still held their line of battle in front of the enemy and within close musketry range.

The Irish Brigade next advanced to the assault. The same gallantry was displayed, but with the same results. Caldwell's brigade was next ordered into action, and, although it behaved with the utmost valor, failed to carry the enemy's position. All the troops then formed one line

---

[33]   Gaffney, P. and D. Gaffney. *The Civil War: Exploring History One Week at a Time*. Page 201

[34]   Nagel, Paul C. *The Lee's of Virginia*. Page 179.

of battle, extending from a point a little distance to the right of Hanover street, in a line nearly parallel to the enemy, with the left thrown back, the extreme left extending about the front of two regiments to the left of the railroad culvert. This line was held during the entire day and until it was relieved, some of the regiments not coming off the field until 10 o'clock the following morning. This line was held for hours after the troops had exhausted their ammunition, and after the ammunition of the killed and wounded within reach had been expended. Shortly after the last of my brigades came into action, it appeared as if the front crest of the enemy's hill might have been taken had there been other troops at hand, for the enemy were at that time running from their rifle-pits and works on the crest directly in front of our right. But by the time Howard's troops were ready to attack, the enemy had repaired this, and making a strong attack at the same time toward our left, it became necessary that a portion of that division should be detached toward that flank. After this hour it appeared to me, although reports were occasionally received that we were gaining ground, which led us to hope it might prove true, that, our object having failed, the only thing to be done was to maintain our front line by constantly supporting it until darkness covered the scene.

The bravery and devotion of the troops could not have been surpassed, as an evidence of which it is but necessary to mention the losses incurred. Out of 5,006 men, the maximum taken into action by me, the loss was 2,013 men, of whom 156 were commissioned officers. It will be observed that the losses in some of the regiments were of unusual severity, such as is seldom seen in any battle, no matter how prolonged. These were veteran regiments, led by able and tried commanders, and I regret to say that their places cannot soon be filled. Although the division failed to carry the enemy's heights, it lost no honor, but held the ground it took, and, under the most discouraging obstacles, retained it until relieved after the action was over. It will be impossible to mention in this report the names of all those who were distinguished."

Meade came through the Battle of Fredericksburg unscathed, but he was nearly killed the day after the battle. As he told his wife, "I was myself unhurt, although a ball passed through my hat so close, that if it had come from the front instead of the side, I would have been a 'goner.' The day after the battle, one of their sharpshooters took deliberate aim at me, his ball passing through the neck of my horse. The one I was riding at the time was a public horse, so that Baldy and Blacky are safe."

For his actions at Fredericksburg, Meade was promoted to major general of volunteers, effective November 29, 1862. Major General Meade was also given command of Hooker's V Corps after Hooker was promoted to "Grand Division" command, overseeing both the III and V Corps.

Chapter 20: The Chancellorsville Campaign

Lee had concluded an incredibly successful year for the Confederates in the East, but the South was still struggling. The Confederate forces in the West had failed to win a major battle, suffering defeat at places like Shiloh in Tennessee and across the Mississippi River. As the war continued into 1863, the southern economy continued to deteriorate. Southern armies were suffering serious deficiencies of nearly all supplies as the Union blockade continued to be effective as stopping most international commerce with the Confederacy. Moreover, the prospect of Great Britain or France recognizing the Confederacy had been all but eliminated by the Emancipation Proclamation.

Given the unlikelihood of forcing the North's capitulation, the Confederacy's main hope for victory was to win some decisive victory or hope that Abraham Lincoln would lose his reelection bid in 1864, and that the new president would want to negotiate peace with the Confederacy. Understandably, this colored Confederate war strategy, and unquestionably Lee's.

In a sense, the Battle of Chancellorsville was a defining moment in the careers of the three Confederates. After the Confederate victory at Fredericksburg, Lee dispatched Longstreet and his corps back to the Virginia Peninsula to protect Richmond and gather food and other much-needed supplies. Although Longstreet accomplished both missions, he was later criticized for having not taken advantage of the opportunity to attack Union positions in the area. As had now become Longstreet's *modus operandi*, to deflect responsibility, he simply responded that he didn't think they could afford the "powder and ball"--an assertion many historians fully doubt. In May of 1863, General Lee ordered Longstreet to rejoin his Army of Northern Virginia in time for a potential battle, but Longstreet's men would not reach Chancellorsville in time.

After the Fredericksburg debacle and the "Mud March" fiasco that left a Union advance literally dead in its tracks, Lincoln fired Burnside and replaced him with "Fighting Joe" Hooker. Hooker had gotten his nickname from a clerical error in a newspaper's description of fighting, but the nickname stuck, and Lee would later playfully refer to him as F.J. Hooker. Hooker had stood out for his zealous fighting at Antietam, and the battle may very well have turned out differently if he hadn't been injured at the head of the I Corps. Now he was in command of a 100,000 man Army of the Potomac, and he devised a complex plan to cross the Rappahannock River with part of his force near Fredericksburg to pin down Lee while using the other bulk to turn Lee's left, which would allow his forces to reach the Confederate rear.

Hooker's plan initially worked perfectly, with the division of his army surprising Lee. Lee was outnumbered two to one and now had to worry about threats on two fronts. Incredibly, Lee once again decided to divide his forces in the face of the enemy, sending Stonewall Jackson to turn the Union army's right flank while the rest of the army maintained positions near Fredericksburg. The Battle of Chancellorsville is one of the most famous of the Civil War, and the most famous part of the battle was Stonewall Jackson's daring march across the Army of the Potomac's flank, surprising the XI Corps with an attack on May 2, 1863. Having ignored warnings of Jackson's march, the XI Corps was quickly routed.

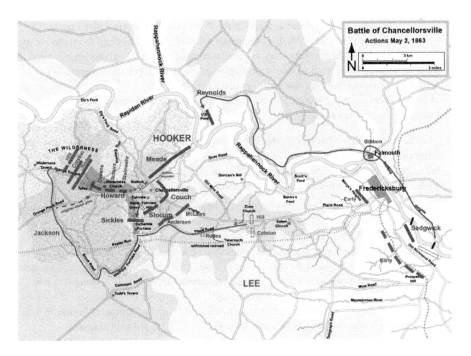

The surprise was a costly success however. Jackson scouted out ahead of his lines later that night and was mistakenly fired upon by his own men, badly wounding him. Jackson's natural replacement, A.P. Hill, was also injured.

Bypassing the next most-senior infantry general in the corps, Brig. General Robert E. Rodes directed Stuart himself to take temporary command of the Second Infantry Corps, a decision Lee seconded when news reached him. Although this change in command effectively ended the flanking attack underway, Stuart proved to be a remarkably adaptive leader and very effective infantry commander, launching a successful, well-coordinated assault against the Union right flank at Chancellorsville the following day. Meanwhile on the other flank, the Confederates evacuated from Fredericksburg but ultimately held the line. Hooker began to lose his nerve, and he was injured during the battle when a cannonball nearly killed him. Historians now believe that Hooker may have commanded part of the battle while suffering from a concussion.

On May 4, as Hooker abandoned the high ground at Hazel Grove in favor of Fairview, Stuart showed particular acumen by immediately taking control of the position and ordering thirty pieces of artillery to bombard the Union positions, not only forcing General Hooker's troops from Fairview (which Stuart then captured for the Confederacy), but essentially decimating the

Union lines while destroying Hooker's headquarters at Chancellor House. Of this well-played turn of events, Stuart wrote: "As the sun lifted the mist that shrouded the field, it was discovered that the ridge on the extreme right was a fine position for concentrating artillery. I immediately ordered thirty pieces to that point, and, under the happy effects of the battalion system, it was done quickly. The effect of this fire upon the enemy's batteries was superb."[35]

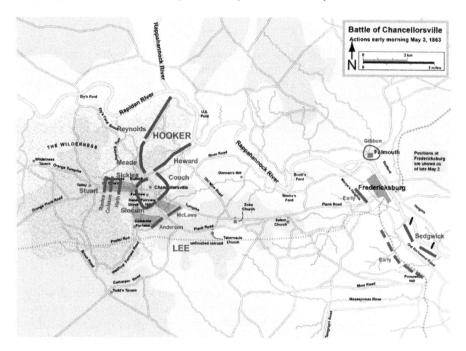

Stuart's effective utilization of a mere 20,000 men to snatch victory from a Union force numbering over 80,000 prompted Confederate General Porter Alexander to comment, "Altogether, I do not think there was a more brilliant thing done in the war than Stuart's extricating that command from the extremely critical position in which he found it."[36]

With Meade's corps kept in reserve for most of the battle, he frustratedly watched the fighting unfold around him. To the last moment, Meade argued with Hooker to resume the attack against Lee, but Hooker had lost his nerve. From May 5-6, Hooker began the delicate process of withdrawing his army, and it was at this point that Hancock and his division were being called

---

[35]   See: Stuart Family Archives.
[36]   Wert, Jeffry D. *Cavalryman of the Lost Cause: A Biography of J.E.B. Stuart.* Page 223.

upon. With men of the II Corps covering the evacuation, Hooker and the artillery crossed first, followed by the infantry on the morning of May 6. However, rains caused the river to rise and threatened to break the pontoon bridges, nearly leaving Hancock and the II Corps separated on the south side of the river after Hooker departed. II Corps commander Couch had been ordered not to continue the battle, but many men in the Army of the Potomac had wanted to keep fighting, and Couch was tempted to actually stay and fight. During the withdrawal, Hancock was wounded yet again.

Due to a smallpox outbreak thought to have been caused by tainted smallpox serum, the 20th Maine was kept out of action from April 17, 1863 through the first week of May. Thus, Colonel Chamberlain and his men missed the Battle of Chancellorsville, but Chamberlain was able to convince Union General Daniel Butterfield to allow his men to be somehow involved -- and was subsequently sent to guard the telegraph line running from Falmouth, Virginia to General Hooker's field headquarters. Chamberlain himself, however, was not content to resign himself to a detail of such "disgust."

On May 5, Chamberlain left his men to their assignment, crossed the Rappahannock River, and joined Union General Charles Griffin's First Division of the Fifth Corps' attack against Confederate General JEB Stuart. Though his horse received a severe wound in the action, Chamberlain rallied the troops, who in the confusion of pounding rain were scrambling back across the pontoon bridges, then for two days steadied the men in the rear guard, enormously impressing General Griffin with his "soldierly qualities". This despite the fact Chamberlain had *technically* disobeyed orders and was there without authorization.

Meade would later privately claim, "Hooker never lost his head, nor did he ever allow himself to be influenced by me or my advice. The objection I have to Hooker is that he did not and would not listen to those around him; that he acted deliberately on his own judgment, and in doing so, committed, as I think, fatal errors. If he had lost his head, and I had been placed in command, you may rest assured a very different result would have been arrived at, whether better or worse for us cannot be told now."

By the end of the battle, the Army of the Potomac had once again been defeated, retreating across the river. But Lee would also lose his "right hand". Jackson had been shot multiple times, twice in the left arm. After being painfully carried back behind the Confederate lines, Jackson had his left arm amputated. When Lee heard of Jackson's injuries, he sent his religious leader Chaplain Lacy to Stonewall with the message, "Give him my affectionate regards, and tell him to make haste and get well, and come back to me as soon as he can. He has lost his left arm, but I have lost my right arm."[37]

---

[37]   Vandiver, Frank E. *Mighty Stonewall*. Page 492.

After the amputation, Stonewall was transported to Thomas C. Chandler's plantation, well behind the battle lines, to convalesce. He seemed to be recovering, and his wife and newborn daughter joined him at the plantation, but his doctors were unaware Jackson was exhibiting common symptoms that indicated oncoming pneumonia. Jackson lay dying in the Chandler plantation outbuilding on Sunday, May 10, 1863 with his wife Anna at his side. He comforted his wife, telling her, "It is the Lord's Day…my wish is fulfilled. I always wanted to die on Sunday." Near the end, a delirious Jackson seemed to have his mind on war, blurting out, "Tell A. P. Hill to prepare for actions! Pass the infantry to the front! Tell Major Hawks…" His final words were "Let us cross over the river, and rest under the shade of the trees."

Although the Confederate Army had won the Battle at Chancellorsville, the loss of "Stonewall" not only diminished the victory but caused a general malaise to befall his men; as well as General Lee.

Chancellorsville was one of the most stunning battles of the Civil War, and not surprisingly there were some serious shakeups in its aftermath as generals pointed the fingers at each other. Hooker had a list of scapegoats, including XI Corps commander Oliver O. Howard, cavalry leader George Stoneman, and General Sedgwick of the VI Corps. Of course, just as many blamed Hooker, including II Corps commander Darius N. Couch, who was so disgusted with Hooker's battle performance that he subsequently transferred out of the Army of the Potomac in protest and headed back to Pennsylvania to lead the state militia. This left Hancock as the new commander of the II Corps.

On May 10, 1863, as Stonewall Jackson lay dying, Meade wrote to his wife, "There is a great deal of talking in the camp, and I see the press is beginning to attack Hooker. I think these last operations have shaken the confidence of the army in Hooker's judgment, particularly among the superior officers. I have been much gratified at the frequent expression of opinion that I ought to be placed in command. Three of my seniors (Couch, Slocum and Sedgwick) have sent me word that they were willing to serve under me. Couch, I hear, told the President he would not serve any longer under Hooker, and recommended my assignment to the command. I mention all this confidentially. I do not attach any importance to it, and do not believe there is the slightest probability of my being placed in command."

In the weeks after the battle, General Hooker had a special plan for the II Corps. Unbeknownst to Hancock at this time, in Hooker's desire to draw General Lee out into the open and away from his entrenchments, Hooker began intentionally isolating Hancock's corps away from the rest of the Union army whenever possible. Having taken an assessment of Lee's troop strength and commanding style, Hooker had become convinced that it would be difficult --virtually impossible --to force Lee to take the offensive unless "good opportunity were offered." Thus, he planned to use Hancock's II Corps as bait.

Considering the distance Lee would have to move his troops to attack the isolated Hancock, Hooker figured he couldn't do so with more than a small complement, and he was certain that Hancock could whip a portion of the Confederate Army under Lee's command. As long as Hooker maintained close communication, he could bring up reinforcements at least as rapidly as the enemy, thus increasing his chances of forcing Lee into an open-field confrontation. By May 22, 1863, Lee had still not taken the bait. As the North was about to discover, Lee had a completely different plan in mind.

Chapter 21: The Pennsylvania Campaign

The Battle of Brandy Station

In the spring of 1863, General Lee discovered that McClellan had known of his plans and was able to force a battle at Antietam before all of General Lee's forces had arrived. General Lee now believed that he could successfully invade the North again, and that his defeat before was due in great measure to a stroke of bad luck. In addition, General Lee hoped to supply his army on the unscathed fields and towns of the North, while giving war ravaged northern Virginia a rest. After Chancellorsville, Longstreet and Lee met to discuss options for the Confederate Army's summer campaign. Longstreet advocated detachment of all or part of his corps to be sent to Tennessee, citing Union Maj. General Ulysses S. Grant's advance on Vicksburg, the critical Confederate stronghold on the Mississippi River. Longstreet argued that a reinforced army under Bragg could defeat Rosecrans and drive toward the Ohio River, compelling Grant to release his hold on Vicksburg. Lee, however, was opposed to a division of his army and instead advocated a large-scale offensive (and raid) into Pennsylvania. In addition, General Lee hoped to supply his army on the unscathed fields and towns of the North, while giving war ravaged northern Virginia a rest.

Knowing that victories on Virginia soil meant little to an enemy that could simply retreat, regroup, and then return with more men and more advanced equipment, Lee set his sights on a Northern invasion, aiming to turn Northern opinion against the war and against President Lincoln. With his men already half-starved from dwindling provisions, Lee intended to confiscate food, horses, and equipment as they pushed north--and hopefully influence Northern politicians into giving up their support of the war by penetrating into Harrisburg or even Philadelphia. Given the right circumstances, Lee's army might even be able to capture either Baltimore or Philadelphia and use the city as leverage in peace negotiations.

In early June, the Army of Northern Virginia occupied Culpeper, Virginia. After their victories at Fredericksburg and Chancellorsville against armies twice their size, Confederate troops felt invincible and anxious to carry the war north into Pennsylvania. Assuming his role as Lee's "Eyes of the Army" for the Pennsylvania Campaign, Stuart bivouacked his men near the Rappahannock River, screening the Confederate Army against surprise Union attacks. Taken with his recent successes, Stuart requested a full field review of his units by General Lee, and on June 8, paraded his nearly 9,000 mounted troops and four batteries of horse artillery for review, also charging in simulated battle at Inlet Station about two miles southwest of Brandy Station. While Lee himself was unavailable to attend the review, some of the cavalrymen and newspaper reporters at the scene complained that all Stuart was doing was "feeding his ego and exhausting the horses." He began to be referred to as a "headline-hunting show-off."

Despite the critics, Stuart basked in the glory. Renowned Civil War historian Stephen Sears described the scene, "The grand review of June 5 was surely the proudest day of Jeb Stuart's thirty years. As he led a cavalcade of resplendent staff officers to the reviewing stand, trumpeters heralded his coming and women and girls strewed his path with flowers. Before all of the spectators the assembled cavalry brigade stretched a mile and a half. After Stuart and his entourage galloped past the line in review, the troopers in their turn saluted the reviewing stand in columns of squadrons. In performing a second "march past," the squadrons started off at a trot, then spurred to a gallop. Drawing sabers and breaking into the Rebel yell, the troopers rush toward the horse artillery drawn up in battery. The gunners responded defiantly, firing blank charges. Amidst this tumult of cannon fire and thundering hooves, a number of ladies swooned in their escorts' arms."[38]

However much Stuart enjoyed "horsing around", there was serious work to be done. The following day, Lee ordered Stuart to cross the Rappahannock and raid Union forward positions, shielding the Confederate Army from observation or interference as it moved north. Already anticipating this imminent offensive move, Stuart had ordered his troops back into formation around Brandy Station. Here, Stuart would endure the first of two low points in his military career: the Battle of Brandy Station, the largest predominantly cavalry engagement of the Civil War.

Union Maj. General Joseph Hooker interpreted Stuart's presence around Culpeper as a precursor to a raid on his army's supply lines. In response, he ordered his cavalry commander, Maj. General Alfred Pleasonton, to take a combined force of 8,000 cavalry and 3,000 infantry on a raid to "disperse and destroy" the 9,500 Confederates. Crossing the Rappahannock River in two columns on June 9,1863 at Beverly's Ford and Kelly's Ford, the first infantry unit caught Stuart completely off-guard, and the second surprised him yet again. Suddenly the Confederates were being battered both front and rear by mounted Union troops.

---

[38]   Sears, Stephen W. *Gettysburg*. Page 64.

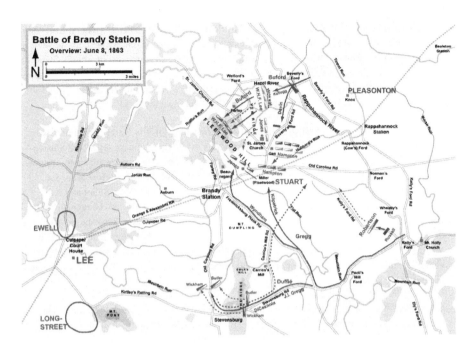

In addition to being the largest cavalry battle of the war, the chaos and confusion that ensued across the battlefield also made Brandy Station unique in that most of the fighting was done while mounted and using sabers. One account of the battle noted, "Of the bodies that littered the field that day, the vast majority were found to have perished by the sword."

After ten hours of charges and countercharges that swept back and forth across Fleetwood Hill (where Stuart had headquartered the night before) involving drawn sabers and revolvers, Pleasonton decided to withdraw his exhausted men across the Rappahannock River. Stuart immediately claimed a Confederate victory because his men had managed to hold the field and inflicted more casualties on the enemy while forcing Pleasonton to withdraw before locating Lee's infantry. But Stuart was trying to save face, and nobody else, including Lee, took his view of the battle. The fact was, the Southern cavalry under Stuart had not detected the movement of two large columns of Union cavalry and had fallen prey to not one but *two* surprise attacks. Two days later the Richmond *Enquirer* reported: "If Gen. Stuart is to be the eyes and ears of the army we advise him to see more, and be seen less. Gen. Stuart has suffered no little in public estimation by the late enterprises of the enemy."[39]

---

[39]   Wert, Jeffry D. *Cavalryman of the Lost Cause: A Biography of J.E.B. Stuart.* Page 251.

Lee was now painfully aware of the increased competency of the Union cavalry, as well as the decline of the seemingly once-invincible Southern mounted armed forces under Stuart.

Lee Invades Pennsylvania

After Chancellorsville, Longstreet and Lee met to discuss options for the Confederate Army's summer campaign. Longstreet advocated detachment of all or part of his corps to be sent to Tennessee, citing Union Maj. General Ulysses S. Grant's advance on Vicksburg, the critical Confederate stronghold on the Mississippi River. Longstreet argued that a reinforced army under Bragg could defeat Rosecrans and drive toward the Ohio River, compelling Grant to release his hold on Vicksburg. Lee, however, was opposed to a division of his army and instead advocated a large-scale offensive (and raid) into Pennsylvania. In addition, General Lee hoped to supply his army on the unscathed fields and towns of the North, while giving war ravaged northern Virginia a rest.

Knowing that victories on Virginia soil meant little to an enemy that could simply retreat, regroup, and then return with more men and more advanced equipment, Lee set his sights on a Northern invasion, aiming to turn Northern opinion against the war and against President Lincoln. Given the right circumstances, Lee's army might even be able to capture either Baltimore or Philadelphia and use the city as leverage in peace negotiations.

In the wake of Jackson's death, Lee reorganized his army, creating three Corps out of the previous two, with A.P. Hill and Richard S. Ewell "replacing" Stonewall. Hill had been a successful division commander, but he was constantly battling bouts of sickness that left him disabled, which would occur at Gettysburg. Ewell had distinguished himself during the Peninsula Campaign, suffering a serious injury that historians often credit as making him more cautious in command upon his return.

During the first weeks of summer of 1863, as Stuart screened the army and completed several well-executed offenses against Union cavalry, many historians think it likely that he had already planned to remove the negative effect of Brandy Station by duplicating one of his now famous circumnavigating rides around the enemy army. But as Lee began his march north through the Shenandoah Valley in western Virginia, it is highly unlikely that is what he wanted or expected.

Before setting out on June 22, the methodical Lee gave Stuart specific instructions as to the role he was to play in the Pennsylvania offensive: as the "Eyes of the Army" he was to guard the mountain passes with part of his force while the Army of Northern Virginia was still south of the Potomac River, and then cross the river with the remainder of his army and screen the right flank of Confederate general Richard Stoddert Ewell's Second Corps as it moved down the Shenandoah Valley, maintaining contact with Ewell's army as it advanced towards Harrisburg.
But instead of taking the most direct route north near the Blue Ridge Mountains, Stuart chose a

much more ambitious course of action.

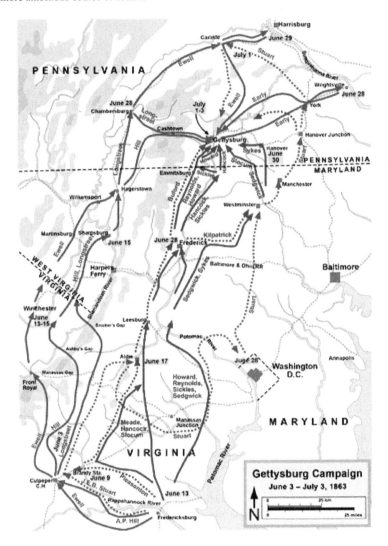

Stuart's ride (the dotted line) during the Gettysburg Campaign

Stuart decided to march his three best brigades (under Generals Hampton and Fitzhugh Lee, and Col. John R. Chambliss) between the Union army and Washington, north through Rockville to Westminster, and then into Pennsylvania--a route that would allow them to capture supplies along the way and wreak havoc as they skirted Washington. In the aftermath, the *Washington Star* would write: "The cavalry chief [Stuart] interpreted his marching orders in a way that best suited his nature, and detached his 9000 troopers from their task of screening the main army and keeping tabs on the Federals. When Lee was in Pennsylvania anxiously looking for him, Stuart crossed the Potomac above Washington and captured a fine prize of Federal supply wagons . . . ."[40]

But to complicate matters even more, as Stuart set out on June 25 on what was probably a glory-seeking mission, he was unaware that his intended path was blocked by columns of Union infantry that would invariably force him to veer farther east than he or Lee had anticipated. Ultimately, his decision would prevent him from linking up with Ewell as ordered and deprive Lee of his primary cavalry force as he advanced deeper and deeper into unfamiliar enemy territory. According to Halsey Wigfall (son of Confederate States Senator Louis Wigfall) who was in Stuart's infantry, "Stuart and his cavalry left [Lee's] army on June 24 and did not contact [his] army again until the afternoon of July 2, the second day of the [Gettysburg] battle."[41]

According to Stuart's own account, on June 29 his men clashed briefly with two companies of Union cavalry in Westminster, Maryland, overwhelming and chasing them "a long distance on the Baltimore road," causing a "great panic" in the city of Baltimore. On June 30, the head of Stuart's column then encountered Union Brig. General Judson Kilpatrick's cavalry as it passed through Hanover--reportedly capturing a wagon train and scattering the Union army--after which Kilpatrick's men were able to regroup and drive Stuart and his men out of town. Then after a twenty-mile trek in the dark, Stuart's exhausted men reached Dover, Pennsylvania, on the morning of July 1 (which they briefly occupied).

Late on the second day of the battle, Stuart finally arrived, bringing with him the caravan of captured Union supply wagons, and he was immediately reprimanded by Lee. One account describes Lee as "visibly angry" raising his hand "as if to strike the tardy cavalry commander."[42] While that does not sound like Lee's style, Stuart has been heavily criticized ever since, and it has been speculated Lee took him to task harshly enough that Stuart offered his resignation. Lee didn't accept it, but he would later note in his after battle report that the cavalry had not updated him as to the Army of the Potomac's movements.

Given great discretion in his cavalry operations before the battle, Stuart's cavalry was too far

[40]   Stepp, John W. & Hill, William I. (editors), *Mirror of War, the Washington Star reports the Civil War*. Page 199.
[41]   Eaton, Clement. *Jefferson Davis*. Page 178.
[42]   Philips, David. *Crucial Land Battles*. Page 75.

removed from the Army of Northern Virginia to warn Lee of the Army of the Potomac's movements. As it would turn out, Lee's army inadvertently stumbled into Union cavalry and then the Union army at Gettysburg on the morning of July 1, 1863, walking blindly into what became the largest battle of the war.

Colonel Joshua Chamberlain

In June 1863, upon the promotion of Union Brig. General Adelbert Ames, and with General Griffin's gleaming recommendation, Ames relinquished command of the 20th Maine to Lt. Colonel Lawrence Chamberlain, promoting him to full colonel of the regiment. The timing proved especially fortuitous, given the momentous campaign that would culminate next month at a sleepy town in southern Pennsylvania.

Meade Takes Command

Though he had privately confided to his wife that he desired command of the Army of the Potomac, Meade never publicly expressed his wishes to those in charge, thus avoiding the political squabbling among generals. On June 28, however, he got his wish.

Before sunrise on that morning, a messenger entered Major General George Meade's field headquarters, shook the sleeping general and said, "I'm afraid I've come to give you some trouble, General."[43] Jumping to his feet, Meade's first thought was that he was being arrested-- probably for arguing with Hooker on the battlefield. Informed that he had replaced Maj. General Joseph Hooker as commander of the Army of the Potomac (Lincoln had passed over his friend, the more qualified John F. Reynolds), Meade at first protested, stating that he didn't want the job. Informed that his promotion was not a "request," Meade hitched up his sagging long underwear, ran his fingers through his thinning hair and said, "Well, I've been tried and condemned without a hearing, and I suppose I shall have to go to the execution."[44] Historians have also speculated that it may well have been Mead's foreign birth that got him selected over Reynolds. As such, he was excluded from running for the U. S. Presidency and therefore posed no future threat to Lincoln, as Reynolds may have if successful. Of course, that doesn't square with reports that Reynolds turned the offer down.

In addition to being informed by Hooker that he was in command, Meade received a telegram from general-in-chief Henry Halleck:

"General:
You will receive with this the order of the President placing you in command of the Army of

---

43   Stevens, Joseph E. *1863: The Rebirth of a Nation.* Page 230.
44   Stevens, Joseph E. *1863: The Rebirth of a Nation.* Page 231.

the Potomac. Considering the circumstances, no one ever received a more important command; and I cannot doubt that you will fully justify the confidence which the Government has reposed in you.

You will not be hampered by any minute instructions from these headquarters. Your army is free to act as you may deem proper under the circumstances as they arise. You will, however, keep in view the important fact that the Army of the Potomac is the covering army of Washington, as well as the army of operation against the invading forces of the rebels. You will therefore manoeuvre and fight in such a manner as to cover the Capital and also Baltimore, as far as circumstances will admit. Should General Lee move upon either of these places, it is expected that you will either anticipate him or arrive with him, so as to give him battle.

All forces within the sphere of your operations will be held subject to your orders.

Harper's Ferry and its garrison are under your direct orders.

You are authorized to remove from command and send from your army any officer or other person you may deem proper; and to appoint to command as you may deem expedient.

In fine, General, you are intrusted with all the power and authority which the President, the Secretary of War, or the General-in-Chief can confer on you, and you may rely on our full support.

You will keep me fully informed of all your movements and the positions of your own troops and those of the enemy, so far as known.

I shall always be ready to advise and assist you to the utmost of my ability.

Very respectfully,

Your obedient servant,

H. W. Halleck, General-in-Chief."

Meade then issued General Orders No. 67:

By direction of the President of the United States, I hereby assume command of the Army of the Potomac.

As a soldier, in obeying this order—an order totally unexpected and unsolicited—I have no promises or pledges to make.

The country looks to this army to relieve it from the devastation and disgrace of a foreign invasion. Whatever fatigues and sacrifices we may be called upon to undergo, let us have in view, constantly, the magnitude of the interests involved, and let each man determine to do his duty, leaving to an all-controlling Providence the decision of the contest.

It is with great diffidence that I relieve in the command of this army an eminent and accomplished soldier, whose name must ever appear conspicuous in the history of its achievements; but I rely upon the hearty support of my companions in arms to assist me in the discharge of the duties of the important trust which has been confided to me.

George G. Meade, Major General, commanding.

When word of Meade's promotion spread around camp, it certainly surprised many men. After all, meade lacked charisma, did not exude confidence, and did not arouse enthusiasm among his men by his presence. In fact, considering the many times he'd been wounded (or nearly wounded), many considered him a danger to his men and to himself. Even his trusty horse "Old Baldy" had been wounded under him at Second Bull Run and again at Antietam. Ultimately, the best thing his men could say about him was that at least he had never made any ruinous mistakes.

Assuming command of the Army of the Potomac on June 28 at Prospect Hall in Frederick, Maryland, (with his second son, George, now part of his staff), Meade had his work cut out for him, though few apparently considered his position. Having to first locate his forces, he then had to review Hooker's strategy, study the most recent intelligence reports, and then determine the appropriate course of action, all the while keeping an eye fixed on Lee. Ultimately disregarding Hooker's plans to strike into the Cumberland Valley, Meade opted to march on Harrisburg, Pennsylvania to move toward the Susquehanna River, keeping his troops between Lee's army and Washinton.

Upon taking command, Meade began drawing up defensive positions around northern Maryland about a dozen miles south of Gettysburg. His proposed line would be referred to as the Pipe Creek Circular, but it would never be implemented due to actions outside of Meade's control.

It is believed that one of the first notices Lee got about the Army of the Potomac's movements actually came from a spy named "Harrison", a man who apparently worked undercover for Longstreet but of whom little is known. Harrison reported that General George G. Meade was now in command of the Union Army and was at that very moment marching north to meet Lee's army. According to Longstreet, he and Lee were supposedly on the same page at the beginning of the campaign. "His plan or wishes announced, it became useless and improper to offer suggestions leading to a different course. All that I could ask was that the policy of the campaign should be one of defensive tactics; that we should work so as to force the enemy to attack us, in such good position as we might find in our own country, so well adapted to that purpose—which might assure us of a grand triumph. To this he readily assented as an important and material adjunct to his general plan." Lee later claimed he "had never made any such promise, and had never thought of doing any such thing," but in his official report after the battle, Lee also noted, "It had not been intended to fight a general battle at such a distance from our base, unless attacked by the enemy.

July 1, 1863

Without question, the most famous battle of the Civil War took place outside of the small town of Gettysburg, Pennsylvania, which happened to be a transporation hub, serving as the center of a wheel with several roads leading out to other Pennsylvanian towns. Lee was unaware of Meade's position when an advanced division of Hill's Corps marched toward Gettysburg on the morning of July 1. The battle began with John Buford's Union cavalry forces skirmishing against the advancing division of Heth's just outside of town. Buford's actions allowed the I Corps of the Army of the Potomac to reach Gettysburg and engage the Confederates, eventually setting the stage for the biggest and most well known battle of the war.

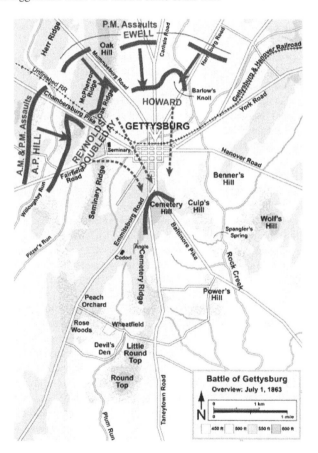

The I Corps was led by Pennsylvanian General John F. Reynolds, an effective general that had been considered for command of the entire army in place of Hooker and was considered by many the best general in the army. Since Lee had invaded Pennsylvania, many believe that Reynolds was even more active and aggressive than he might have otherwise been, and as he was at the front positioning his men, he was shot and killed. With his death, command of the I Corps fell upon Maj. Gen. Abner Doubleday, the Civil War veteran wrongly credited for inventing baseball.

Meanwhile, General Oliver O. Howard and his XI Corps came up on the right of the I Corps, eager to replace the stain the XI Corps had suffered at Chancellorsville thanks to Stonewall Jackson. As a general battle began to form northwest of town, news was making its way back to Meade several miles away that Reynolds had been killed, and that a battle was developing.

Meade had been drawing up a proposed defensive line several miles away from Gettysburg near Emmitsburg, Maryland, but when news of the morning's fighting reached him, Meade sent II Corps commander Winfield Scott Hancock ahead to take command in the field, putting him in temporary command of the "left wing" of the army consisting of the I, II, III and XI Corps. Meade also charged Hancock with determining whether to fight the general battle near Gettysburg or to pull back to the line Meade had been drawing up. Hancock would not be the senior officer on the field (Howard outranked him), so the fact that he was ordered to take command of the field demonstrates how much Meade trusted him.

As Hancock headed toward the fighting, and while the Army of the Potomac's I and XI Corps engaged in heavy fighting, they were eventually flanked from the north by Ewell's Confederate Corps, which was returning toward Gettysburg from its previous objective. After a disorderly retreat through the town itself, the Union men began to dig in on high ground to the southeast of the town. When Hancock met up with Howard, he told the XI Corps commander, "I think this the strongest position by nature upon which to fight a battle that I ever saw." When Howard agreed, Hancock replied, "Very well, sir, I select this as the battle-field."

As the Confederates sent the Union corps retreating, Lee arrived on the field and saw the importance of the defensive positions the Union men were taking up along Cemetery Hill and Culp's Hill. Late in the afternoon, Lee sent discretionary orders to Ewell that Cemetery Hill be taken "if practicable", but ultimately Ewell chose not to attempt the assault. Lee's order has been criticized because it left too much discretion to Ewell, leaving historians to speculate on how the more aggressive Stonewall Jackson would have acted on this order if he had lived to command this wing of Lee's army, and how differently the second day of battle would have proceeded with Confederate possession of Culp's Hill or Cemetery Hill. Discretionary orders were customary for General Lee because Jackson and Longstreet, his other principal subordinate, usually reacted to them aggressively and used their initiative to act quickly and forcefully. Ewell's decision not to attack, whether justified or not, may have ultimately cost the Confederates the battle.

General Ewell

With so many men engaged and now taking refuge on the high ground, Meade, who was an engineer like Lee, abandoned his previous plan to draw up a defensive line around Emmittsburg a few miles to the south. After a council of war, the Army of the Potomac decided to defend at Gettysburg.

Day 1 by itself would have been one of the 20 biggest battles of the Civil War, and it was a tactical Confederate victory. But the battle had just started, and thanks to the actions of Meade and Hancock, the largest battle on the North American continent would take place on the ground of their choosing.

July 2, 1863

By the morning of July 2, Major General Meade had put in place what he thought to be the optimal battle strategy. Positioning his now massive Army of the Potomac in what would become known as the "fish hook", he'd established a line configuration that was much more compact and maneuverable than Lee's, which allowed Meade to shift his troops quickly from inactive parts of the line to those under attack without creating new points of vulnerability. Moreover, Meade's army was taking a defensive stance on the high ground anchored by Culp's Hill, Cemetery Hill, and Cemetery Ridge. Meade also personally moved the III Corps under Maj. General Daniel Sickles into position on the left of the line.

On the morning of July 2, Meade was determined to make a stand at Gettysburg, and Lee was determined to strike at him. That morning, Lee decided to make strong attacks on both Union flanks while feinting in the middle, ordering Ewell's corps to attack Culp's Hill on the Union right while Longstreet's corps would attack on the Union left.

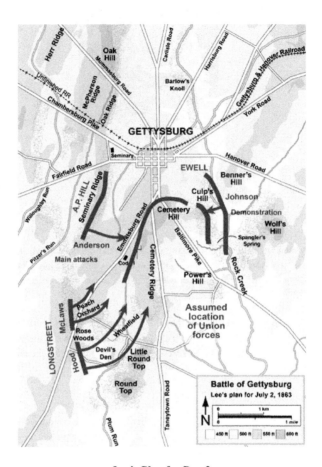

Lee's Plan for Day 2

As it turned out, both attacks would come too late. Though there was a controversy over when Lee ordered Longstreet's attack, Longstreet's march got tangled up and caused several hours of delay. Lost Cause advocates attacking Longstreet would later claim his attack was supposed to take place as early as possible, although no official Confederate orders gave a time for the attack. Lee gave the order for the attack around 11:00 a.m., and it is known that Longstreet was reluctant about making it; he still wanted to slide around the Union flank, interpose the Confederate army between Washington D.C. and the Army of the Potomac, and force Meade to attack them. Between Longstreet's delays and the mixup in the march that forced parts of his corps to double back and make a winding march, Longstreet's men weren't ready to attack until about 4:00 p.m.

Longstreet's biographer, Jeffrey Wert, wrote, "Longstreet deserves censure for his performance on the morning of July 2. He allowed his disagreement with Lee's decision to affect his conduct. Once the commanding general determined to assail the enemy, duty required Longstreet to comply with the vigor and thoroughness that had previously characterized his generalship. The concern for detail, the regard for timely information, and the need for preparation were absent." Edwin Coddington, whose history of the Gettysburg Campaign still continues to be considered the best ever written, described Longstreet's march as "a comedy of errors such as one might expect of inexperienced commanders and raw militia, but not of Lee's ' War Horse' and his veteran troops." Coddington considered it "a dark moment in Longstreet's career as a general."

Writing about Day 2, Longstreet criticized Lee, insisting once again that the right move was to move around the Union flank. "The opportunity for our right was in the air. General Halleck saw it from Washington. General Meade saw and was apprehensive of it. Even General Pendleton refers to it in favorable mention in his official report. Failing to adopt it, General Lee should have gone with us to his right. He had seen and carefully examined the left of his line, and only gave us a guide to show the way to the right, leaving the battle to be adjusted to formidable and difficult grounds without his assistance. If he had been with us, General Hood's messengers could have been referred to general Headquarters, but to delay and send messengers five miles in favor of a move that he had rejected would have been contumacious. The opportunity was with the Confederates from the assembling on Cemetery Hill. It was inviting of their preconceived plans. It was the object of and excuse for the invasion as a substitute for more direct efforts for the relief of Vicksburg. Confederate writers and talkers claim that General Meade could have escaped without making aggressive battle, but that is equivalent to confession of the inertia that failed to grasp the opportunity."

As Longstreet's men began their circuitous march, Sickles took it upon himself to advance his entire corps one half mile forward to a peach orchard, poising himself to take control of higher ground. Some historians assert that Sickles had held a grudge against Meade for taking command from his friend Joseph Hooker and intentionally disregarded orders. It has also been speculated by some historians that Sickles moved forward to occupy high ground in his front due to the devastation unleashed against the III Corps at Chancellorsville once Confederates took high ground and operated their artillery on Hazel Grove. Sickles and Meade would feud over the actions on Day 2 in the years after the war, after Sickles (who lost a leg that day) took credit for the victory by disrupting Lee's attack plans. Historians have almost universally sided with Meade, pointing out that Sickles nearly had his III Corps annihilated during Longstreet's attack.

Whatever the reasoning for Sickles' move, this unauthorized action completely undermined Meade's overall strategy by effectively isolating Sickles' corps from the rest of the Union line and exposing the Union left flank in the process. By the early afternoon of July 2, nothing but the fog of war was preventing the Confederates from turning and crushing Sickles' forces, then moving to outflank the entire Union Army.

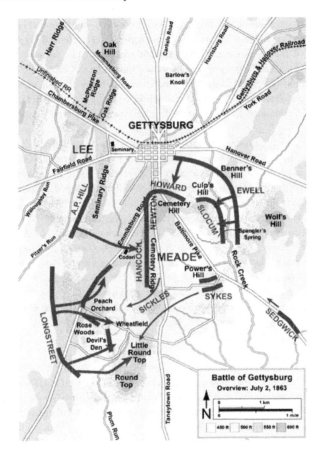

With General George Meade once again in command, Hancock and the II Corps was positioned on Cemetery Ridge, roughly in the center of the Union line. Since Lee intended to strike at both Union flanks, theoretically Hancock's men should very well not have been engaged at all on the second day of the battle. But as a result of the fact Sickles had moved his men so far out of position, it created a major gap in the Union line and brought the III Corps directly into Longstreet's path. Longstreet's assault commenced by smashing into Sickles III Corps, engaging them in a peach orchard, wheat field, and Devil's Den, an outcropping of boulders that provided the Confederates prime cover.

When it became obvious that Sickles' III Corps was in dire straits, the chaos in that sector acted like a vacuum that induced both sides to pour more men into the vicinity. Moreover, when Sickles was injured, command of the III Corps fell upon II Corps commander Hancock as well. As Meade tried to shuffle reinforcements to his left, Hancock sent in his II Corps' First Division (under Brig. General John C. Caldwell) to reinforce the III Corps in the wheat field. The fighting in the wheat field was so intense that Caldwell's division would be all but annihilated during the afternoon.

At the same time, men from Confederate General A. P. Hill's corps made their advance toward the Union center, forcing the Army of the Potomac to rally defenses and rushed unit to critical spots to patch the holes. With Hill in his front and Longstreet's attack to his left, Hancock was in the unenviable position of having to attempt to resist Confederate advances spread out over a few miles, at least until more and more reserves could be rushed over from the other side of the Union line to the army's left flank. At one point, Hancock ordered a regiment to make what was essentially a suicidal bayonet charge into the face of Hill's Confederates on Cemetery Ridge. Hancock sent the First Minnesota to charge a Confederate brigade four times its size. One of the Minnesota volunteers, one William Lochren later said, "Every man realized in an instant what the order meant -- death or wounds to us all; the sacrifice of the regiment to gain a few minutes time and save the position, and probably the battlefield -- and every man saw and accepted the necessity of the sacrifice."[45] While extremely costly to the regiment (the Minnesotans suffered 87% casualties, the worst of any regiment at Gettysburg), this heroic sacrifice bought time to organize the defensive line and kept the battle from turning in favor of the Confederates. Hancock would write of them, "I cannot speak too highly of this regiment and its commander in its attack, as well as in its subsequent advance against the enemy, in which it lost three-fourths of the officers and men engaged."

As Longstreet's assault on the Union left continued, his line naturally got more and more entangled as well. As Longstreet's men kept moving to their right, they reached the base of Little Round Top and Round Top, two rocky hills south of Gettysburg proper, at the far left. When Meade's chief engineer, Brig. General Gouverneur Warren, spotted the sun shining off the bayonets of Longstreet's men as they moved toward the Union left, it alerted the Army of the Potomac of the need to occupy Little Round Top, high ground that commanded much of the field.

With Warren having alerted his superiors to the importance of Little Round Top, Strong

45   Davis, Kenneth C. *The Civil War: Everything You Need to Know About America's Greatest Conflict but Never Learned.* Page 301.

Vincent's brigade moved into position, under orders from Warren to "hold this ground at any costs," As part of Strong Vincent's brigade, Chamberlain's 20th Maine was on the left of the line, and thus Chamberlain's unit represented the extreme left of the Army of the Potomac's line.

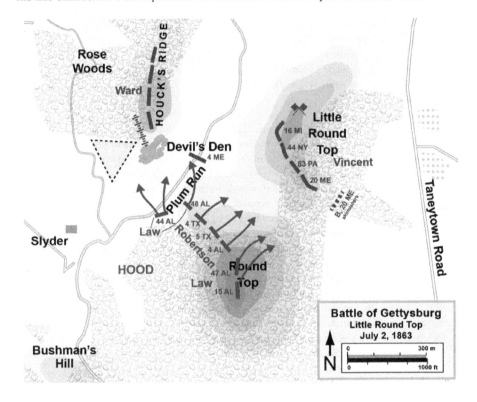

Vincent

In front of Vincent's brigade was General Evander Law's advancing Alabama Brigade (of Hood's Division). Law ordered 5 regiments to take Little Round Top, the 4th, 15th, and 47th Alabama, and the 4th and 5th Texas, but they had already marched more than 20 miles just to reach that point. They were now being asked to charge up high ground on a muggy, hot day.

Nevertheless, the Confederates made desperate assaults against Little Round Top, even after being repulsed by the Union defenders several times. In the middle of the fighting, after he saw Confederates trying to push around his flank, Chamberlain stretched his line until his regiment was merely a single-file line, and he then had to order his left (southernmost) half to swing back, thus forming an angle in their line in an effort to prevent a flank attack. Despite suffering heavy losses, the 20th Maine held through two subsequent charges by the 15th Alabama and other Confederate regiments for nearly 2 hours.

Even after repulsing the Confederates several times, Chamberlain and his regiment faced a serious dilemma. With casualties mounting and ammunition running low, in desperation, Chamberlain *claimed* to have ordered his left wing to initiate an all-out, pivoting bayonet charge. With the 20th Maine charging ahead, the left wing wheeling continually to make the charging line swing like a hinge, thus creating a simultaneous frontal assault and flanking maneuver, they ultimately succeeded in not only taking the hill, but capturing 100 Confederate soldiers in the process. Chamberlain suffered two slight wounds in the battle, one when a shot ricocheted off his sword scabbard and bruised his thigh, another when his right foot was struck by a piece of shrapnel. With this success, Chamberlain was credited with preventing the Union flank from being penetrated and keeping the Confederates from pouring in behind Union lines.

Ultimately, it was the occupation and defense of Little Round Top that saved the rest of the

Union line at Gettysburg. Had the Confederates commanded that high ground, it would have been able to position artillery that could have swept the Union lines along Cemetery Ridge and Cemetery Hill, which would have certainly forced the Army of the Potomac to withdraw from their lines. Chamberlain would be awarded the coveted Congressional Medal of Honor for "daring heroism and great tenacity in holding his position on the Little Round Top against repeated assaults, and carrying the advance position on the Great Round Top", and the 20th Maine's actions that day became one of the most famous attacks of the Battle of Gettysburg and the Civil War as a whole.

But did it really happen that way? Though historians have mostly given Chamberlain the credit for the order to affix bayonets and make the charge down Little Round Top, and Chamberlain received the credit from Sharaa's *The Killer Angels* and the movie *Gettysburg*, some recent researchers have claimed that Lt. Holman S. Melcher initiated the charge. According to Chamberlain however, Melcher had requested permission to make an advance to help some of his wounded men, only to be told by Chamberlain that a charge was about to be ordered anyway.

Melcher

While Chamberlain's men held the extreme left, the rest of Vincent's brigade struggled desperately to the right, and Vincent himself would be mortally wounded in the fighting. The Confederates had advanced as far as Devil's Den, but Warren continued to bring reinforcements to Little Round Top to hold off Confederate attempts on the high ground. For the rest of the battle, even after the Confederates were repulsed from Little Round Top, their snipers in Devil's Den made the defenders of Little Round Top miserable. Confederate sharpshooters stationed around Devil's Den mortally wounded General Stephen Weed, whose New York brigade had arrived as reinforcements, and when his friend, artilleryman Lt. Charles Hazlett leaned over to comfort Weed or hear what he was trying to say, snipers shot Hazlett dead as well.

The fighting on the Union left finally ended as night fell. George Sykes, the commander of the V Corps, later described Day 2 in his official report, "Night closed the fight. The key of the battle-field was in our possession intact. Vincent, Weed, and Hazlett, chiefs lamented throughout the corps and army, sealed with their lives the spot intrusted to their keeping, and on which so much depended.... General Weed and Colonel Vincent, officers of rare promise, gave their lives to their country."

While the Army of the Potomac managed to desperately hold on the left, Ewell's attack against Culp's Hill on the other end of the field met with some success in pushing the Army of the Potomac back. However, the attack started so late in the day that nightfall made it impossible for the Confederates to capitalize on their success. Ewell's men would spend the night at the base of Culp's Hill and partially up the hill, but it would fall upon them to pick up the attack the next morning.

That night, Meade held another council of war. Having been attacked on both flanks, Meade and his top officers correctly surmised that Lee would attempt an attack on the center of the line the next day. Moreover, captured Confederates and the fighting and intelligence of Day 2 let it be known that the only Confederate unit that had not yet seen action during the fighting was George Pickett's division of Longstreet's corps.

July 3, 1863

If July 2 was Longstreet's worst day of the Civil War, July 3 was almost certainly Robert E. Lee's. After the attack on July 2, Longstreet spent the night continuing to plot potential movements around Little Round Top and Big Round Top, thinking that would again get the Confederate army around the Union's flank. Longstreet himself did not realize that a reserve corps of the Union army was poised to block that maneuver.

Longstreet did not meet with Lee on the night of July 2, so when Lee met with him the following morning he found Longstreet's men were not ready to conduct an early morning attack, which Lee had wanted to attempt just as he was on the other side of the lines against Culp's Hill. With Pickett's men not up, however, Longstreet's corps couldn't make such an attack. Lee later wrote that Longstreet's "dispositions were not completed as early as was expected."

On the morning of July 3, the Confederate attack against Culp's Hill fizzled out, but by then Lee had already planned a massive attack on the Union center, combined with having Stuart's cavalry attack the Union army's lines in the rear. A successful attack would split the Army of the Potomac at the same time its communication and supply lines were severed by Stuart, which would make it possible to capture the entire army in detail.

There was just one problem with the plan, as Longstreet told Lee that morning: no 15,000 men who ever existed could successfully execute the attack. The charge required marching across an open field for about a mile, with the Union artillery holding high ground on all sides of the incoming Confederates. Longstreet ardently opposed the attack, but, already two days into the battle, Lee explained that because the Army of the Potomac was here on the field, he must strike at it. Longstreet later wrote that he said, "General Lee, I have been a soldier all my life. It is my opinion that no fifteen thousand men ever arrayed for battle can take that position."[46] Longstreet proposed instead that their men should slip around the Union forces and occupy the high ground, forcing Northern commanders to attack them, rather than *vice versa*.

Realizing the insanity of sending 15,000 men hurtling into all the Union artillery, Lee planned to use the Confederate artillery to try to knock out the Union artillery ahead of time. Although old friend William Pendleton was the artillery chief, the artillery cannonade would be supervised by Edward Porter Alexander, Longstreet's chief artillerist, who would have to give the go-ahead to the charging infantry because they were falling under Longstreet's command. Alexander later noted that Longstreet was so disturbed and dejected about ordering the attack that at one point he tried to make Alexander order the infantry forward, essentially doing Longstreet's dirty work for him.

A short time later, Confederate General George Pickett, commander of one of the three divisions under General Longstreet, prepared for the *Lee-designed* charge (henceforth known as "Pickett's Charge") aimed at the Union center. With his men in position, Pickett asked Longstreet to give the order to advance, but Longstreet would only nod, fearing that "to verbalize the order may reveal his utter lack of confidence in the plan." And while most of the men participating in that charge had been led to believe that the battle was nearly over and that all that remained was to march unopposed to Cemetery Hill, in actually, those men were unwittingly walking into a virtual massacre.

As Longstreet had predicted, from the beginning the plan was an abject failure. As Stuart's cavalry met its Union counterparts near East Cavalry Field, a young cavalry officer named George Custer convinced division commander Brig. General David McMurtrie Gregg to allow his brigade to stay and fight, even while Custer's own division was stationed to the south out of the action.

---

[46]   Gaffney, P. and D. Gaffney. *The Civil War: Exploring History One Week at a Time*. Page 282.

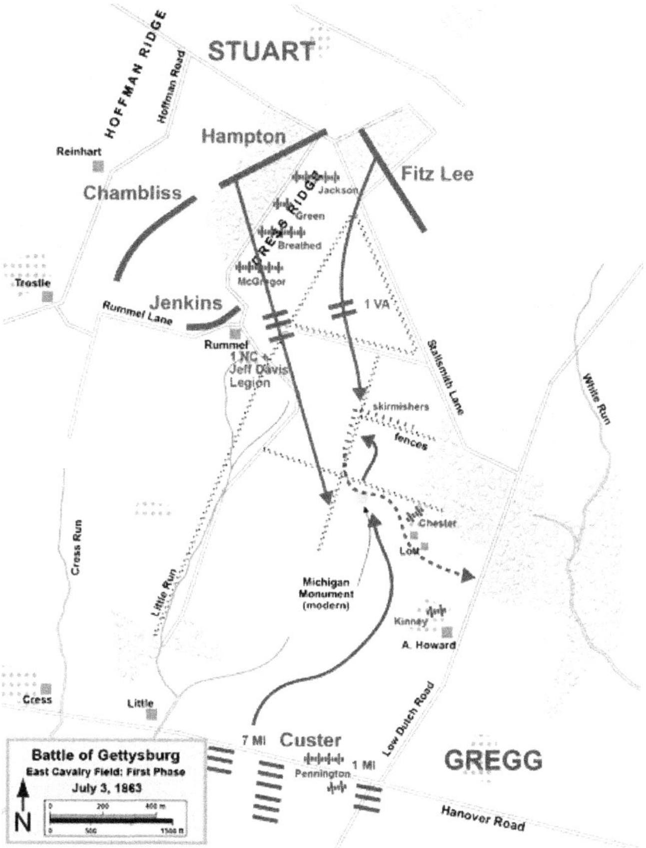

STUART
HOFFMAN RIDGE
Hoffman Road
Hampton
Reinhart
Fitz Lee
Chambliss
Jackson
Green
Breathed
McGregor
Trostle
Jenkins
Rummel Lane
1 VA
Rummel
1 NC + Jeff Davis Legion
Stallsmith Lane
White Run
skirmishers
fences
Chester
Cress Run
Michigan Monument (modern)
Little Run
Kinney
A. Howard
Cress
Little
Low Dutch Road
7 MI
Custer
1 MI
Pennington
GREGG
Hanover Road
Battle of Gettysburg
East Cavalry Field: First Phase
July 3, 1863
N

The fighting at East Cavalry Field turned out to be Custer's best known action of the Civil War, and it was his brigade that bore the brunt of the casualties in repulsing Stuart's cavalry. Right as the Confederates were starting the artillery bombardment ahead of Pickett's Charge, Stuart's men met Gregg's on the field.

After Stuart's men sent Union skirmishers scurrying, Gregg ordered Custer to counterattack with the 7th Michigan Cavalry Regiment. Custer led the charge personally, exhorting his men with the rallying cry, "Come on you Wolverines!" In the ensuing melee, which featured sabers and close range shooting, Custer had his horse shot out from under him, at which point he took a bugler's horse and continued fighting. Ultimately, his men sent Stuart's cavalry retreating, forcing Stuart to order in reinforcements.

Stuart's reinforcements sent the 7th Michigan in retreat, but now Custer rallied the 1st Michigan regiment to charge in yet another counterattack, with the same rallying cry, ""Come on you Wolverines!" Both sides galloped toward each other and crashed head on, engaging in more fierce hand-to-hand combat. Eventually, the Union held the field and forced Stuart's men to retreat.

Custer's brigade lost over 200 men in the attack, the highest loss of any Union cavalry brigade at Gettysburg, but he had just valiantly performed one of the most successful cavalry charges of the war. Custer wasn't exactly humble about his performance, writing in his official report after the battle, "I challenge the annals of warfare to produce a more brilliant or successful charge of cavalry."

As Stuart was in the process of being repulsed, just after 1:00 p.m. 150 Confederate guns began to fire from Seminary Ridge, hoping to incapacitate the Union center before launching an infantry attack, but they mostly overshot their mark. The artillery duel could be heard from dozens of miles away, and all the smoke led to Confederate artillery constantly overshooting their targets. Realizing that the artillery was meant for them as a way of softening them up for an infantry charge, Hancock calmly rode his horse up and down the line of the II Corps, both inspiring and assuring his men with his own courage and resolve.

During the massive Confederate artillery bombardment that preceded the infantry assault, Hancock was so conspicuous on horseback reviewing and encouraging his troops that one of his subordinates pleaded with him that "the corps commander ought not to risk his life that way." Hancock reportedly replied, "There are times when a corps commander's life does not count."

Eventually, Union artillery chief Henry Hunt cleverly figured that if the Union cannons stopped firing back, the Confederates might think they successfully knocked out the Union batteries. On top of that, the Union would be preserving its ammunition for the impending charge that everyone now knew was coming. When they stopped, Lee, Alexander, and others mistakenly concluded that they'd knocked out the Union artillery.

A short time later, Confederate General George Pickett, commander of one of the three divisions under General Longstreet, prepared for the charge that would forever bear his name, even though he commanded only about a third of the force and was officially under Longstreet's direction. With his men in position, Pickett asked Longstreet to give the order to advance, but Longstreet could only nod, fearing that "to verbalize the order may reveal his utter lack of confidence in the plan."

Thus, about 15,000 Confederates stepped out in sight and began their charge with an orderly march starting about a mile away, no doubt an inspiring sight to Hancock and the Union men directly across from the oncoming assault.

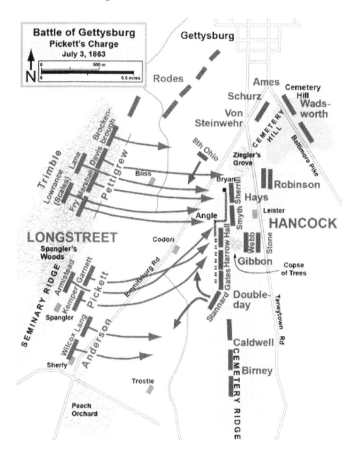

As the Confederate line advanced, Union cannon on Cemetery Ridge and Little Round Top began blasting away, with Confederate soldiers continuing to march forward. One Union soldier later wrote, "We could not help hitting them with every shot . . . a dozen men might be felled by one single bursting shell."[47] By the time Longstreet's men reached Emmitsburg Road, Union artillery switched to firing grapeshot (tin cans filled with iron and lead balls), and as the

---

[47] Gaffney, P. and D. Gaffney. *The Civil War: Exploring History One Week at a Time*. Page 283.

Confederate troops continued to approach the Union center, Union troops positioned behind the wall cut down the oncoming Confederates, easily decimating both flanks. And while some of the men did mange to advance to the Union line and engage in hand-to-hand combat, it was of little consequence.

In the midst of the fighting, as he was conferring with one of his brigadier generals, General Stannard, Hancock suddenly felt a searing pain in his thigh. He had just been severely wounded when a bullet struck the pommel of his saddle and entered his inner right thigh, along with wood splinters and a large bent nail. Helped from his horse by his aides, he removed the saddle nail himself and applied a tourniquet, colorfully swearing at his own men while demanding that they not let him bleed to death. Nevertheless, he refused to remove himself to the rear until the offensive had concluded.

After about an hour, nearly 6,500 Confederates were dead or wounded, five times that of the Union, with all 13 regimental commanders in Pickett's division killed or wounded. In the aftermath of the defeat, General Longstreet stated, "General Lee came up as our troops were falling back and encouraged them as well as he could; begged them to reform their ranks and reorganize their forces . . . and it was then he used the expression . . . 'It was all my fault; get together, and let us do the best we can toward saving which is left to us.'"[48] Longstreet never resisted an opportunity to distance himself from failure and direct it towards someone else, even Lee.

Today Pickett's Charge is remembered as the American version of the Charge of the Light Brigade, a heroic but completely futile march that had no chance of success. In fact, it's remembered as Pickett's Charge because Pickett's Virginians wanted to claim the glory of getting the furthest during the attack in the years after the war. The charge consisted of about 15,000 men under the command of James Longstreet, with three divisions spearheaded by Pickett, Trimble, and Pettigrew. Trimble and Pettigrew were leading men from A.P. Hill's corps, and Hill was too disabled by illness that day to choose the men from his corps to make the charge. As a result, some of the men who charged that day had already engaged in heavy fighting.

The charge suffered about a 50% casualty rate, as the Confederates marched into hell. The men barely made a dent in the Union line before retreating in disorder back across the field, where Lee met them in an effort to regroup them in case the Union counterattacked. At one point, Lee ordered Pickett to reform his division, to which Pickett reportedly cried, "I have no division!"

---

48   Davis, Kenneth C. *The Civil War: Everything You Need to Know About America's Greatest Conflict but Never Learned*. Page 306.

Pickett

One of the Virginians who marched straight into Hancock's II Corps was his old friend Lewis A. Armistead, who was leading one of Pickett's brigades. Armistead famously led his brigade with his hat atop his sword, serving as a visual cue for his men, and they actually breached the II Corps' line, making it about as far as any Confederate got. In the fighting, Armistead was mortally wounded and captured, dying days later.

Who's to Blame?

After the South had lost the war, the importance of Gettysburg as one of the "high tide" marks of the Confederacy became apparent to everyone, making the battle all the more important in the years after it had been fought. Former Confederate comrades like Longstreet and Jubal Early would go on to argue who was responsible for the loss at Gettysburg (and thus the war) in the following decades. Much of the debate was fueled by those who wanted to protect Lee's legacy, especially because Lee was dead and could not defend himself in writing anymore. However, on July 3, Lee insisted on taking full blame for what occurred at Gettysburg, telling his retreating men, "It's all my fault." Historians have mostly agreed, placing the blame for the disastrous Day 3 on Lee's shoulders. Porter Alexander would later call it Lee's "worst day" of the war.

However, after the war, former Confederates would not accept criticism of Lee, and blame for the loss at Gettysburg was placed upon other scapegoats. Although it was not immediately apparent where the blame rested for such a devastating loss, not long after the Battle of Gettysburg two names kept surfacing: cavalry leader General "Jeb" Stuart and General James Longstreet; Stuart blamed for robbing Lee of the "eyes" he needed to know of Union movement, and Longstreet for delaying his attack on Round Top Hills the second day and acting too slowly in executing the assault on the Union left flank.

Though credited with devoting his full attention to the Confederate cause upon his arrival, many historians attribute the catastrophic loss to the absence of Stuart and his cavalry. Immediately becoming the most devastating event of Stuart's military career, in his official report General Lee's wrote, " . . . the absence of the cavalry rendered it impossible to obtain accurate information. By the route [we] pursued, the Federal Army was interposed between [my] command and our main body, preventing any communication with [Stuart] until his arrival at Carlisle. The march toward Gettysburg was conducted more slowly than it would have been had the movements of the Federal Army been known." Some of Stuart's subordinates would come to his defense after the war, and Lee deserves some blame for allowing his subordinates so much discretion, which may have worked with Stonewall Jackson but backfired spectacularly with Ewell and Stuart. After the war, Stuart's subordinate, General Thomas L. Rosser stated what many were already convinced of, "On this campaign, [Stuart] undoubtedly, make the fatal blunder which lost us the battle of Gettysburg."[49]

Controversy over Lee's Retreat

From a military perspective, Meade had made efficient use of his subordinates (particularly Generals John F. Reynolds and Winfield S. Hancock) during this three-day, course-changing battle, ultimately executing some of the most effective battleline strategies of the War. In short, Meade had successfully commanded the forces that repulsed Lee's Army and effectively won what most historians consider the battle that changed the course of the Civil War and ultimately resulted in a Confederate defeat.

While nobody questions that Meade's strategy at Gettysburg was strong, he was heavily criticized by contemporaries for not pursuing Lee's army more aggressively as it retreated. Chief-of-staff Daniel Butterfield, who would call into question Meade's command decisions and courage at Gettysburg, accused Meade of not finishing off the weakened Lee. Meade would later state that as his army's new commander, he was uncertain of his troops' capabilities and strength, especially after a battle that had just resulted in over 20,000 Union casualties. Moreover, heavy rains made pursuit almost impossible on July 4, and Lee actually invited an attack during the retreat, hoping Meade would haphazardly attack strongly fortified positions.

Though historians now mostly credit Meade with making proper decisions in the wake of the battle, Lincoln was incredibly frustrated when Lee successfully retreated south. On July 14, Lincoln drafted a letter that he ultimately decided not to send to Meade, who never read it in his lifetime:

---

[49]   Wert, Jeffry D. *Cavalryman of the Lost Cause: A Biography of J.E.B. Stuart.* Page 300.

"I have just seen your despatch to Gen. Halleck, asking to be relieved of your command, because of a supposed censure of mine. I am very--very--grateful to you for the magnificent success you gave the cause of the country at Gettysburg; and I am sorry now to be the author of the slightest pain to you. But I was in such deep distress myself that I could not restrain some expression of it. I had been oppressed nearly ever since the battles at Gettysburg, by what appeared to be evidences that yourself, and Gen. Couch, and Gen. Smith, were not seeking a collision with the enemy, but were trying to get him across the river without another battle. What these evidences were, if you please, I hope to tell you at some time, when we shall both feel better. The case, summarily stated is this. You fought and beat the enemy at Gettysburg; and, of course, to say the least, his loss was as great as yours. He retreated; and you did not, as it seemed to me, pressingly pursue him; but a flood in the river detained him, till, by slow degrees, you were again upon him. You had at least twenty thousand veteran troops directly with you, and as many more raw ones within supporting distance, all in addition to those who fought with you at Gettysburg; while it was not possible that he had received a single recruit; and yet you stood and let the flood run down, bridges be built, and the enemy move away at his leisure, without attacking him. And Couch and Smith! The latter left Carlisle in time, upon all ordinary calculation, to have aided you in the last battle at Gettysburg; but he did not arrive. At the end of more than ten days, I believe twelve, under constant urging, he reached Hagerstown from Carlisle, which is not an inch over fifty-five miles, if so much. And Couch's movement was very little different.

Again, my dear general, I do not believe you appreciate the magnitude of the misfortune involved in Lee's escape. He was within your easy grasp, and to have closed upon him would, in connection with our other late successes, have ended the war. As it is, the war will be prolonged indefinitely. If you could not safely attack Lee last Monday, how can you possibly do so South of the river, when you can take with you very few more than two thirds of the force you then had in hand? It would be unreasonable to expect, and I do not expect you can now effect much. Your golden opportunity is gone, and I am distressed immeasurably because of it.

I beg you will not consider this a prosecution, or persecution of yourself As you had learned that I was dissatisfied, I have thought it best to kindly tell you why."

Still, Meade was promoted to brigadier general in the regular army and was officially awarded the Thanks of Congress, which commended Meade "... and the officers and soldiers of [the Army of the Potomac], for the skill and heroic valor which at Gettysburg repulsed, defeated, and drove back, broken and dispirited, beyond the Rappahannock, the veteran army of the rebellion."

Hancock was unquestionably one of the Union heroes at Gettysburg, but his recognition was slow in coming. In the months after the battle, the U.S. Congress thanked Meade and Howard without listing Hancock. Eventually, Major General Hancock later received the Thanks of the U. S. Congress for "gallant, meritorious, and conspicuous share in that great and decisive victory."

As usual, Hancock shared the credit with his men, writing in his post-battle report:

"To speak of the conduct of the troops would seem to be unnecessary, but still it may be justly remarked that this corps sustained its well-earned reputation on many fields, and that the boast of its gallant first commander, the late Maj. Gen. E. V. Sumner, that the Second Corps had "never given to the enemy a gun or color," holds good now as it did under the command of my predecessor, Major-General Couch. To attest to its good conduct and the perils through which it has passed, it may be stated that its losses in battle have been greater than those of any other corps in the Army of the Potomac, or probably in the service, notwithstanding it has usually been numerically weakest."

Chapter 22: The End of 1863

The Army of Northern Virginia Holds the Line

By September 9, 1863, General Lee had reorganized his cavalry, creating a cavalry corps for Stuart with two divisions of three brigades each. In the Bristoe Campaign (in Virginia), Stuart was assigned to lead a broad turning movement in an attempt to access General Meade's rear, but Meade skillfully withdrew his army without providing the opportunity. On October 13, Stuart stumbled into the rear guard of the Union III Corps near Warrenton, resulting in Lee having to send General Ewell's corps to rescue him; Stuart managed to hide his troopers in a wooded ravine until the unsuspecting III Corps moved on. And then on October 14, as Meade withdrew towards Manassas Junction, brigades from the Union II Corps fought a rearguard action against Stuart's cavalry and a division of Brig. General Harry Hays near Auburn, with Stuart's cavalry effectively bluffing Union General Gouverneur K. Warren's infantry and narrowly evading disaster.

After the Confederate debacle at Bristoe Station and an aborted advance on Centreville, Virginia, Stuart's cavalry shielded the withdrawal of Lee's army from Manassas Junction, after which Union General Judson Kilpatrick's cavalry pursued Stuart's cavalry along the Warrenton Turnpike--but were lured into an ambush near Chestnut Hill and routed. Kilpatrick was the one Civil War officer who may have been even more flamboyant than Stuart.

And in a confrontation fought on October 19, 1863 that became known as the "Buckland Races" (and likened to a fox hunt), Stuart and Maj. General Wade Hampton's cavalry succeeded in not only routing Kilpatrick's cavalry, they pursued it at full-gallop for five miles to Haymarket and Gainesville, eventually forcing it to scatter. At this point, the Southern press began to reconsider its harsh criticism of Stuart.

Chickamauga

In June of 1863, Union general William Rosecrans marched southeast toward Chattanooga, Tennessee, in pursuit of Confederate general Braxton Bragg, intending to "drive him into the sea." By this point, both the Union and Confederates had realized how uniquely important Chattanooga was as the rail and road gateway to all points south of the Ohio River and east of the Mississippi River.

In mid-September, the Union Army under General Rosecrans had taken Chattanooga, but rather than be pushed out of the action, Bragg decided to stop with his 60,000 men and prepare a counterattack south of Chattanooga at a creek named Chickamauga. To bolster his fire-power, Confederate President Jefferson Davis sent 12,000 additional troops (some sources say as many as 60,000) under the command of Lieutenant General Longstreet. In only nine days, Longstreet had successfully moved his entire corps by rail to come to Bragg's aid.

On the morning of September 19, 1863, Bragg's men assaulted the Union line, which was established in a wooded area thick with underbrush along the river. That day and the morning of the next, Bragg continue to pummel Union forces, with the battle devolving from an organized succession of coordinated assaults into what one Union soldier described as "a mad, irregular battle, very much resembling guerilla warfare on a vast scale in which one army was bushwhacking the other, and wherein all the science and the art of war went for nothing."[50]

Late that second morning, Rosecrans was misinformed that a gap was forming in his front line, so he responded by moving several units forward to shore it up. What Rosecrans didn't realize, however, was that in doing so he accidentally created a quarter-mile gap in the Union center, directly in the path of an eight-brigade (15,000 man) force led by Longstreet. Described by one of Rosecrans' own men as "an angry flood," Longstreet's attack, which historians are split on whether it was skill or luck, was successful in driving one-third of the Union Army to the crossroads of Rossville, five miles north, with Rosecrans himself running all the way to Chattanooga where he was later found weeping and seeking solace from a staff priest.

The destruction of the entire army was prevented by General George H. Thomas, who rallied the remaining parts of the army and formed a defensive stand on Horseshoe Ridge. Union units spontaneously rallied to create a defensive line on their fall-back point at Horseshoe Ridge-- forming a new right wing for the line of Maj. General George H. Thomas, who had now assumed overall command of the remaining forces. And although the Confederates launched a series of well-executed (albeit costly) assaults, Thomas and his men managed to hold until nightfall, when they made an orderly retreat to Chattanooga while the Confederates occupied the surrounding heights, ultimately besieging the city. Dubbed "The Rock of Chickamauga", Thomas's heroics ensured that Rosecrans' army was able to successfully retreat back to Chattanooga.

In the aftermath of the Battle of Chickamauga, Longstreet blamed the number of men lost during what would be the bloodiest battle of the Western Theater on Bragg's incompetence, also criticizing him for refusing to pursue the escaping Union army. He later stated to Jefferson Davis, "Nothing but the hand of God can help as long as we have our present commander."[51] Bragg owed his position to being a close friend of Jefferson Davis's, and one of the criticisms often lodged at Davis by historians is that he played favorites to the detriment of the South's chances. Even after he reluctantly removed Bragg from command out West, he would bring

---

[50]   Gaffney, P. and D. Gaffney. *The Civil War: Exploring History One Week at a Time.* Page 305.
[51]   Gaffney, P. and D. Gaffney. *The Civil War: Exploring History One Week at a Time.* Page 306.

Bragg to Richmond to serve as a military advisor.

Bragg

Following the victory at Chickamauga, Longstreet departed on an independent mission to expel the Union army from Knoxville, Tennessee--operations that would fail due to what Longstreet explained away as "weakened forces and disagreeable subordinates." Longstreet then took a position at Gordonsville, Virginia where he was poised to protect against Union invasion via the Shenandoah Valley, or quickly reunite with the main body of Lee's Army of Northern Virginia should the main thrust of Union movement advance towards Fredericksburg. On May 4, 1864, upon finding out that his long-time friend General Ulysses S. Grant was now in command of the Union Army, Longstreet confided to his fellow officers, "He will fight us every day and every hour until the end of the war."[52]

Chapter 23: The Overland Campaign

Meade and Grant

For the remainder of the fall of 1863, during both the Bristoe Campaign (the Battle of Auburn on October 13–14, Battle of Bristoe Station on October 14, Battle of Buckland Races on October 19, and Battle Across the Rappahannock on November 7), and during the Mine Run Campaign (Battle Mine Run on November 27--December 2), Meade was repeatedly outmaneuvered by Lee, subsequently withdrawing after fighting minor, inconclusive battles due to his reluctance to attack Lee's entrenched positions.

---

[52]   Rhea, Gordon C. *The Battle of the Wilderness May 5–6, 1864.* Page 42.

With Lee continuing to hold off the Army of the Potomac in a stalemate along the same battle lines at the end of 1863, Lincoln shook things up. In March 1864, Grant was promoted to lieutenant general and given command of all the armies of the United States. His first acts of command were to keep General Halleck in position to serve as a liaison between Lincoln and Secretary of War Edwin Stanton. And though it's mostly forgotten today, Grant technically kept General Meade in command of the Army of the Potomac, even though Grant attached himself to that army before the Overland Campaign in 1864 and thus served as its commander for all intents and purposes.

In May 1864, with Grant now attached to the Army of the Potomac, the Civil War's two most famous generals met each other on the battlefield for the first time. Lee had won stunning victories at battles like Chancellorsville and Second Bull Run by going on the offensive and taking the strategic initiative, but Grant and Lincoln had no intention of letting him do so anymore. Grant ordered General Meade, "Lee's army is your objective point. Wherever Lee goes, there you will go also."

By 1864, things were looking so bleak for the South that the Confederate war strategy was simply to ensure Lincoln lost reelection that November, with the hope that a new Democratic president would end the war and recognize the South's independence. With that, and given the shortage in manpower, Lee's strategic objective was to continue defending Richmond, while hoping that Grant would commit some blunder that would allow him a chance to seize an opportunity.

When Lt. General Ulysses S. Grant was appointed General-in-Chief of all Union Armies in March of 1864, Meade offered to resign, stating that considering the grave importance of the situation, he would not stand in the way of Grant choosing the right man for the job--Sherman, for example. He offered to serve in wherever capacity Grant thought him best suited. Grant, however, who had known Meade somewhat from the Mexican-American War, assured Meade that he had no intentions of replacing him, later writing that Meade's willingness to sacrifice his position for the good of the Union gave him more respect for Meade than his victory at Gettysburg.

But even though Grant would later write that Meade had made a good first impression, and Meade wrote to his wife, "I am much pleased with Grant, and most agreeably disappointed in his evidence of mind and character, Grant immediately set out to control Meade by curtailing his independence of command--even setting up his headquarters with Meade for the remainder of the war. This arrangement was no doubt due in no small way to the lackluster performance the Army of the Potomac had delivered thus far under General Halleck--according to both President Lincoln and Secretary of War Edwin M. Stanton. And while Meade could hardly be held accountable for the Army's less-than-stellar showing thus far, Grant was out to prove that the Army under his command could and would be far more successful against Lee than his predecessor. Thus, as Meade's chief-of-staff General Humphrey wrote regarding their command arrangement, "It was as if two officers commanded the same army and naturally caused some vagueness and uncertainty as to the exact sphere of each."[53] As Meade would later put it in a letter to his wife during the Overland Campaign, "The papers are giving Grant all the credit of what they call successes; I hope they will remember this if anything goes wrong." Unbeknownst to Meade, whose surly demeanor annoyed the press, journalists attached to the Army of the Potomac agreed amongst each other only to mention Meade when reporting about defeats, an arrangement Meade never knew about.

But their commanding arrangement wasn't the only source of friction between the two commanders. In waging a "war of attrition" against Lee in his Overland Campaign, Grant was willing to sustain previously unacceptable losses, knowing that the Union Army had replacement soldiers readily available--while the Confederate Army did not. Meade, despite his aggressive performance in lesser commands early in the War, had now become a more cautious general; more concerned about the futility of attacking entrenched positions that invariably wasted human lives and accomplished little. Most of the bloody repulses his army would suffer in the Overland Campaign would be ordered by Grant.

Grant

[53]   Catton, Bruce. *Grant Takes Command*. Page 156.

Additionally, Meade was frequently frustrated by the preferential treatment Grant gave subordinates he brought from the Western Theater to the Army of the Potomac, particularly Maj. General Philip Sheridan, who Grant brought in to command the army's cavalry. While Meade had insisted that Sheridan's troopers perform the traditional (and vital) cavalry functions of reconnaissance, screening, and guarding Union Army's trains, the equally short-tempered Sheridan objected, telling Meade that his talents were wasted on outpost duty and better applied to pursuing General "Jeb" Stuart. After several heated clashes, Grant sided with Sheridan, obliging Meade to defer to Grant's judgment. Thus, Meade's own effort and resolve to end the War are largely overshadowed by Grant's greater scheme. Meade would later write to his brother-in-law, Henry Cram, "Grant is not a mighty genius, but he is a good soldier of great force of character . . . His prominent quality is unflinching tenacity of purpose, which blinds him to opposition and obstacles--certainly a great quality in a commander, when controlled by judgment; but a dangerous one otherwise."[54]

Hancock and Chamberlain Recuperate

Forced out of action for the next six months after Gettysburg, Hancock performed recruiting duty in Norristown, and though he eventually resumed command, he would suffer the effects of his Gettysburg wound for the duration of his life.

By November of 1863, Hancock had started to question his resolve to remain part of the Union War effort. Long past were his "Superb" moments, he'd now been wounded four times, his Gettysburg wound stubbornly refused to heal, and independent command seemed no closer than it had several engagements before. There were rumors that General Meade might be relieved of duty, and that he was in line to replace him, but he also began to wonder if his promotions had been more appeasement than acknowledgment of his leadership abilities. Additionally, his once proud II Corps had been reduced to a mere shadow of itself, now bloated with "bounty men." Decidedly tired of serving the army and receiving so little glory, he remarked to a colleague, "We do not get any of the credit, considering the fighting we do."[55]

Hancock had a good point, especially when he could point to the treatment Meade received in the wake of the battle. Although the Army of the Potomac had been victorious at Gettysburg, Lincoln was still upset at what he perceived to be General Meade's failure to trap Robert E. Lee's Army of Northern Virginia in Pennsylvania. When Lee retreated from Pennsylvania without much fight from the Army of the Potomac, Lincoln was again discouraged, believing Meade had a chance to end the war if he had been bolder. Though historians dispute that, and the Confederates actually invited attack during their retreat, Lincoln was constantly looking for more

---

[54]   Catton, Bruce. *Grant Takes Command.* Pages 409--410.

[55]   Catton, Bruce. *Grant Takes Command.* Page 431.

aggressive fighters to lead his men.

Meanwhile, in the fall of 1863, following the Battle of Gettysburg, Colonel Chamberlain left his regiment to heal from wounds sustained at Little Round Top and a case of malaria, not rejoining his regiment until May of 1864. On June 6, Brig. General Gouverneur Warren appointed Chamberlain commander of the new First Brigade of General Charles Griffin's division (a brigade of six battle-hardened veteran Pennsylvania regiments), pushing to have him promoted to brigadier general, saying, "Colonel Chamberlain is one whose services and sufferings entitle him to the promotion and I am sure his appointment would add to my strength even more than the reinforcement of a thousand men."[56] These sentiments were echoed by Generals Griffin, Barnes, and Bartlett as well.

The Battle of the Wilderness

On May 4, 1864, Grant launched the Overland Campaign, crossing the Rapidan River near Fredericksburg with the 100,000 strong Army of the Potomac, which almost doubled Lee's hardened but battered Army of Northern Virginia. It was a similar position to the one George McClellan had in 1862 and Joe Hooker had in 1863, and Grant's first attack, at the Battle of the Wilderness, followed a similar pattern. Nevertheless, Lee proved more than capable on the defensive.

From May 5-6, Lee's men won a tactical victory at the Battle of the Wilderness, which was fought so close to where the Battle of Chancellorsville took place a year earlier that soldiers encountered skeletons that had been buried in (too) shallow graves in 1863. Moreover, the woods were so thick that neither side could actually see who they were shooting at, and whole brigades at times got lost in the forest. Still, both armies sustained heavy casualties while Grant kept attempting to move the fighting to a setting more to his advantage, but the heavy forest made coordinated movements almost impossible.

Though ultimately one of the most horrendous battles of the war (where wounded men literally burned to death in fires ignited by rifle fire sparking the underbrush), by the end of the first day, Union forces still held control of vital intersections. That night, Grant ordered General Hancock and his Second Corps to "throw everything he had into an assault on the Confederate right at dawn."[57]

The next day, as Hancock rode up and down the line establishing order and preparing his men for battle, he was approached by Grant's personal aid, General Horace Porter, who later

---

[56]   Wallace, Willard M. *Soul of the Lion: A Biography of General Joshua L. Chamberlain.* Page 126.
[57]   McPherson, James M. *Ordeal by Fire: The Civil War and Reconstruction.* Page 448.

described the "knightly corps commander," writing, "His face was flushed with the excitement of victory, his eyes were lighten by the fire of battle, his flaxen hair was thrust back from his temples, his right are was extended to its full length in pointing out certain positions . . . his commanding form towered still higher as he rose in his stirrups to peer through the openings in the woods. It was enough to inspire the troops he led to deeds of unmatched heroism."[58] Clearly, Hancock was poised for a major victory.

Hancock's May 6, dawn assault initially went well, successful in driving Confederate forces back to Lee's command post a mile away. By one account, "in his wake along the line of his advance, the enemies dead were everywhere visible; his wounded strewn the road; prisoners had been captured, and battle-flags had been taken."[59] However, he wasn't the only one pressing an assault; Lee was determined to launch an attack in the same sector using Longstreet's corps. Longstreet ordered the advance of six brigades by heavy skirmish lines--four to flank the Union right and two against the front--which allowed his men to deliver continuous fire into the enemy while proving elusive targets themselves. After a confusing exchange of gunfire in a heavily-wooded area, Longstreet launched a powerful flanking attack along the Orange Plank Road against Hancock's II Corps that greatly surprised it and nearly drove it off the field.

---

[58]   Porter, Horace. *Campaigning with Grant*. Pages 57--58.
[59]   Porter, Horace. *Campaigning with Grant*. Page 58.

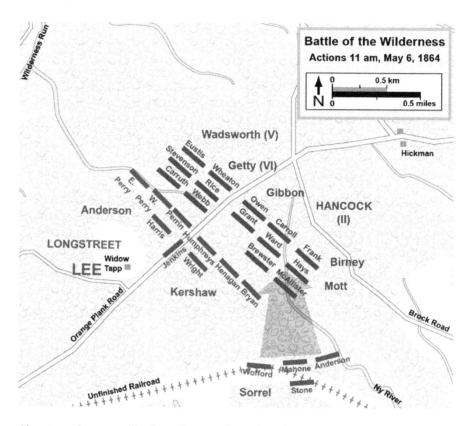

Battle of the Wilderness

Actions 11 am, May 6, 1864

Almost exactly a year earlier, just miles away from where the Battle of the Wilderness was fought, Stonewall Jackson was mortally wounded by fire from his own men. Longstreet nearly suffered the same fate. During the assault, Longstreet was himself wounded — accidentally shot by one of his own men – with the ball passing through the base of his neck and lodging in his shoulder. To assure his men, Longstreet raised his hat as he was being carried off the field, but with Longstreet incapacitated, the momentum of the attack was lost, forcing General Lee to delay further action until units could be realigned. This setback gave Hancock and his corps sufficient time to reorganize, and they were able to hold their position until night fell.

By the end of the day, the battle ended at virtually the same place it had started that morning, except now, thousands of men lay dead. Confederate General Edward Porter Alexander later spoke of the loss of Longstreet at the critical juncture of the battle, saying, "I have always believed that, but for Longstreet's fall, the panic which was fairly underway in Hancock's Corps would have been extended and have resulted in Grant's being forced to retreat back across the

Rapidan."[60]

The Confederates had won a tactical victory at a staggering cost, inflicting 17,000 casualties on Grant and suffering 11,000 of their own. Grant disengaged from the battle in the same position as Hooker before him at Chancellorsville, McClellan on the Virginian Peninsula, and Burnside after Fredericksburg. His men got the familiar dreadful feeling that they would retreat back across the Rapidan toward Washington, as they had too many times before. This time, however, Grant made the fateful decision to keep moving south, inspiring his men by telling them that he was prepared to "fight it out on this line if it takes all Summer."[61]

The Battle of Yellow Tavern

On May 9, 1864, the day after General Grant lost to General Lee the race to occupy Spotsylvania, Virginia (the second major battle of Grant's Overland Campaign), Grant caught wind that Sheridan had been boasting that if he were allowed to concentrate all his cavalry, he could easily whip JEB Stuart's cavalry. General Meade was less impressed with Sheridan's boasts, arguing with Sheridan that he was not screening the army and performing reconnaissance as traditional cavalry units were intended. To that, Sheridan replied that he could "whip Stuart" if Meade let him. Meade informed Grant of that exchange, to which Grant, far more trusting of Sheridan, replied, "Well, he generally knows what he is talking about. Let him start right out and do it."

Sheridan and his men only required a few days to make the Stuart problem go away once and for all. Given this discretion, Sheridan immediately organized a raid against Confederate supply and railroad lines close to Richmond, knowing it would force Stuart to come running out to confront him. Leaving just one regiment behind for routine patrol (about 1,000 men), Sheridan set out with about 13,000 mounted soldiers organized into columns stretching 13 miles. On May 9, the largest cavalry force ever seen in the Eastern Theater, along with 32 artillery pieces, arched southeast intending to slip behind Lee's army with three goals: to disrupt Lee's supply lines by destroying railroad tracks and supplies; to threaten the Confederate capital of Richmond; and most significantly for Sheridan, to take Stuart out of the war.

Moving aggressively to the southeast, Sheridan crossed the North Anna River and seized Beaver Dam Station on the Virginia Central Railroad, then circled wide around Lee's right, so wide that he had Lee virtually encircled before he was detected. General Stuart responded by sending 3,000 men ahead and raced to join them. As Stuart rode to meet the enemy, accompanied by his aide, Maj. Andrew R. Venable, they stopped briefly to see Stuart's wife,

[60]   Alexander, Edward P. (Gallagher, Gary W. editor). *Fighting for the Confederacy: The Personal Recollections of General Edward Porter Alexander.* Page 360.
[61]   Fellman, Michael. *The Making of Robert E. Lee.* Page 167.

Flora, and his children, Jimmie and Virginia. Venable later wrote, "He told me he never expected to live through the war, and that if we were conquered, that he did not want to live."[62]

At noon on May 11, 1864, the two forces met at Yellow Tavern, an abandoned inn six miles north of Richmond, Virginia. Not only did the Union outnumber the Confederates (ten to one by some estimates), it had superior firepower--armed with newly-developed rapid-firing Spencer carbine rifles.

After a spirited resistance by Confederate troops from the low ridge bordering the road to Richmond that lasted over three hours, the First Virginia Cavalry pushed the advancing Union soldiers back from the hilltop as Stuart, mounted on horseback in his conspicuous attire, rallied his men and encouraged them to keep pushing forward. While Union men of the Fifth Michigan Cavalry were steadily retreating, one of them, 48 year old sharpshooter John A. Huff, found himself only about 20 yards away from the vaunted and easily recognizable Stuart. Huff turned and shot Stuart with his .44-caliber pistol, sending a bullet slicing through his stomach and exiting his back, just right of his spine. In excruciating pain, an ambulance took Stuart to the home of his brother-in-law Dr. Charles Brewer, in Richmond, to await his wife's arrival.

The following day, before Flora could reach his side, at 7:38 p.m., Stuart died. In his final moments, Stuart ordered his sword and spurs be given to his son. His dying words were: "I am resigned; God's will be done."[63] He was just 31 years old.

The death of Stuart brought a cloud of gloom to the South, said to be second only to that following the death of General "Stonewall" Jackson. Having known Stuart well before the war, Lee took the news of his death very hard, and witnesses observed him break down upon learning of Stuart's fate. Lee himself noted, "Among the gallant soldiers who have fallen in this war, General Stuart was second to none in valor, in zeal, and in unfaltering devotion to his country. To military capacity of a high order and all the nobler virtues of the soldier he added the brighter graces of a pure life, guided and sustained by the Christian's faith and hope. The mysterious hand of an all-wise God has removed him from the scene of his usefulness and fame. His grateful countrymen will mourn his loss and cherish his memory. To his comrades in arms he has left the proud recollection of his deeds and his inspiring influence of his example."[64]

Following her husband's death, his wife Flora donned black mourning garb which she wore for the remaining 59 years of her life.

---

[62]   Wert, Jeffry D. *Cavalryman of the Lost Cause: A Biography of J.E.B. Stuart*. Page 349.
[63]   Wert, Jeffry D. *Cavalryman of the Lost Cause: A Biography of J.E.B. Stuart*. Pages 361--362.
[64]   Lee, Robert E., Jr. *Recollections and Letters of General Robert E. Lee by Captain E. Lee, His Son.*

Stuart's grave

A short time later, Sheridan released an official report of the incident, making no mention of Stuart: "[I] reached North Anna river without serious opposition. During the night [I] destroyed the enemy's depot at Beaver river, three large trains of cars numbering one hundred, two fine locomotives, one hundred thousand pounds of bacon and other stores amounting in all to one million and a half of rebel rations; also, the telegraph and railroad track for about ten miles . . . recaptured three hundred and seventy-eight of our men. . . ."[65]

---

[65]   Stepp, John, W. and Hill, William I. (editors). *Mirror of War, The Washington Star*

Thrilled by Sheridan's accomplishment (which included the death of Stuart), from that time on, Grant provided him men and horses, rest, and resources as needed. Assured of those resources, the no-nonsense Sheridan routinely shot horses that could no longer function at peak performance. Nevertheless, Sheridan's raid during May has been criticized by some, including Overland Campaign historian Gordon Rhea, who argues, "By taking his cavalry from Spotsylvania Court House, Sheridan severely handicapped Grant in his battles against Lee. The Union Army was deprived of his eyes and ears during a critical juncture in the campaign. And Sheridan's decision to advance boldly to the Richmond defenses smacked of unnecessary showboating that jeopardized his command."

Battle of Spotsylvania Court House

Using the Union V Corps under Major General Gouverneur K. Warren, Grant moved forward in a series of flanking maneuvers that continued to move the army steadily closer to Richmond. But Lee continued to parry each thrust. The next major battle took place at Spotsylvania Court House from May 8-21, with the heaviest fighting on May 12 when a salient in the Confederate line nearly spelled disaster for Lee's army.

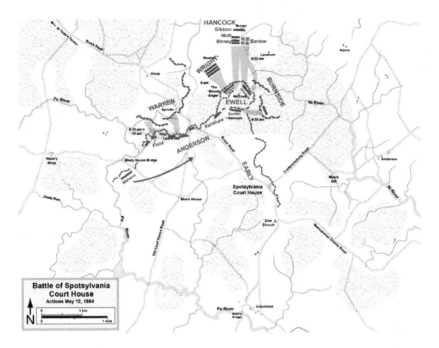

Battle of Spotsylvania
Court House
Actions May 12, 1864

Under General Grant's direct orders, at 4:30 a.m. on May 12, 1864, Hancock's II Corps burst out through the rain and fog, leading a large-scale assault at Spotsylvania Court House that caught the Confederates completely by surprise. Breaking through Lee's front line at "the mule shoe" with relative ease, Hancock's corps effectively split the Confederate Army in half--capturing approximately twenty guns and 2,800 prisoners in the process, the majority of General Jackson's legendary "Stonewall Brigade".

In their zeal, however, the Union forces lost their cohesion, allowing the Confederates to launch an exuberant counterattack that resulted in savage, unrelenting fighting in the rain lasting hours, while bodies piled up on both sides. (Men were literally trampled under the mud as soldiers advanced to take the place of their fallen comrades.) Fighting raged around the "Bloody Angle" for hours, with soldiers fighting hand to hand before the Confederates finally dislodged the Union soldiers. At midnight, the Confederates finally abandoned "Mule Shoe," but Grant had failed to break Lee's defenses as planned.

Following the tactically inconclusive Battle of Spotsylvania Courthouse, during which Grant failed repeatedly to break the Confederate line, Grant requested that Meade be promoted to major general of the Regular Army. In a telegram to Secretary of War Edwin Stanton dated May

13, 1864, Grant stated, "Meade has more than met my most sanguine expectations. He and Sherman are the fittest officers for large commands I have come in contact with." Though honored, Meade felt slighted that his well-deserved promotion was processed after those of Sherman and Sheridan (especially since Sheridan was his subordinate). However, his date of rank meant that at war's end he was outranked only by Grant, Halleck, and Sherman.

Sheridan

Cold Harbor

For the next two weeks, Grant pursued Lee, sending a number of his commanders to outmaneuver Lee's army; attempting to disrupt Lee's supply lines and threaten his rear, thus forcing him out of the trenches to fight, or further retreat.

Lee's army continued to stoutly defend against several attacks by the Army of the Potomac, but massive casualties were inflicted on both sides. After Spotsylvania, Grant had already incurred about 35,000 casualties while inflicting nearly 25,000 casualties on Lee's army. Grant, of course, had the advantage of a steady supply of manpower, so he could afford to fight the war of attrition. It was a fact greatly lost on the people of the North, however, who knew Grant's track record from Shiloh and saw massive casualty numbers during the Overland Campaign. Grant was routinely criticized as a butcher.

As fate would have it, the only time during the Overland Campaign Lee had a chance to take the initiative was after Spotsylvania. During the fighting that came to be known as the Battle of North Anna, Lee was heavily debilitated with illness. Grant nearly fell into Lee's trap by splitting his army in two along the North Anna before avoiding it.

By the time the two armies reached Cold Harbor near the end of May 1864, Grant incorrectly thought that Lee's army was on the verge of collapse. Though his frontal assaults had failed spectacularly at places like Vicksburg, Grant believed that Lee's army was on the ropes and could be knocked out with a strong attack. The problem was that Lee's men were now masterful at quickly constructing defensive fortifications, including earthworks and trenches that made their positions impregnable. While Civil War generals kept employing Napoleonic tactics, Civil War soldiers were building the types of defensive works that would be the harbinger of World War I's trench warfare. This was an innovation that Meade had clearly recognized a considerable time in advance of other Civil War generals, thus explaining his reluctance to make frontal assaults on well-fortified positions.

On June 3, 1864, sensing he could break Lee's army, Grant ordered a full out assault at dawn in the hopes of catching the rebels before they could fully entrench. Although Meade generally performed effectively under Grant's supervision during the Overland Campaign, but a few instances of decidedly bad judgment served to mar his prior substantial record. During the Battle of Cold Harbor, Meade inadequately supervised his corps commanders and did not insist they perform reconnaissance before mounting what would prove to be a famously disastrous frontal attack.

Although the story of Union soldiers pinning their names on the back of their uniforms in anticipation of death at Cold Harbor is apocryphal, the frontal assault on June 3 inflicted thousands of Union casualties in about half an hour. In just minutes, 7,000 Union soldiers were killed or wounded as 30,000 Confederate soldiers successfully held the line against 50,000 Union troops, losing just 1,500 men in the process. With another 12,000 casualties at Cold Harbor, Grant had suffered about as many casualties in a month as Lee had in his entire army at the start of the campaign. Grant later admitted, "I have always regretted that the last assault at Cold Harbor was ever made...No advantage whatever was gained to compensate for the heavy loss we sustained." At the same time, however, Meade understood Grant's strategy, writing to his wife the day after Cold Harbor, "How long this game is to be played it is impossible to tell; but in the long run, we ought to succeed, because it is in our power more promptly to fill the gaps in men and material which this constant fighting produces."

Chapter 24: The Siege of Petersburg

Early Fighting Around Petersburg

Although Grant's results were widely condemned, he continued to push toward Richmond. After the Confederate victory at Cold Harbor, General P.G.T. Beauregard attempted in vain to convince his superiors that Grant's next move would be to cross the James River and attempt to seize Petersburg, the main railroad hub of the Confederacy situated just miles away from

Richmond. Beauregard proved prophetic; after Cold Harbor, Grant managed to successfully steal an entire day's march on Lee and crossed the James River, moving on the Confederacy's primary railroad hub at Petersburg with two Union Army corps totaling 16,000 men on June 15.

Incredibly, the war was saved right then and there by the quick and skillful defense of Petersburg organized by Beauregard and his 5,400 men, outnumbered 3 to 1 by the Union attackers. With Union forces breathing down their necks, Beauregard sent urgent messages to both Lee and the War Department asking for immediate reinforcements, despite serious doubts they could reach him in time. After the war, when the back and forth messages were publicly published, one historian noted, "Nothing illustrates better the fundamental weakness of the Confederate command system than the weary series of telegrams exchanged in May and early June between Davis, Bragg, Beauregard, and Lee. Beauregard evaded his responsibility for determining what help he could give Lee; Davis and Bragg shirked their responsibility to decide, when he refused. The strangest feature of the whole affair was that, in the face of Lee's repeated requests, nobody in the high command thought to order Beauregard to join Lee."

Meanwhile, for three days Union General William "Baldy" Smith seized Confederate artillery and occupied Confederate trenches, winning key positions that gave him and his troops unobstructed entrance into Petersburg. With each passing day, Beauregard assumed retreat was inevitable. But then just as events reached the critical point, Smith lost his nerve and decided to wait for reinforcements before launching his main attack, giving Confederate troops ample time to arrive and successfully fend off a series of assaults characterized as "poorly coordinated" and "driven home without vigor." Ultimately, Lee managed to get his Army of Northern Virginia to Beauregard before the Union could muster a proper attack.

On June 18, still in the early days of what would be a 9 month siege, Union General Meade ordered a general assault of Confederate lines. Leading his Fifth Corps, Colonel Chamberlain rushed ahead of the other Union units, successfully capturing what had been a strongly-defended Confederate position colloquially known as, "Fort Hell." While initially defending the position from a crest above the ground fighting, Chamberlain received orders to lead his men in a frontal charge. His orders were to form a two-column brigade and "not to stop and fire" since this would slow their advance and expose them longer; to try to "carry the defenses with their bayonets."

With his horse shot out from under him in the first minutes, Chamberlain led the charge as directed on foot, with the defense quickly becoming bitter and the casualties heavy. When his color-bearer was shot dead at his side, Chamberlain picked up and hoisted the standard, holding the flag in one hand, his saber in the other. Realizing that his men could not hear his order to "oblique to the left," he waved his saber and flag into the air to gain their attention, essentially making a target of himself. At that moment, a "Minie" ball slammed into his right hip, ripped through his body, and exited through the other hip. Steadying himself with his sword, he continued to direct his men before collapsing to the ground unconscious from loss of blood.

Taken back behind the lines, the profusely-bleeding Colonel Chamberlain was given up for dead by the field surgeons, who were all certain his wound was mortal. After being notified by Warren, General Grant promoted him to brigadier general on the spot, the only battlefield promotion of that elevated rank of the Civil War, stating, "He has been recommended for promotion for gallant and efficient conduct on previous occasion and yesterday led his brigade against the enemy under most destructive fire. He expresses the wish that he may receive the recognition of his services by promotion before he dies for the gratification of his family and friends."

On what was assumed his "deathbed," not only did Chamberlain pen a farewell message to his wife, the U. S. Army listed him as killed in action and published his obituary. Remarkably, Chamberlain began to gradually recover, and to the surprise of all, he was back in command by November. Even when he was urged to resign by many, including wife Fanny, Chamberlain vowed to serve until the war's end and stayed in the army.

By June 20, Grant had called off all attacks and opted to make a siege of Petersburg. And while Beauregard was credited with preventing a Union occupation -- the saving of Petersburg deemed his greatest military achievement -- Grant had nonetheless succeeded in occupying a fixed position that would greatly limit Lee's movement and give Grant the upper hand. Although Beauregard's actions had saved Petersburg from occupation -- and probable destruction -- they resulted in a ten-month siege of the city that ultimately proved successful for the North anyway.

On July 27, 1864, Major General Hancock's II Corps coordinated with General Philip Sheridan's cavalry, crossing north of the James River at Deep Bottom (July 27–29) in an attempt to sever railroad lines in the Shenandoah Valley linking General Lee and General Jubal Early; an attempt that fell quite short in managing to only penetrate the outer Confederate lines.

On August 12, 1864, Hancock was promoted to brigadier general in the Regular Army, and from August 14-20 made another attempt to disrupt Lee's lines at Deep Bottom, only to fail again. Due to the heat and high number of new recruits, the battle was ultimately a Union defeat. With luck already seeming to be running against him, Hancock would now face the only significant military defeat of the Civil War.

On August 25, 1864, while his II Corps moved south of the city, tearing up track along the Wilmington and Weldon Railroad, Confederate Maj. General Henry Heth launched a successful assault against the Union position at Reams' Station, in Dinwiddie County, Virginia, ultimately crushing Hancock's II Corps and taking many of his men prisoner. This humiliating defeat not only tarnished an otherwise distinguished military career, it robbed him of any hope of securing an independent command and playing a prominent role in the remainder of the War. After suffering yet another beating at the Battle of Burgess Mill on October 27-28, in November of 1864 Hancock made the decision to resign from field duty.

Distraught from his mortifying defeat at Reams' Station, increasingly concerned that Grant's "war of attrition" was resulting in unreasonable Union casualties (to which he was contributing), and still suffering pain from his Gettysburg wound, Hancock resigned his field commission to convalesce in Washington, D. C. where he served out the War very much as he'd begun it: leading a recruiting effort.

The siege lines of Petersburg kept Lee completely pinned down and stretched his army. As Lee continued to maintain a tenuous grip there, Sherman's men in the West defeated Joseph E. Johnston and John Bell Hood in the Atlanta Campaign and then marched to sea, capturing Savannah by Christmas. Sherman's successes helped ensure Lincoln was reelected, ensuring the war would go on. Although he'd lost the use of his right arm and could not speak above a whisper, in October of 1864, Longstreet reassumed command of his corps and joined Lee's forces at Petersburg, Virginia. At Cedar Creek on October 19, Union General Philip Sheridan executed a stunning victory over Longstreet, capturing 43 pieces of Confederate artillery and taking numerous prisoners--including Confederate general Stephan Dodson.

Lee had almost no initiative, at one point futilely sending Jubal Early with a contingent through the Shenandoah Valley and toward Washington D.C. in an effort to peel off some of Grant's men. Though Early made it to the outskirts of Washington D.C. and Lincoln famously became the only president to come under enemy fire at Fort Stevens, the Union's "Little Phil" Sheridan pushed Early back through the Valley and scorched it.

The Battle of the Crater

During the initial days of the Siege of Petersburg (which ultimately lasted from June 9, 1864 to March 25, 1865), Meade oversaw an ambitious plan to dig a long mine shaft beneath the Confederate lines so that explosive charges could be planted directly under Elliott's Salient, a fortification in the middle of the Confederate First Corps line. If successful, this would not only kill all the Confederate soldiers in the surrounding area, it would open a considerable gap in Confederate defenses.

The men began work on the shaft on June 25, 1864, though Grant regarded the project as just a means to keep the men occupied and Meade said he didn't think there was any chance of it succeeding. Nevertheless, the worked progressed for the next month while several battles ensued in the surrounding area in an attempt to force General Lee out into the open.

On July 27, Meade was directed to order the completed shaft to be loaded with three hundred twenty kegs of gunpowder, with the plan calling for the mine to be detonated between 3:30 and 3:45 am on the morning of July 30. But on the morning of the 30th when the fuse was lit by civil engineer Union Lieutenant Colonel Henry Pleasants, nothing happened. As minutes passed, no explosion occurred, and the impending dawn creating a threat to the men at the staging points.

After almost an hour had passed and the plan all but aborted, two volunteers from the Forty-eighth Regiment agreed to crawl into the tunnel. Discovering that the fuse had burned out at one of the splices, they proceeded to splice in a length of new fuse and relight it. Finally, at 4:44 a.m. the charges exploded, resulting a massive shower of earth, smoke, broken timbers, and fragmented weaponry that left a deep crater 260 by 60 feet and 30 feet deep. The crater, which is still visible today, immediately wiped out 278 Confederate soldiers and so shocked the remaining troops that they did not even return fire for the next 15 minutes. Even Union soldiers stood paralyzed as blackened body parts rained from the sky and the heads and limbs of half-buried men "wriggled in the loose earth."

Meade had approved Burnside's plan for the battle, but Burnside had intended to lead the attack with a black division that was specifically drilled just for this action. Fearing how the attack would be portrayed with the use of black soldiers, Meade instructed Burnside to substitute an untrained white division in place as the lead attackers.

Stunned -- they had, after all, witnessed the largest manmade explosion in the Western Hemisphere up to that time -- Union troops proceeded to enter the crater instead of fanning out or heading for critical high ground as ordered. Additionally, an unforeseeable result of the explosion was the creation of a 30 foot high wall of dirt from behind which the Confederates could now level a point-blank counterassault against the 15,000 Union soldiers approaching. Infuriated by such a ruthless method of attack, as well as the use of black troops in the assault, over the next few hours the Confederates proceeded to slaughter the Union troops, who were essentially trapped in an earthen fishbowl.

Grant considered the assault "the saddest affair I have witnessed in the war."

Breaking Lee's Lines

Although the Battle of the Crater was the best known battle of the siege, and a Union debacle at that, by the beginning of 1865 the Confederacy was in utter disarray. The main Confederate army in the West under John Bell Hood had been nearly destroyed by General Thomas's men at the Battle of Franklin in late 1864, and Sherman's army faced little resistance as it marched through the Carolinas. Although Confederate leaders remained optimistic, by the summer of 1864 they had begun to consider desperate measures in an effort to turn around the war. From

1863-1865, Confederate leaders had even debated whether to conscript black slaves and enlist them as soldiers. Even as their fortunes looked bleak, the Confederates refused to issue an official policy to enlist blacks. It was likely too late to save the Confederacy anyway.

By the time Lincoln delivered his Second Inaugural Address in March 1865, the end of the war was in sight. That month, Lincoln famously met with Grant, Sherman, and Admiral David Porter at City Point, Grant's headquarters during the siege, to discuss how to handle the end of the war.

George P.A. Healy's famous 1868 painting, "The Peacemakers", depicts the meeting at City Point

After a long and painful period of recovery, Brigadier General Lawrence Chamberlain returned to active duty, taking command of the Union Army's lead brigade at the Battle of Lewis' Farm on March 29, 1865, fighting that would eventually evolve into the Battle of Five Forks on April 1). Leading the main assault against Confederate Lt. General Richard H. Anderson, Chamberlain was wounded yet again, struck by a bullet that penetrated his horse's neck before hitting a leather case he carried in his breast pocket, then grazed his ribs and exited his back, knocking him off his horse. As Anderson sent two brigades to intercept Chamberlain, in the confusion his men lost considerable ground before Chamberlain managed to remount his horse, rally his troops, and then lead a spirited counterattack that captured the enemy's earthworks and lead to a stunning victory.

Lee's siege lines at Petersburg were finally broken on April 1 at the Battle of Five Forks, which is best remembered for General George Pickett (best remembered for Pickett's Charge) enjoying a cod bake lunch while his men were being defeated. Historians have attributed it to unusual environmental acoustics that prevented Pickett and his staff from hearing the battle despite their close proximity, not that it mattered to the Confederates at the time. Between that and Gettysburg, Pickett and Lee were alleged to have held very poor opinions of each other by the end of the war, and there is still debate as to whether Lee had ordered Pickett out of the army during the Appomattox campaign.

In the aftermath of this pivotal battle, despite being credited with breaking Lee's line and forcing Lee's retreat, Sheridan was infuriated with the less-than-stellar actions of his Fifth Corps commander, Maj. General Gouverneur K. Warren. Citing that he had hesitated to press the attack and was not at the front of his columns as expected, Sheridan removed him from command, virtually ruining the general's military career. This action drew considerable criticism (both at that time and later in history), but not from Grant, who concurred that hesitation could not win the war, and gave Sheridan written permission to relieve Warren if he felt it was justified for the good of the service. A court inquiry, however, disagreed; later determining that Sheridan was unjustified in the handling of this matter.

Nevertheless, the following day, Generals Grant and Meade ordered a general assault against the weakened Petersburg lines by the Second, Ninth, Sixth, and Twenty-fifth Corps. That day, April 2, 1865, Lee abandoned Petersburg, and thus Richmond with it.

Chapter 25: The End of the Civil War

The days between April 2 and April 9, 1865 have been characterized as "ferocious marching for both armies as fierce little battles took place that never blossomed into the last full-scale action so many expected." Lee's battered army began stumbling toward a rail depot in the hopes of avoiding being surrounded by Union forces and picking up much needed food rations. While Grant's army continued to chase Lee's retreating army westward, the Confederate government sought to escape across the Deep South. On April 4, President Lincoln entered Richmond and toured the home of Confederate President Jefferson Davis.

Though stiff and sore from his recent wounds, Major General Chamberlain remained in command and in westward pursuit of Lee's Army of Northern Virginia. On April 2, Chamberlain's army swept across the Southside railroad and captured the last Confederate train out of Richmond, cutting off Lee's supplies. Then, as Confederate resistance increased, Chamberlain used his troops (and a brigade under General Edgar Gregory) to dislodge any enemy resisters.

From April 3 to April 4, Chamberlain marched his troops some 35 miles to Jetersville--where it was supposed the final battle would take place. On April 6, when it was discovered that General Lee had slipped away, Chamberlain marched his men 32 miles that day and almost as many the next, as part of forces intending to outmaneuver, or, at a minimum, box Lee in with no escape. On April 6, 1865, the Civil War took a major step towards its conclusion. At a place described as a "soggy little crossing in a bottomland ninety miles from nowhere" known as Sayler's Creek, the Army of the Potomac overtook part of Lee's army under General Ewell and proceeded to effectively decimate nearly half of it, taking many prisoners (including Ewell himself).

After Sayler's Creek, Sheridan's report, dated April 7, read, "If the thing is pressed I think that Lee will surrender," prompting Lincoln to send an immediate dispatch to Grant saying, "Let the *thing* be pressed."[66] That same day, April 7, 1865, Grant sent Lee the first official letter demanding Lee's surrender. In it Grant wrote, "The results of the last week must convince you of the hopelessness of further resistance on the part of the Army of Northern Virginia in this struggle. I feel it is so, and regret it as my duty to shift myself from the responsibility of any further effusion of blood by asking of you the surrender of that portion of the Confederate States army known as the Army of Northern Virginia."[67] Passing the note to General Longstreet, now his only advisor, Longstreet said, "Not yet."[68] But by the following evening during what would be the final Confederate Council of War (and after one final attempt had been made to break through Union lines), Lee finally succumbed, stating regretfully, "There is nothing left me but to go and see General Grant, and I had rather die a thousand deaths."[69]

Communications continued until April 9, at which point Lee and Grant two met at Appomattox Court House. When Lee and Grant met, the styles in dress captured the personality differences perfectly. Lee was in full military attire, while Grant showed up casually in a muddy uniform. The Civil War's two most celebrated generals were meeting for the first time since the Mexican-American War. As fate would have it, Meade and Hancock would not be present at the surrender ceremony, while Chamberlain played a conspicuous role.

---

[66]   Lincoln, Abraham (D. E. Fehrenbacher, editor). *Abraham Lincoln: Speeches and Writings 1859--1865.* Page 696.

[67]   Horn, Stanley F. (editor). *The Robert E. Lee Reader.* Page 436.

[68]   Davis, Kenneth C. *The Civil War: Everything You Need to Know About America's Greatest Conflict but Never Learned.* Page 402.

[69]   Davis, Kenneth C. *The Civil War: Everything You Need to Know About America's Greatest Conflict but Never Learned.* Page 402.

The McLean Parlor in Appomattox Court House. McLean's house was famously fought around during the First Battle of Bull Run, leading him to move to Appomattox.

The Confederate soldiers had continued fighting while Lee worked out the terms of surrender, and they were understandably devastated to learn that they had surrendered. Some of his men had famously suggested to Lee that they continue to fight on. Porter Alexander would later rue the fact that he suggested to Lee that they engage in guerrilla warfare, which earned him a stern rebuke from Lee. As a choked-up Lee rode down the troop line on his famous horse Traveller that day, he addressed his defeated army, saying, "Men, we have fought through the war together. I have done my best for you; my heart is too full to say more."

On Palm Sunday, April 9, 1865, Union general Charles Griffin summoned Major General Chamberlain to his headquarters. With most of the surrender terms worked out, General Grant had insisted on a formal surrender of the Confederate arms and colors before a representative portion of the Union Army; General Chamberlain was to have the honor of receiving the Confederate infantry surrender at Appomattox Court House.

When the procession of defeated Confederates marched past the ranks of Union troops, the ever-chivalrous Chamberlain ordered his men to attention and saluted the defeated "Rebels." Chamberlain later described the scene in his memoirs about the final campaigns of the Civil War, *The Passing of the Armies*: "[General John] Gordon, at the head of the marching column, outdoes us in courtesy. He was riding with downcast eyes and more than pensive look; but at this clatter of arms he raises his eyes and instantly catching the significance, wheels his horse with that superb grace of which he is master, drops the point of his sword to his stirrup, gives a command, at which the great Confederate ensign following him is dipped and his decimated brigades, as they reach our right, respond to the 'carry.' All the while on our part not a sound of trumpet or drum, not a cheer, nor a word nor motion of man, but awful stillness as if it were the passing of the dead."

Did it really happen the way Chamberlain described it? When Gordon wrote his own memoirs, he referred to Chamberlain as "one of the knightliest soldiers of the Federal Army." But Gordon himself never mentioned this anecdote until after he read Chamberlain's account nearly 40 years after the event. While Chamberlain's description of the event has generally been accepted as accurate, there remains a trace of uncertainty.

Appomattox is frequently cited as the end of the Civil War, but there still remained several Confederate armies across the country, mostly under the command of General Joseph E. Johnston, who Lee had replaced nearly 3 years earlier. On April 26, Johnston surrendered all of his forces to General Sherman. Over the next month, the remaining Confederate forces would surrender or quit. The last skirmish between the two sides took place May 12-13, ending ironically with a Confederate victory at the Battle of Palmito Ranch in Texas. Two days earlier, Jefferson Davis had been captured in Georgia.

By the time Lee had surrendered, Meade could sense how the history of both Appomattox and the Civil War would be written, and how it would not be in his favor. The day after Lee's surrender, Meade wrote his wife, "I have been quite sick, but I hope now, with a little rest and quiet, to get well again. I have had a malarious catarrh, which has given me a great deal of trouble. I have seen but few newspapers since this movement commenced, and I don't want to see any more, for they are full of falsehood and of undue and exaggerated praise of certain individuals who take pains to be on the right side of the reporters. Don't worry yourself about this; treat it with contempt. It cannot be remedied, and we should be resigned. I don't believe the truth ever will be known, and I have a great contempt for History. Only let the war be finished, and I returned to you and the dear children, and I will be satisfied."

Meade was also forthcoming with his wife about how he felt regarding Grant and Sheridan by the end of the war. "Grant I do not consider so criminal; it is partly ignorance and partly selfishness which prevents his being aware of the effects of his acts. With Sheridan it is not so. His determination to absorb the credit of everything done is so manifest as to have attracted the attention of the whole army, and the truth will in time be made known. His conduct towards me has been beneath contempt, and will most assuredly react against him in the minds of all just and fair-minded persons."

At the same time, Hancock was not present for the surrender ceremony. Hancock served in the Middle Military Division until the end of the war, never receiving an independent command, but effective March 13, 1865, was promoted to brevet major general in the Regular Army for his service at Spotsylvania. A year later, in 1866, the War Department recognized his contribution to the Civil War by making his wartime rank of major general in the Regular Army permanent.

Hancock was almost certainly the greatest corps commander the Army of the Potomac had during the Civil War, and given how much more successful and competent he proved than others who actually led that army, it didn't escape many's notice that he was never given an independent command. In his famous memoirs, Ulysses S. Grant noted, "Hancock stands the most conspicuous figure of all the general officers who did not exercise a separate command. He commanded a corps longer than any other one, and his name was never mentioned as having committed in battle a blunder for which he was responsible. He was a man of very conspicuous personal appearance.... His genial disposition made him friends, and his personal courage and his presence with his command in the thickest of the fight won for him the confidence of troops serving under him. No matter how hard the fight, the 2d corps always felt that their commander was looking after them."

Chapter 26: Lee's Post-War Years

As a civilian for the first time in 40 years, the Proclamation of Amnesty and Reconstruction of 1865 prevented citizen Lee from holding public office even though he was many times encouraged to enter politics; he was, after all, a celebrity.

Even so, he applied for a complete personal pardon as provided for by the proclamation, hoping to set an example for other leading Southerners. In a paperwork snafu involving the required Oath of Allegiance, however, Lee did not receive his pardon in his lifetime, but a general amnesty did restore his right to vote. It wasn't until 1975 that a National Archive employee ran across Lee's sworn oath and Congress retroactively restored his American citizenship.

Although offered many prestigious positions, Lee opted to spend his final years as president of Washington College in Lexington, Virginia. While there, he raised the school's level of scholarship and established schools of commerce and journalism. With a growing fan club of sorts, young men from all across the South flocked to what became known as "General Lee's school," later christened Washington and Lee University.

While many statesmen of the South remained "unreconstructed" and spread bitterness, resentment, and hatred after the Confederacy's defeat, Lee openly urged his students and friends to maintain the peace and accept the outcome of the war. As a true "Washingtonian" and believer in what America represented as a whole, he spent his final years doing what he could to restore the political, economic, and social life of the South, urging all to "Make your sons Americans."

Lee had frequently been ill during the Civil War, and though he began collecting papers and records with which to write memoirs about the Civil War, his health began to quickly fail in early 1870. Lee died on October 12, 1870 of a stroke, outlived by his frail wife Mary, who died November 5, 1873. Lee was buried in the chapel he built on campus in Lexington, Virginia, along with his other family members; a building often referred to as "The Shrine of the South," a spot visited by thousands each year.

Lee's home has been preserved in Arlington National Cemetery, near Washington, D.C. Lee's birthday, January 19, is observed as a legal holiday in most Southern states. Lee represents Virginia in Statuary Hall in the Capitol in Washington.

Lee's Arlington House

Chapter 27: Meade's Post-War Years

Personal Life

Although it was most likely not evident to his military comrades, George Meade was wholly devoted to his wife and children. Though known as "a damned old goggle-eyed snapping turtle" to his men, his foul temperament apparently never spilled over into his correspondences home. In a letter written to his daughter in the spring of 1862, he wrote, "I think a great deal about you, and all the other dear children. I often picture to myself as I last saw you—yourself, Sarah, and Willie lying in bed, crying because I had to go away, and while I was scolding you for crying, I felt like crying myself.

It is very hard to be kept away from you, because there is no man on earth that loves his children more dearly than I do, or whose happiness is more dependent on being with his family. Duty, however, requires me to be here, to do the little I can to defend our old flag, and whatever duty requires us to do, we should all, old and young, do cheerfully, however disagreeable it may be."[70]

Clearly, Meade was unwilling or unable to expose this softer side in his professional life. In his letters he spoke often of fulfilling duty, ironic sentiments from a man who had been so reluctant to spend his life in the Army. Perhaps he felt duty required being more stoic and insensitive.

Reconstruction

After the Civil War, Major General George Meade was mustered out of the Volunteer Service but continued to serve in the Regular Army as the fourth highest ranking officer in the U. S Army. Meade was assigned to Reconstruction duty in the South, as many Union officers were right at the end of the war.

On January 2, 1868, Meade was called to Atlanta to handle Reconstruction efforts, and on January 10 of that year, he replaced Maj. General John Pope as Governor of the Third Military District in Atlanta. His service appears to have been completed without incident or particular distinction.

Following Reconstruction duty, Meade successively commanded the military division of the Atlantic, headquartered in Philadelphia (where at his request, he could remain with his family while overseeing military affairs), the Department of East, the Third Military District (encompassing Georgia, Alabama, and Florida), and the Department of the South.

One of his last official acts occurred on May 31, 1872, when he spoke at the dedication of the monument to the Civil War dead of the Twenty-First Ward (Roxborough/Manayunk) of Philadelphia.

Meade was also active in Philadelphia civic affairs, overseeing charity work and service to veterans, their widows and orphans. In 1866, he became Commissioner of Fairmount Park in Philadelphia, a post he held till his death.

Major General George Gordon Meade was living with his wife and family in Philadelphia when on October 31, 1872, he was struck down by a violent pain in his side. Once taken ill, Meade's health quickly faded, with him ultimately dying of pneumonia (weakened by his many battle wounds) on November 6, 1872.

---

[70]   Meade George G. Jr. *The Life and Letters of George Gordon Meade.*

Scientist, inventor, scholar, soldier, gentleman of highest virtue, and a true patriot, before his life ended, he received an honorary doctorate in law (LL.D.) from Harvard University.

In Memoriam

On October 31, 1872, at the age of 57, George Gordon Meade died in Philadelphia from complications of his battle wounds, succumbing to pneumonia. Buried in Laurel Hill Cemetery in Philadelphia, in attendance at his funeral were President of the United States Ulysses S. Grant and his cabinet, numerous civil and military dignitaries, throngs of admiring citizens, as well as war comrades and veterans of past American wars. Meade's favorite horse and Civil War mount, "Old Baldy," marched in the funeral procession riderless.

Old Baldy

("Baldy" was subsequently presented to blacksmith John Davis of Jenkintown, Pennsylvania. Dying on December 16, 1882, he was over thirty years old and had survived his master by ten years.)

On January 7, 1886, 13 years after his death, his wife Margaretta died at the age of 71.

Homage

Recognized as a scientist, inventor, and scholar, Meade's scientific achievements were acknowledged by various institutions, including the American Philosophical Society and the

Philadelphia Academy of Natural Sciences.

The citizenry of Philadelphia gifted his widow, Margaretta, the house at 1836 Delancey Place where the couple had lived. Today, the house still has the designation "Meade" over the door, but it is now divided into apartments.

There are numerous memorial statues dedicated to Meade throughout Pennsylvania, including statues at Gettysburg National Military Park and Fairmount Park in Philadelphia.

The United States Army's Fort George G. Meade in Maryland is named in his honor, as well as Meade County, Kansas, and Meade County, South Dakota.

The "Old Baldy" Civil War Round Table in Philadelphia is named in honor of Meade's famous horse.

In World War II, the United States liberty ship SS George G. Meade was named in his honor.

Meade's likeness can be found on the one-thousand-dollar Treasury note (also called Coin note), Series 1890 and 1891.

General Meade was honored for his service in the Mexican-American War with the presentation of a bejeweled sword by the city of Philadelphia.

The General George G. Meade school, located in Philadelphia, is named in his honor.

The General Meade Society

Founded in 1996 by Meade enthusiasts and based in the Greater Philadelphia area, the *General Meade Society* is an organization dedicated to the memory and deeds of the "hero of Gettysburg," General George G. Meade.

The *General Meade Society* gathers annually on December 31 to celebrate the anniversary of the general's birth. Since 2001, the *Society* has also sponsored activities that include tours of Meade-related sites in Philadelphia; seminars featuring speakers who discuss Meade's life, services, and career; adoption and maintenance of the Meade Monument and the site he chose as his headquarters at Gettysburg; a scholarship drive for the General George G. Meade school in Philadelphia; and an annual birthday commemoration at his gravesite in Philadelphia's historic Laurel Hill Cemetery.

Chapter 28: Hancock's Post-War Years

Reconstruction

At the close of the Civil War, General Hancock was assigned to supervise the execution of the people convicted in the conspiracy to assassinate President Abraham Lincoln. Murdered on April 14, 1865 by John Wilkes Booth, by May 9 of that year, a military commission had already been convened to try the accused. Though Booth himself was already dead, tracked to a farm in Virginia where he was killed by Sergeant Boston Corbett on April 26, the trial of his co-conspirators had proceeded quickly, with President Andrew Johnson ordering the hangings of the convicted to be carried out on July 7.

Though reluctant to execute some of the less-culpable conspirators, particularly Mary Surratt, Hancock carried out his orders, later writing that "every soldier was bound to act as I did under similar circumstances."[71] Surratt became the first woman executed by the United States federal government, and though he carried out orders, Hancock was criticized for opposing her execution.

After the Lincoln hangings, Hancock was assigned command of the newly-organized Middle Military Department, headquartered in Baltimore, Maryland. In 1866, on Grant's recommendation, Hancock was promoted to major general and later that year transferred to Fort Leavenworth, Kansas to assume command of the Military Department of the Missouri, which included the states of Missouri, Kansas, Colorado, and New Mexico.

Soon after arriving, General William Tecumseh Sherman assigned Hancock to lead an expedition to negotiate peace with the Cheyenne and Sioux, with whom relations had taken a turn for the worse after the Sand Creek Massacre on November 29, 1864. 700 Colorado Territory militia had attacked and destroyed a village of friendly Cheyenne and Arapaho, killing and mutilating an estimated 150 Native Americans, about two-thirds of whom were women and children. After a bad start, negotiations got even worse after Hancock ordered the burning of an abandoned Cheyenne village in central Kansas, after which an armed confrontation ensued. Though there was little actual loss of life on either side, Hancock failed to establish order, with relationships remaining strained.

By January of 1867 it had become apparent around Washington, D. C. that President Andrew Johnson considered Reconstruction a "mad, infamous revolution," and intended to oppose Congress at every turn. Radical Republicans responded by getting the House of Representatives to pass a resolution calling for an immediate impeachment investigation. In February, an official statement was issued regarding Johnson's attitude: "If [Johnson] fails to execute the laws, in

---

[71]   Tucker, Glenn. *Hancock the Superb*. Page 272.

their spirit as well as in their letter . . . the President may, after all, come to be regarded as an 'obstacle' which must be 'deposed.'"[72]

Unhappy with the way Republican generals were governing the South under Reconstruction, in mid-1867, President Johnson reassigned General Hancock to New Orleans, placing him in charge of the Fifth Military District, which encompassed Texas and Louisiana. Almost immediately, Hancock ingratiated himself with the White conservative population by issuing his General Order #40 on November 29, 1867, expressing his support of Johnson's policies and declaring that so long as a state of peace exists in his district, he would not interfere with civil authorities. In essence, this meant no soldiers would be posted at polling places to protect black voters. To the South and Democrats of the North, this suggested that although Hancock had opposed the South's secession from the United States, he now supported leniency toward the defeated Confederates.

Immediately condemned by Radical Republicans in Washington and wholeheartedly approved by President Johnson, Hancock then proceeded to act on his declaration, denying local Republican politicians' requests to use his power to overturn elections and court verdicts in their favor, while also letting it be known that open insurrection would be militarily suppressed. This resulted in Hancock's popularity within the Democratic Party growing to such an extent that he was considered the Presidential nominee frontrunner in the 1868 election. And although Hancock collected a significant number of delegates at the 1868 convention, his presidential aspirations went unfulfilled, with Ulysses S. Grant elected the 18th President of the United States.

Heading West Again

With Ulysses S. Grant's 1868 election to the White House, the Republicans gained a firm hold on Washington politics, and General Hancock transferred once again. This time, he was sent away from the sensitive Reconstruction issues to the isolated post that was the Department of Dakota, covering Minnesota, Montana, and the Dakotas.

As with his previous Western command, Hancock began his duty with a conference of the regional Native American tribal leaders, but this time he was much more successful in establishing a state of peace. Less than two years later, however, in 1870, peace was broken when an army expedition massacred a Blackfeet settlement, and relations worsened as whites were granted government sanctioning to encroach into the Sioux's Black Hills in violation of the 1868 Treaty of Fort Laramie guaranteeing the Lakota ownership of the Black Hills, including land and hunting rights in South Dakota, Wyoming, and Montana. Still, Hancock managed to avert all-out war, and most of Hancock's time in Western command was peaceful.

---

[72]   McPherson, James M. *Ordeal by Fire: The Civil War and Reconstruction.* Page 568.

During his Western tour of duty, General Hancock was afforded the unique opportunity to contribute to the creation of Yellowstone National Park. In August of 1870, Hancock ordered the Second Cavalry at Fort Ellis to provide a military escort for General Henry D. Washburn's exploration of the Yellowstone Region--henceforth known as the Washburn-Langford-Doane Expedition. In 1871, during Captain John W. Barlow's subsequent exploration of the Yellowstone region, Barlow formally named a summit on what would become the southern boundary of the Park, "Mount Hancock" in honor of the general's contribution.

Command in the East

In November of 1872, after General Meade died, General Hancock became the U. S. Army's senior major general, with Grant making him the new Commander of the Division of the Atlantic, headquartered at Fort Columbus on Governors Island, New York City. Although the new command covered a vast expanse of U. S. territory (the entire settled northeast area of the country), his command was militarily uneventful with the exception of the army's involvement in the Great Railroad Strike of 1877.

At the time of his death on February 9, 1886, Hancock was still in command of the Military Division of the Atlantic

Political Aspirations

On February 1, 1867, Hancock received word that his father had died. Then in 1875, 1879, 1884, respectively, Hancock's daughter Ada, his mother Elizabeth, and his son Russell died.

In 1867, Hancock published what is believed to be his only completed work, *Reports of Major General W. S. Hancock Upon Indian Affairs.*

Though seldom overt about his interest, while serving in his military capacity in New York City in command of Governor's Island, Hancock did his best to foster his political connections and apparent interest in the Presidency. Subsequently, in the first ballot at the Democratic Convention of 1876, Hancock initially received considerable support, only to be swept from the field by New York Governor Samuel J. Tilden on the second ballot. When Republican Rutherford B. Hayes finally took the election, Hancock and his Democratic supporters set their sights on 1880. Considering the electoral crisis of 1876 (the Tilden/Hayes Presidential election was one of the most disputed in American history) and the end to Reconstruction in 1877, Democrats figured the political atmosphere surrounding the 1880 election would offer the best opportunity for a Democratic victory in a generation.

Although Hancock had considerable Democratic support in the 1877 Presidential election, he was unable to attract the majority of delegates needed. In 1880, however, Hancock's chances improved when President Hayes announced that he would not seek a second term and Democratic favorite Samuel J. Tilden declined to run again due to failing health. Still, that year Hancock faced a line-up of renowned public figures, including Stephen Johnson Field, Thomas A. Hendricks, Thomas F. Bayard, and Allen G. Thurman, all vying for the Presidential nomination.

Ultimately, Democrats decided that Hancock's neutral position on the monetary "gold standard" issue, combined with his continued support of the South (stated in his General Order #40) meant that Hancock more than any other candidate had nationwide appeal. Thus when the Democratic Convention assembled in Cincinnati in June 1880, Hancock led on the first ballot but did not get the requisite two-thirds votes until the second. Ultimately, Winfield Scott Hancock became the 1880 Democratic Presidential nominee, pitted against Republican James A. Garfield.

Garfield

Although Hancock's stance toward "maintenance of the civil authorities in their natural and rightful dominion", as spelled out in his General Order #40, endeared Hancock to the majority of Democrats, Garfield's campaigners painted the Democrats as "unsympathetic to the plight of industrial laborers," a group that would benefit by a high protective tariff. In the end, the "tariff issue" succeeded in cutting Democratic support in the industrialized Northern states, which were essential to establishing a Democratic majority. Ultimately failing to carry any of the Northern states except New Jersey, Hancock lost the election to James Garfield, who won just 39,213 more votes than Hancock.

Final Days

Following the election of 1880, Hancock left politics behind and continued in his capacity as commander of the Division of the Atlantic until his death in 1886.

In 1881 he was elected president of the National Rifle Association, stating, "The object of the NRA is to increase the military strength of the country by making skill in the use of arms as prevalent as it was in the days of the Revolution."[73]

From 1878 until his death, Hancock was a Charter Director and the first president of the Military Service Institution of the United States, and from 1879 until his death, he was commander-in-chief of the Military Order of the Loyal Legion of the United States Veterans Organization.

In 1885 Hancock made his last major public appearance, presiding over the funeral of Ulysses S. Grant. That same year, he made a much less publicized visit to Gettysburg, Pennsylvania.

On February 9, 1886, Hancock died at Governors Island.

In 1887, Hancock's wife, Almira, published *Reminiscences of Winfield Scott Hancock*.

Accolades

In his lifetime, General Winfield Scott Hancock received a commemorative service plate from the citizens of Pennsylvania for his years of service, a sword from the U. S. Sanitary Commission of St. Louis, Missouri, and an official "thanks" from the Congress of the United States.

In Memoriam

On February 9, 1886, Winfield Scott Hancock died at Governors Island, New York City, just five days short of his 62nd birthday, the victim of an infected carbuncle complicated by diabetes. He was buried in Montgomery Cemetery in West Norristown Township, Montgomery County, Pennsylvania, near Norristown, Pennsylvania.

Homage

General Winfield Scott Hancock is memorialized in a number of equestrian statues and portrait representations:

---

[73]   Kopel, David, et al. "The Hero of Gettysburg: Winfield Scott Hancock's Shot Straight."

An equestrian statue on East Cemetery Hill on the Gettysburg Battlefield.

A portrait statue, part of the Pennsylvania Memorial at Gettysburg.

An *alto-relievo* (relief sculpture) depicting Hancock's wounding during "Pickett's Charge" on the New York State Monument at Gettysburg.

An equestrian statue located at Pennsylvania Avenue and 7th Street, NW in Washington, D. C.

An equestrian statue atop the Smith Civil War Memorial in Fairmount Park, Philadelphia, Pennsylvania.

A monumental bronze bust in Hancock Square, New York City, created by sculptor James Wilson Alexander MacDonald.

Hancock's likeness also adorns U. S. currency, on the $2 Silver Certificate series of 1886. Approximately 1500-2500 of these bills survive today, most in numismatic collections. Hancock's bill is ranked #73 on a list of the "100 Greatest American Currency Notes," published by Bowers and Sundman.

Chapter 29: Longstreet's Post-War Years

Shortly after the end of the Civil War, James Longstreet was appointed the Adjutant General of the Louisiana State Militia by the Republican Governor of that state, and by 1872 became Major General in command of all New Orleans militia and state police forces.

In 1874, one of his most controversial post-War incidents occurred during protests of election irregularities, when an armed force of 8,400 "White League" members advanced on the State House. Longstreet, in command of a 3,600 man force comprised of Metropolitan Police, city police, and African-American militia troops armed with two Gatling guns and a battery of artillery, foolishly rode into the crowd of protesters and was promptly pulled from his horse, shot, and taken prisoner. Emboldened by his capture, the 'White League' then charged, causing many of Longstreet's men to flee or surrender, with 38 men ultimately killed and 79 wounded, prompting Federal troops to be called in to restore order.

Longstreet's use of Black troops during this disturbance increased his denunciations by anti-Reconstructionists.

Longstreet in later years

During the post-War Reconstruction, Longstreet fell drastically out of public favor. His political attitudes, criticism of Lee at Gettysburg (who Longstreet referred to as "Marse Robert," a term of endearment reserved for friends), and outspoken admiration for Radical Republican and former Union commander Ulysses S. Grant (who became the 18th President of the United States in 1869) only amplified the ire and resentment of the Southern people.

Moving to New Orleans, Longstreet took a position as an insurance company president but was soon ousted. Having joined the Republican Party, "Lincoln's Party", directly after the War, he found that all his employment (and personal) opportunities were limited to Republican prospects, which dried up after the Democrats assumed control. Thus he was forced to accept positions as postmaster, U. S. Marshall, and in 1880, Ambassador to Turkey (an appointment provided by President Grant). Then from 1896 (or 1898) until his death in 1904, he served as U. S. Commissioner of Railroads.

In June of 1867, Longstreet was asked by a reporter from a local newspaper how Louisiana should respond to the new Federal mandate that required former Confederate states to give Blacks the vote. Longstreet responded that the South should obey; that *might makes right.* "The ideas that divided political parties before the war, upon the rights of the States, were thoroughly discussed by our wisest statesmen, and eventually appealed to the arbitrament of the sword. The decision was in favor of the North . . . and should be accepted."[74] Longstreet was immediately denounced as a traitor by many Southerners; some speculating that he had been a traitor all along. In his 1896 memoirs, he wrote that the day after he made that statement, "old comrades passed me on the streets without speaking."

In 1884, Longstreet relocated to Gainesville, Georgia, where he went into semi-retirement on a 65 acre farm his neighbors referred to mockingly as "Gettysburg," where he raised turkeys, grew orchards, and set up vineyards on terraced ground, all while writing his memoirs.

On April 9, 1889 (the 24th anniversary of Lee's surrender at Appomattox), a devastating fire occurred (which many saw simply as *come-uppance*) that destroyed Longstreet's house and most of his personal possessions, including his personal Civil War documents and memorabilia (which partly explains why so little written about his youth still exists). Then in December of that year, Maria Louise Garland, his wife of 40 years, died.

On September 8, 1897, the 76 year old Longstreet married his second wife, the 34 year old Helen Dortch of Atlanta, Georgia. Although Longstreet's children are said to have reacted poorly to the marriage, by all accounts, Helen was a devoted wife and avid supporter of James' legacy after his death. Helen would outlive James by 58 years, dying in 1962 at the age of 99.

In his final years, the American people, for the most part, seems to have forgotten about the post-War controversies and once again recognized Longstreet as a principal leader during the Civil War; once again recognizing him as the field commander who had once warranted the designation of Lee's "War Horse", even though it was a term he personally despised. He and General George Pickett remained friends to his final days.

In 1896, James Longstreet published his memoirs, *From Manassas to Appomattox*. While considered overtly defensive in tone and containing numerable inconsistencies, contradictions, half-truths, and outright lies, it is nonetheless viewed today as an important source of insight into the Civil War, this portion of American history, and of course, James Longstreet himself.

On January 2, 1904 at the age of nearly 83, Longstreet died while visiting Gainesville. He was buried in Alta Vista Cemetery, Hall County, Georgia.

An indication of how long it has taken for Longstreet to get the credit he deserved for his participation in the war can be found in the fact that only recently was a monument to Longstreet constructed at Gettysburg. There is no special recognition at Hollywood Cemetery in Richmond, Virginia (although there are for George Pickett and "Jeb" Stuart), and most, if not all, Confederate Generals are buried in Hollywood rather than Gettysburg National Cemetery.

---

[74]   Gaffney, P. and D. Gaffney. *The Civil War: Exploring History One Week at a Time.* Page 442.

According to *The Confederate Image: Prints of the Lost Cause*, "There [is] nothing mysterious about the scarcity of portraits of General Longstreet . . . it seems a near-miracle that two survive," (a lithograph by J. L. Giles and an engraving made in France by Goupil et cie.)[75] As this text explains, the production of such prints "was determined by postwar myth as much as wartime performance, and there was good reason to shunt Longstreet aside for other heroes."

While it is true that for a brief period of time after Stonewall Jackson's death, General Longstreet held a command of great importance that *could* have led to assuming Jackson's former status as unequivocal champion of the South -- second only to Robert E. Lee -- immediately following the War, he quickly embraced what he termed "practical reconstruction and reconciliation," stating, "The sword has decided in favor of the North . . . [and Northern principles] cease to be principles and become law."[76] After becoming an avowed Republican and Grant supporter in 1869 (as well as devout Catholic), the vast majority of Southerners shunned him. (It is most likely that the Giles lithograph was made before that date, before he was widely deemed a traitor.)

Chapter 30: Chamberlain's Post-War Years

Personal Life

Upon his return from the War, one of Lawrence's first projects was to expand the house he'd bought near Bowdoin College campus in 1861. With his family and social life considerably expanded, he found that his old house was too small, so he enlarged it by a somewhat unique method: he raised it and added a new ground floor.

With 20 rooms now available, for the remainder of his life, Lawrence entertained a veritable *who's-who* of distinguished War celebrities, including Generals Sherman, Grant, Sheridan, McClellan, Porter, Warren, Ayers, Schurz, Griffin, and Howard. Additionally, statesmen, businessmen, and politicians frequented his home to discuss the matters of the day, including Senators Charles Sumner, Pitt Fessenden, and Morrill, and Secretary of State James G. Blaine. World-famous poet Henry Wadsworth Longfellow even stayed there when he came back for his 50th class reunion at Bowdoin in 1875.

Beginning with his first year in office as governor of Maine and continuing to the end of his life, Chamberlain was active in the Grand Army of the Republic and made many visits to Gettysburg, giving speeches at soldiers' reunions despite suffering continual pain from his 1864 wounds.

---

75   Neely, Mark E., Holzer, Harold & Boritt, Gabor S. *The Confederate Image.* Page 201.
76   Neely, Mark E., Holzer, Harold & Boritt, Gabor S. *The Confederate Image.* Page 201.

In November of 1900, Chamberlain decided that a trip abroad may improve his incessant health issues, so he took a leave of absence from his various responsibilities to travel to Italy and then Egypt, where he took up residence in Cairo. There, to his surprise, he took an interest in Egyptian history and religion, even making a serious study of the Koran. While there he also established friendships with British proconsul in Egypt, Lord Cromer, as well as the distinguished Moslem leader, Fordure, who was said to have been the direct linear descendant of the Prophet Mohammed.

Shortly after his return to the United States, on October 18, 1905, Lawrence's wife Fanny died after several years of blindness and serious illness, at the age of 79.

Political Career

In June of 1866, Chamberlain resigned his army commission and returned to his academic duties at Bowdoin College, though his tenure was brief. Deciding to capitalize on his immense post-War popularity, Chamberlain left academia to venture into politics. Running on the Republican ticket, he was elected the 32nd governor of Maine, and he served four consecutive one-year terms between 1867 and 1871. His victory in 1866 set the record for margin of victory when he trounced Democratic opponent Eben F. Pillsbury, 62% to 37%. It was a record he would himself beat in 1868.

Proving a somewhat controversial governor, during his time in office he was frequently opposed by those angered by his support for capital punishment and his refusal to create a special police unit to enforce the prohibition of alcohol.

Academic Career

Serving first for a brief period immediately after the War, and then after leaving political office, Chamberlain returned to Bowdoin College in 1871 to resume teaching and lecturing. He was subsequently appointed president of the college, a position he held until 1883 when he was forced to resign due to recurring health problems related to wounds sustained at Petersburg. Though it was not widely known in his lifetime, from the time of his wound in 1864 until his death, he was forced to wear a catheter bag, and underwent six unsuccessful operations to correct the original wound and stop recurring fevers and infections.

From 1867 to 1871, Chamberlain also served as an *ex-officio* trustee of nearby Bates College.

Federal Service

In January of 1880, a bitter dispute erupted between two Maine factions concerning the newly-elected governor of Maine, Republican Party nominee Daniel F. Davis. In the general election,

Davis had won more votes than his opponent, but he had not won more than 50% of the total votes cast as required. Davis was named as the legal governor only after the Maine Legislature was called upon to decide who would serve as governor. In the interim, however, the Maine State House was occupied by a band of armed men demanding justice.

To help settle the dispute, the outgoing governor, Alonzo Garcelon, summoned Chamberlain, now the commander of the Maine militia, to take charge. Chamberlain sent home the armed men and arranged for the Augusta police to maintain control, remaining in the State House himself for most of the 12 period it took for the Maine Supreme Judicial Court to decide who the rightful governor was.

During his stay in the State House, there were ongoing threats of assassination and kidnap, and on one occasion, the angry mob stormed through the gates of the State House bent on killing him. Confronting the unruly mob, Chamberlain told them, "Kill me if you must, but I have faced death before and deserve it now no more than ever!"[77] Finding many veterans of the Civil War among the crowd who were ready to defend Chamberlain with their lives, the mob finally dispersed and agreed to await the official decision, but not before both sides offered to appoint him Senator for siding with them.

Having gratified neither side in the dispute, Chamberlain did not become Senator, and his career in state politics ended.

Business Endeavors

From 1885 until his death in 1914, Chamberlain engaged in a number of business activities, including real estate speculation in Florida, as well as investing in a college of art in New York and a number of hotels and railroads. From 1900 to 1901, he served as a Federally-appointed Surveyor of the Port of Portland, Maine, receiving an annual salary of $4500.

Author and Lecturer

While writing several books about Maine, education, as well as his Civil War memoir, *The Passing of the Armies*, Chamberlain traveled the country, lecturing about his Civil War experiences. Unlike War colleagues Grant and Sherman who promoted the idea that "war is hell" and very distasteful business, Chamberlain stressed a more idealized and philosophical perspective, that war can also be seen as being about courage and compassion; where an individual is tested in battle and his fate is given entirely to Providence.

Accolades

---

[77]   Sell, Bill. *Civil War Chronicles: Leaders of the North and South*. Page 51.

In 1893, 30 years after the battle that made the 20th Maine nationally famous, Major General (retired) Lawrence Joshua Chamberlain was awarded the Congressional Medal of Honor for his actions at Gettysburg. The citation commends him for his "Daring heroism and great tenacity in holding his position on the Little Round Top against repeated assaults, and carrying the advance position on the Great Round Top."

Other Interests

Chamberlain became a founding member of the Maine Institution for the Blind (founded around 1903), in Portland, Maine, now called The Iris Network. His wife Fanny was herself blind in her final years, and Chamberlain served on the first Board of Directors.

Military Life, Later Years

In 1898, at the age of 70, Lawrence Chamberlain volunteered for duty as an officer in the Spanish-American War. Rejected for duty, he called it one of the major disappointments of his life.

Chamberlain later in life, wearing all his military decorations

Death and Homage

On February 24, 1914 at the age of 85, Chamberlain died in Portland, Maine of residual effects of his wartime wounds, and he was buried in Pine Grove Cemetery in Brunswick, Maine. At his bedside was Dr. Abner Shaw of Portland, one of the two surgeons who had operated on him in the Petersburg campaign 50 years prior. He was among the last Civil War veterans to die from wounds incurred during the war itself.

Chamberlain's home, located across from Bowdoin College campus, is now the Joshua L. Chamberlain Museum and is owned by the Pejepscot Historical Society, which also maintains an extensive research collection on Chamberlain memorabilia. On display is the "Minie" ball that almost ended his life at Petersburg, as well as Don Troiani's famous rendition of the charge at Little Round Top. Tours of the home are conducted by knowledgeable volunteers from late May until mid-October.

U. S. Route 1A is carried across the Penobscot River between Bangor and Brewer, Maine by the Joshua Chamberlain Bridge, a four lane steel plate girder bridge opened in 1959.

Though known almost exclusively as "Lawrence" throughout his life, and referred to as such in most surviving biographical literature, his grave marker lists him as Joshua Lawrence Chamberlain, and he is acknowledged as Joshua L. Chamberlain by several entities and institutions, including the Pejepscot Historical Society of Brunswick, Maine.

Chapter 31: Lee's Legacy

War and Peace

History speaks of Robert E. Lee as man of peace, a man of compassion, a man responsibility. But above all, it speaks of a pragmatic man with an all-pervasive sense of duty.

Although Lee saw war as a disintegrating and largely unnecessary response to social disapproval--an act of disloyalty that fundamentally undermines a society's stability--as a military man, Lee spent most of his mature life waiting for the next war; the next battle.

Lee hadn't chosen a career in law or politics or even farming (as he'd often said he'd prefer), he'd chosen the life of a soldier; a military strategist whose job it was to enable his side to overcome the opposition through cunning, ingenuity, and deception. And for all his moral and ethical aversion to armed dissention, in reality, his natural abilities and formidable training in accomplishing these goals weren't fully utilized in times of peace, only in times of war.

As a practical man who as a boy had watched his family suffer and disintegrate due to his father's irresponsibility, Lee had vowed never to subject his family to the same financial embarrassment and social indignation. And although history records Lee as a man of principles, more to the heart it seems, he was a man of duty. A man of peace who relied upon conflict. And it seems likely that he was torn between these two principles for most of his life.

Freedom for "The People"

Modern history describes Lee as a man who gave his loyalty, his industry, to the causes of the South although fundamentally, he opposed the enslavement of his fellow man. More flattering accounts emphasize that he'd actually given up his slaves long before the Civil War began.

More accurately, however, it wasn't so much that he'd "given up" his slaves as participated in slave-rental. And while Lee was never known to refer to human chattel as "slaves" or even the more popular, "darkies" (preferring instead, "the people"), Lee is quoted as saying, "The best men of the South have long desired to do away with the institution [of slavery] and were quite willing to see it abolished. But the question has ever been, 'What will you do with the freed people?'"[78]

As records show, in late 1857, Lee inherited 63 slaves from his father-in-law, George Washington Parke Curtis. Though technically the property of his wife, Mary, responsibility for their care and maintenance ultimately fell to Lee as Master of the plantation. And while the principled Lee may have been repulsed by the idea of further subjugating these men, woman, and children under his charge, the pragmatic Lee, the dutiful Lee, knew that he could never provide for his family in the true Southern spirit--the way his wife Mary had long been accustomed--

---

[78]   Blount, Jr., Roy. *Robert E. Lee.* Page 202.

without supplementing his officer's pay.

He needed to not only make certain that his wife and children wouldn't be left to their own devices should he die or be killed, but consider the immediate issues at hand: by the time his son Curtis started boarding school, tuition cost three hundred dollars a year; nearly a fourth of a captain's pay. Thus, as his family grew in size, so too did the necessity to compromise his principles. But as one story from his younger days demonstrates, for Lee, the issue couldn't have been nearly that cut and dry.

As the account is told, following the passing of his mother Anne, Lee's sister Mildred inherited responsibility for Nat, an elderly house servant and coachman, who in his old age, apparently suffered tuberculosis. On the advise that warmer climate might make Nat's final days more pleasant, the twenty-two year old Lee took Nat along with him to his post on Cockspur Island, where he is said to have nursed him with all the tenderness of a son through his final days. Thus, it seems that Lee's sense of responsibility and humanity rose far beyond simply supporting or opposing slavery. He genuinely saw his charges as *people*.

In the end, while the principled Lee may have seen slavery as an abomination against mankind--something he'd put an end to and something that would have pleased his wife who by this time had become an anti-slavery advocate--the practical Lee saw it as a necessary evil; a means to an end. The dutiful Lee found a way to compromise.

Champion of a Lost Cause

Ironically, though he had no use for post-war politics, Lee's legacy was crafted and embroiled in it. Though Lee accepted the South's loss, unreconstructed rebels continued to "fight" the Civil War with the pen, aiming to influence how the war was remembered. Much of this was accomplished by the Southern Historical Society, whose stated aim was the homogenization of Southern white males. But longstanding feuds between former generals found their way into the papers, and the feuds were frequently based on regional differences. These former Confederates looked to their idealized war heroes as symbols of their suffering and struggle. Based in Richmond, the Society's ideal Southern white male embodied the "Virginian" essence of aristocracy, morality and chivalry. The Society's ideal male, of course, was Robert E. Lee. David Blight credits the Society for creating a "Lee cult" that dominates public perception to this day. Writing about this perception of Lee, Charles Osbourne described the perception as "an edifice of myth built on the foundation of truth...the image became an icon."

With Lee being pushed forward as the quintessential Southern man, he began to be treated as the ideal man and ideal leader. This sentiment eventually began to influence Northern views of the man as well. An equestrian statue of Lee that was unveiled in Richmond in 1890 sparked an outburst of sentimentality that affected the North as well as the South. Reporting on the unveiling of the Lee statue, the *New York Times* referred to the memory of Lee as a "possession of the American people" and called the monument a "National possession." As far west as Minnesota, it was noted that the "Lee cult" was "in vogue." Not all Northerners shared the sentimental appreciation of the Lee cult. Frederick Douglass found that he could "scarcely take up a newspaper…that is not filled with nauseating flatteries of the late Robert E. Lee."

Few men in American history--perhaps, General George Armstrong Custer, General Douglas MacArthur, and General George S. Patton--can be so clearly defined by their military accomplishments as Robert E. Lee. Though by most accounts he was a loving and attentive husband and father, a family man with tiny feet who loved to have his children tickle them, that part of him pales in comparison to his demonstration of duty. Even as the leader of a failed cause, his sense of humility and selflessness gives him an extraordinarily unique and unparalleled place in American history.

As a soldier, Lee's strongest attribute was his natural ability to access a military situation and quickly devise an effective strategy. He excelled in his capacity to anticipate an opponent's moves and then outmaneuver them--often with inferior numbers and resources at his dispose. Never did he settle to meet the enemy on even tactical terms, and by most measure, he was unparalleled in American military history as a battlefield strategist.

Although field entrenchments had been used as a method of defense long before the founding of America, Lee refined this ancient science into a fine, fluid, and adaptive art--one that's studied today on university campuses across the land. He was a guerilla fighter with the mental agility of a ballerina; the optimal warrior in this place and time in American history when that was precisely what was called for. This, added to his power to arouse unparalleled devotion in his men, provided--quite handily--the South's greatest chance to end their war victoriously. Quite remarkable for a man who'd often remarked that all he really ever wanted to be was a farmer.

Still, Lee was far from perfect, despite the attempts of the Southern Historical Society to defend his war record as fault free, at the expense of some of his subordinates. Given that the Confederacy lost the war, some historians have pointed out that Lee was often too eager to engage in offensive warfare. After all, Lee scored large and smashing victories at places like Chancellorsville that deprived him of more manpower against opponents that could afford casualties more than he could. Moreover, for the engineer who used tactics to successfully defend against typical Civil War tactics, he all too often engaged in the same futile offensive tactics himself, none more costly than Pickett's Charge.

More objective analysts, including those among Lee's contemporaries like Longstreet and Porter Alexander, pointed out that despite these kinds of criticisms, it was Lee's daring tactics and successes that extended the Civil War so many years. Pointing out how many more casualties Lee's armies inflicted compared to those he lost, many of his subordinates compared him favorably to Napoleon, even if Lee never won the necessary complete victory.

One can only wonder what Lee would've accomplished with equal manpower and resources.

Historian

Much of what we know today about the Civil War comes from letters, government correspondences, and journal entries made by the soldiers involved, both Confederate and Union. Although Lee was never able to write memoirs, he was prolific letter writer, contributed abundantly to all three. Even in the heat of battle, it seems, his first impulse was to document his thoughts; express in words the complexities of his emotional state, mental reasoning, and assessment of the situation as he saw it. These correspondences provide invaluable insight not just into Lee the man, Lee the soldier, and Lee the husband and father, but insight into a period of American history which for the most part only received serious, unbiased reporting years after the fact.

Lee as Icon

Described by biographer Roy Blount, Jr. as "a sort of precursor-cross between England's Cary Grant and Virginia's Randolph Scott"--and perhaps the most beautiful person in America--Robert E. Lee is perhaps the most written-about character of the Civil War era, next to President Lincoln himself. Depicted as a handsome war hero, unifying national figure in the aftermath of a war-torn country, and a symbol of what is noble and just in the American spirit, Lee's image has evolved over time.

After Lee's death, former Maryland slave, writer, and statesman Frederick Douglass wrote, "[I]t would seem . . . that the soldier who kills the most men in battle--even in a bad cause--is the greatest Christian and entitled to the highest place in heaven."[79] Some 37 years later on the eve of the Celebration of the Hundredth Anniversary of Lee's birth, President Theodore Roosevelt wrote, "[Lee] stood that hardest of all strains, the strain of bearing himself well through the gray evening of failure; and therefore out of what seemed failure he helped to build the wonderful and mighty triumph of our national life, in which all his countrymen, north and south, share."[80] And now approaching a century and a half after his death, history has shown an iconic evolution from mere post-war personality to what biographer Thomas L. Connelly terms a man considered a

---

[79]   Blount, Jr., Roy. *Robert E. Lee.* Page 2.
[80]   Blount, Jr., Roy. *Robert E. Lee.* Page 2.

"military genius and a spiritual leader, the nearest thing to a saint that the white South has possessed."[81]

There can be no doubt that Lee's lasting legend is a combination of both fact and fiction; myth and understatement. As was common in 19th century America, heroes weren't always born--they were sometimes made. And it seems likely that what we now know of Lee was a carefully constructed conglomeration of both. In fact, immediately following his death, a group of Virginians led by general Jubal Early began a campaign to make Lee a national idol, a campaign that undoubtedly flavored 19th century biographies attempting to paint a fair yet colorful portrait of the iconic war hero. Immediately after the war, Grant was initially the most *popular* Civil War figure, but he was soon eclipsed.

As someone once astutely observed, 'Desperate times call for desperate measures,' and for many, America suffered no more desperate times than when brothers were called upon to take arms against bothers. And if survival of such an unnatural ordeal required the glorification--even exaggeration--of one who seemed to do it best, then we can hardly condemn those who may have sought to assure their success. But by any measure, Robert E. Lee was indeed an extraordinary individual who demonstrated through actions what we have come to define as the "American Spirit." In the face of unprecedented adversity, he repeatedly stood up, stepped forward, and sacrificed himself for the greater good. And that's why he holds the place in American history that he does.

Chapter 32: Meade's Legacy

Either by intent or lack of interest, there is much about George Gordon Meade's life that remains unknown. His years in Spain, early home life, and early schooling are little more than blank pages or simply glossed over by historians in the rush to discuss his Civil War service. Even his time at West Point is little more than a footnote in the annals of the Academy. Surprisingly, even renowned Civil War historian Bruce Catton--who has written numerous, extensive works on the Civil War--devotes comparatively little copy to Meade's early life, reporting his participation in the Civil War with few of the details afforded other key players.

Although General George Gordon Meade significantly influenced the events and outcome of the Civil War, most obviously at Gettysburg, he is neither well-known nor well-respected as one of the War's great commanders outside his home city of Philadelphia. As historian Joseph Stevens aptly points out, "He performed well enough to merit steady advancement, but not so brilliantly as to draw undue attention to himself."[82]

---

[81]   Blount, Jr., Roy. *Robert E. Lee.* Page 2.
[82]   Stevens, Joseph E. 1863: The Rebirth of a Nation. Page 234.

Among the many factors that negatively impacted Meade's reputation was his diminishing responsibilities during the final battles of the conflict, due largely to his somewhat contentious relationship with General Ulysses S. Grant, his increasingly acerbic predisposition regarding his fellow officers (and civilians), and his hostility toward the press, who became so exasperated with Meade's incessant hostility that they ultimately agreed to only report his failures. Even so, historians are quick to spotlight his actions at Gettysburg and his loyal service to Grant, despite Grant's obvious objective to limit his involvement.

As a result of the somewhat complicated circumstances surrounding Meade's command of the Army of the Potomac, his ultimate contributions to the Civil War have been the focus of ongoing controversy, both in his time and in retrospect. Accused of not being aggressive enough in pursuing Confederate forces, and of being reluctant to attack on occasion, Meade continues to languish in the shadow of the considerably more aggressive Grant.

Other factors worked against him, including public opinion tainted by his infamous short temper (several of his subordinates referred to him as "a damned old google-eyed snapping turtle"), his appearance (he was viewed as singularly unattractive: tall, scrawny, balding with scaly skin, a beak-like nose, and seemingly permanent scowl), and his bad relationship with the press (he ran several reporters out of camp for writing unflattering or intelligence-compromising reports and even had a reporter tied backwards on a mule which he seny scurrying out of camp with a slap on the rump). Even Meade's own personal aide, Theodore Lyman, once said of him, "I don't know any thin old gentleman . . . who when he is wrathy, exercises less of Christian charity than my well-beloved chief!"[83]

Over time, more recent historical accounts portray Meade in a somewhat more positive light than a century ago, especially for the manner he commanded at Gettysburg. Furthermore, historians today now commend his decisions to entrench when possible and not launch frontal assaults on fortified positions.

Private Perspective

Throughout the war, Meade kept a regular correspondence with his wife Margaretta, and as demonstrated throughout this narrative, his private letters reveal something of Meade the man-- and perhaps shine a bit of light on the method behind his seeming madness.

Appearing energetic and exacting in his letters, Meade made no apologies for his impatience concerning what he saw as "stupidity, negligence, and laziness" among the ranks and on the battlefield. Serious and sincere about successfully completing the tasks to which he was assigned, tasks he often saw as repugnant and inhumane, under the stress of active campaigning

---

[83]   Lanning, Michael Lee. *The Civil War 100*. Page 96.

or the heat of battle he often reacted with (well-publicized) outbursts of rage or annoyance. And while his temperament and demeanor certainly rubbed many people the wrong way, as his personal aide Theodore Lyman explained, while his manner was hard on people, "[Meade's] decisions were always founded in good reason, and it got results. By worrying and flaring out unexpectedly on various officers, he did manage to have things pretty shipshape."[84]

Significantly, although he privately expressed great ambition and vanity frequently, Meade made no attempts to make himself popular, generally kept to himself, and made it a rule not to speak to members of the press, which (like today) could break the career of someone who was essentially a "celebrity." Characterized as a "completely unassuming man," Col. Philip DeTrobriand, a brigade commander in the Third Corps, said of Meade, "[He] was more reserved than audacious, more modest than presumptuous, on which account he treated his corps commanders more as friends than as inferiors."[85]

In the end, General George Gordon Meade's war record may have been best summed up by his most famous superior. In his *Memoirs*, Ulysses S. Grant wrote, "General Meade was an officer of great merit, with drawbacks to his usefulness that were beyond his control. He was brave and conscientious, and commanded respect of all who knew him. He was unfortunately of a temper that would get beyond his control at times. No one saw this better than he himself, and no one regretted it more. This made it unpleasant at times, even in battle, for those around him to approach him even with information."[86] Thus, it could be argued that ultimately, Meade was his own worst enemy. But that should not detract from his apparent accomplishments and significant contributions. He was there to fight a war, and he simply performed the best way he knew how.

Chapter 33: Longstreet's Legacy

Criticisms

For decades after his death, Longstreet, who was called "Old Pete" by his troops and "Old War Horse" by Lee, was viewed primarily through his arguments with other Confederate generals, his own analyses, and his memoirs. In sum, he was viewed very unflatteringly. To an extent this continues. As historians have since discovered, once weighted against known historical facts, Longstreet's descriptions not only contain flights of fantasy and self-aggrandizing (as autobiographical accounts are prone to do), they contain gross inaccuracies, distortions, and outright lies. Many of his descriptions of events simply did not, *could* not, have occurred as he states. He exaggerates his combat record, grossly overrates his reputation as a corps leader, and boasts of a level of confidence with Lee that simply did not exist. Thus as is academically

---

[84]   Civil War Women website, "Margaretta Sergeant Meade."
[85]   Civil War Women website, "Margaretta Sergeant Meade."
[86]   Lanning, Michael Lee. *The Civil War 100*. Page 96.

prudent in such cases, Longstreet's version of history in the memoirs is largely discounted.

Some continue to assert that Longstreet was too selfish and had too high an opinion of himself. To these people, a cursory evaluation of Longstreet's service record makes it clear that whether or not one holds him responsible for the South's defeat at Gettysburg, his behavior there was not an isolated--or even *out-of-character*--incident. It was, in fact, just another episode in a long pattern of behavior at odds with a man entrusted with the second-highest position in the Confederate Army. Even as early as the Battle of Seven Pines on May 31, 1862, though not a particularly significant battle for Longstreet, he'd already begun to reveal ambitions that far exceeded his limitations. Though initially appearing to be a simple unwillingness to cooperate, the underlying disconnect manifested again at Second Manassas (where he responded dangerously slow and was reluctant to attack), his attempted siege of Suffolk (which weighed heavily against him until Lee and Jackson's victory at Chancellorsville overshadowed his lack of good judgment), and then at Knoxville (where his failure was categorically written off as just "one of the winter of 1863-1864 disasters").

Long before Gettysburg, Longstreet was characterized by his men and commanders as "congenitally resistant to hurry himself,"[87] resistant to change of orders (even from his supreme commander, Lee), and disliked to overextend his men (once bivouacked, he allowed his men to prepare three-days' rations before breaking camp, even when they were supposed to stick to a timetable). In fact, his designation as Lee's "old reliable" appears to have been bestowed by someone who had never actually worked with him or had to rely upon him.

Similarly, Longstreet's clash with A. P. Hill, then Jackson, Hood and Toombs, were indicative of his unwillingness to accept that he was not the center of attention; not the one destined for greatness. And, of course, as the War progressed, Longstreet's propensity to find fault (and start feuds) with Lafayette McLaws (who he tried to have court-martialed), Evander Law (who he tried to have arrested), Charles Field, and ultimately, Lee himself, was highly indicative of the self-possessed illusion Longstreet was living (and fighting) under. While always quick to reprimand any subordinate who questioned his orders, he clearly hesitated to resist orders from his superiors on occasions. In his Gettysburg account, Longstreet had the impudence to blame Lee for "not changing his plans" based on Longstreet's "want of confidence in them."

Was Longstreet an Opportunist?

On the surface, it's easy to assume that Longstreet paid his dues and earned his advancement in the Confederate Army. And in that he was one of the final hold-outs who resisted surrender to the Union until the South was out of options, it's also easy to assume that his loyalty--at least

---

[87]   Dowdey, Clifford. *Lee's Last Campaign: The Story of Lee & His Men against Grant--1864.* Page 134.

during the conflict--was to the Southern cause. But many historians believe that assumption may be ill-conceived.

As a captain in the U. S. Army, Longstreet transferred to the paymaster department in order to achieve a higher rank and pay, that of major, having "denounced all dreams of military glory." Subsequently, (by the majority of accounts), when he enlisted in the Confederate Army, he did not join the troop complement of any particular state--as most soldiers loyal to their state did--he applied directly for the paymaster post, thus securing for himself rank and privilege.

In that Longstreet arrived at Richmond from a New Mexican garrison *via* Texas, arriving later than most officers who came from various army outposts, he *coincidentally* arrived in the War Office at precisely the time a brigadier general was being selected for three regiments of Virginia volunteers. The result of this *coincidence* was that Longstreet started as a brigadier general when most of his peers (some of whom were better experienced) were starting as colonels. This meant that at promotion time, he made major general while they were only making brigadier. Thus, when Lee took control and was forming his two corps, Longstreet's seniority made him next in line for command (alongside "Stonewall" Jackson). But from several military historians' perspectives, he was not the best qualified--just *coincidentally* in the right place at the right time.

Charges of Traitor

After General Robert E. Lee died in October of 1870, a group of ex-Confederates led by General Jubal Early (who had led a division in Ewell's corps at Gettysburg) publicly criticized Longstreet for ignoring orders and delaying his attack on the second day of the Battle on July 2, 1863. But while many former Confederates held Longstreet accountable for not following orders, Early took it one step further, arguing that Longstreet -- not Lee -- was responsible for the Confederate defeat (deemed a "tactical disaster" by most) that by most accounts was the beginning of the end for the Confederacy.

In his memoirs, however, Longstreet defended himself, saying that the blistering post-War attacks concerning Gettysburg were merely "payback for supporting Black suffrage", thus shifting the blame back to Lee. He wrote, "[Lee] knew that I did not believe that success was possible . . . he should have put an officer in charge who had more confidence in his plan."[88] He went on to say that Lee should have given the responsibility to Early, thus justifying his insubordination.

It's also important to note that Lee himself never made any post-War statements to suggest that he held Longstreet responsible for the Confederacy's demise.

A More Positive Perspective

Despite what many considered to be some critical military and personal failures and shortcomings, General James Longstreet is regarded by many today as one of the best, if not *the* best, tactical commanders on either side of the War, even though he did not do well in independent command. Although his emphatic belief that the Confederacy should fight a "strategic offensive-tactical defensive" war was in direct conflict with his commanders (including General Lee), some historians (including Jeffry D. Wert) believe that had Lee followed Longstreet's advice, it is quite likely that not only would the Southern army have endured longer, it possibly would have won the war.

While historians and scholars will continue to disagree on Longstreet's ultimate level of negligence (or incompetence), everyone agrees that he did have a profound effect on the War. And even those who have criticized him have pointed out how thoroughly competent he was

---

[88]   Gaffney, P., and D. Gaffney. *The Civil War: Exploring History One Week at a Time.* Page 442.

when battle was actually joined. Biographer Jeffry Wert wrote "Longstreet ... was the finest corps commander in the Army of Northern Virginia; in fact, he was arguably the best corps commander in the conflict on either side." Richard L. DiNardo wrote, "Even Longstreet's most virulent critics have conceded that he put together the best staff employed by any commander, and that his de facto chief of staff, Lieutenant Colonel G. Moxley Sorrel, was the best staff officer in the Confederacy."

Longstreet's reputation has also been on the upswing in the past few decades, due in no small part to Michael Shaara's 1974 novel *The Killer Angels*, which portrayed Longstreet in a more flattering light. That novel was the basis for the 1993 film *Gettysburg*, which has also helped rehabilitate Longstreet's legacy and helped make clear to the public how instrumental he was during the war. In 1982, Thomas L. Connolly and Barbara L. Bellows published *God and General Longstreet*, which took the Lost Cause proponents like Early to task for their blatant fabrications (such as the one that Lee ordered Longstreet to attack in the early morning of Day 2 of Gettysburg), helping make clear the extent of historical revision propagated by the Lost Cause. In doing so, they cast Longstreet as a sympathetic victim of circumstances and sectional and political hostility.

The Lee Factor

No analysis of Longstreet's contribution to the Civil War would be just or complete without first recognizing the leadership methodology Lee used in guiding his commanders. As many historians point out, in that Lee had not personally trained his field commanders, he was forced to accept these men as they came. Accordingly, Lee's leadership style was designed to promote the individual man's initiative (which most cite as a weakness in his leadership), encouraging them to explore their fullest potential through independent thought.

Thus, Lee did not dictate precise orders (which by his reasoning would have denied each leader's creative participation and sharing of responsibility) but offered what was generally perceived as suggestions or *discretionary* orders. This loose approach to leadership obliged Lee to depend heavily upon each of his field commander's judgment, which, as it turned out, was often in conflict with his own. While some commanders, like "Stonewall" Jackson, urged aggressive and quick movements, others, like Longstreet, preferred defensive tactics. In fact, many historians believe the only reason Longstreet may have blundered during Day 2 of Gettysburg is because Lee gave a discretionary order to a conservative general (Ewell), who refused to take the initiative and attack Culp's Hill on the first night of the battle. Had Jackson survived Chancellorsville and received the same order, he might have made the attack, and if it succeeded there never would have been a 3 day battle at Gettysburg.

For that reason, many military historians contend that as supreme field commander of the Confederate forces, Lee should have adapted his leadership style to best serve the Southern interests, or removed Longstreet at the first sign that he could not be depended upon to follow Lee's lead.

Chapter 34: Hancock's Legacy

Few men were as admired as Hancock the Superb from a civilian or military perspective. In 1880, President Hayes noted, "If, when we make up our estimate of a public man, conspicuous both as a soldier and in civil life, we are to think first and chiefly of his manhood, his integrity, his purity, his singleness of purpose, and his unselfish devotion to duty, we can truthfully say of Hancock that he was through and through pure gold."

Although Winfield Scott Hancock's father, Benjamin, had hoped his son would choose a life-path other than the military, it seems reasonable to assume that his future was in no small way led by the glorious name bestowed upon him at birth: Winfield Scott, the famed patriot and general of many American wars. And in that Winfield showed so early, even as a boy, glimpses of martial discipline, perhaps he had always foreseen himself in the military commander role. Even so, although his apparent skills and propensities put him at the center of the most pivotal battles in the Eastern Theater, including Gettysburg, he was never entrusted with a command of his own. Many historians ask if his greater potential had gone unnoticed, or if he had simply accomplished all that he was capable of accomplishing.

Despite having disagreed with Grant's "war of attrition" and post-War treatment of the South, Grant had glowingly commended Hancock and pointed out that he was the most "conspicuous" of general officers who were not given an independent command. As one who made little overt effort to bring glory or attract recognition to his military career, perhaps Winfield Scott Hancock had assumed his efforts and accomplishments (as well as sacrifices) would speak for themselves, and he would be rewarded accordingly. There can be little doubt that after being dubbed "Hancock the Superb" so early in the game by commanding officer General McClellan after his showing at the Battle of Williamsburg, Hancock assumed independent command was in his future, perhaps following the next battle.

But when recognition still didn't arrive by November of 1863, Hancock began to question his resolve to remain part of the war effort. Even after displaying exemplary soldiering at Fredericksburg and Gettysburg, and having been promoted to major general for "gallant, meritorious, and conspicuous share in that great and decisive victory"--greater command still eluded him. He must have recognized that his efforts were often overshadowed by the flamboyant "glory seekers" and political generals who owed their position to good connections.

The "McClellan Effect"?

Some historians have speculated that Hancock was a victim of other's perceived failures, none more prominent than McClellan. After all, with the exception of Gettysburg, Hancock's superb performances and effective generalship in the Army of the Potomac still ended in tactical draws or Union defeats.

From September 1861 (when Hancock entered the War) until November 1862, Winfield Scott Hancock served under Maj. General George B. McClellan, until President Lincoln removed McClellan from command for repeatedly showing reluctance to aggressively pursue Lee's Army. Although McClellan was meticulous in his planning and preparations, he was always reluctant to move until he felt things were just right, which was difficult because he was chronically overestimating the strength of enemy units. Thus, even when he did engage in pitched battles, McClellan frequently kept large portions of his army in reserve rather than send them into an offensive action. Such was the case at the Battle of Williamsburg as well as the Battle of Antietam.

While the Battle of Williamsburg (fought on May 5, 1862) was deemed militarily inconclusive (with some historians giving a slight edge to the Union), the only reason it did not end in a clear-cut Union victory was because McClellan refused to follow up on "Hancock the Superb's" brilliant showing and allowed the Confederate forces to retreat unscathed rather than pursue and deliver as much damage as his army was capable. Similarly, at the Battle of Antietam (fought on September 17, 1862), despite greatly outnumbering Lee's Army, McClellan was unwilling to send in his reserves to exploit breaks in the Confederate line, in the end, he simply allowed Lee to execute a tactical evacuation, avoiding potential annihilation, instead of pursuing and taking advantage of his clear military advantage. And even with General Hancock assuming command of the First Division, Second Corps, clearly prepared for battle, General McClellan ordered Hancock and his men to maintain their position rather than take the offensive.

Lincoln and the North deemed McClellan's Peninsula and Maryland Campaigns a failure and a missed opportunity respectively, Though Lincoln fired McClellan in November 1862, some historians have suggested McClellan was not removed from command soon enough to prevent irreparable damage to Hancock's career. On the Peninsula and at Antietam, Hancock's success was either not exploited, or Hancock was not given opportunities to prove himself further. On top of that, as a long-time general officer in the Army of the Potomac, he was naturally associated with its costly defeats.

Hancock will always be remembered for his amazing performance at Gettysburg, but did the "McClellan Effect" ultimately taint Hancock's chances for solo command? That is something about which historians can only speculate. But had he not been associated with a series of missed opportunities, he may have been provided the opportunity to live up to his "Hancock the Superb" cognomen and gone down in history as one of the Civil War's primary players, rather than just a "superb" supportive one.

Chapter 35: Stuart's Legacy

Stuart's Image

As a military man, few would dispute that "Jeb" Stuart was a born leader. He refined cavalry tactics (and even invented new ones as needed) and perfected the role of the cavalry as a reconnaissance and intelligence-gathering unit. And while content to play a supportive--even subordinate--role in battle, he repeatedly proved quite adept at taking charge and executing strategic moves fellow officers had not even considered. In fact, in all areas of military service, he garnered the highest of honors for his keen instincts, soldierly genius, and ever-readiness to step boldly into the fray. Stuart clearly attracted the notice of his opponents; Army of the Potomac Corps Commander John Sedgwick (who was also killed during the Overland Campaign) called Stuart, "the greatest cavalry officer ever foaled in America."

Still, he was a man of paradox who while not necessarily *misunderstood* in his lifetime, was seemingly never fully *known*.

Outwardly, Stuart was the embodiment of reckless courage, magnificent manhood, and unconquerable virility; a man who could wear--without drawing suspicion of instability--the flamboyant adornments of a classic cavalier. It was once written that his black plume and hat caught up with a golden star, seemed the proper frame for a knightly face. In that same vein, people were always aware that Stuart was engaging in public relations even then, and Civil War historian Jeff Wert captured it well: "Stuart had been the Confederacy's knight-errant, the bold and dashing cavalier, attired in a resplendent uniform, plumed hat, and cape. Amid a slaughterhouse, he had embodied chivalry, clinging to the pageantry of a long-gone warrior. He crafted the image carefully, and the image befitted him. He saw himself as the Southern people envisaged him. They needed a knight; he needed to be that knight." Stuart, in effect, was the very essence of the Lost Cause.

Yet inwardly, he was guarded about how his lighthearted, boyish silliness in camp might be misinterpreted; a laugh was always at his lips and a song behind it, and he would frequently lead an *impromptu* march with his banjo-player strumming at his side. As he rode down the lines at Chancellorsville, the commander of an army and successor to "Stonewall" Jackson, he is said to have sung a rollicking, "Old Joe Hooker, come out of the Wilderness."

Thus, he left it to those who really knew him to clarify that he never indulged in vices thought common to wartime soldiers (like drinking and tobacco), was never profane, and even abstained from card-playing. More importantly, perhaps, though frequently presented with opportunities for female companionship (something largely accepted in times of war for men far from home), he was a faithful husband and father, and said to be one of the purest of hearts the South ever produced.

Testament

Somewhat ironically, one of the first (and most enduring) accounts written about "Jeb" Stuart was not written by a Virginian--or even a Southerner--but by Johann August Heinrich Heros von Borcke (July 23, 1835--May 10, 1895), a German-American born of an aristocratic Prussian family who offered his services to the Confederate Army during the Civil War. A large, powerfully built and courageous man who joined Stuart's ranks in May of 1862, a mutual respect and admiration is said to have developed between the two men over the course of the two years they served together. Von Borcke was also present at some of the war's most noteworthy campaigns, including Stuart's famous ride around McClellan's army, the Battle of Fredericksburg, and the Battle of Yellow Tavern, where Stuart was mortally wounded. Von Borcke was nearly killed by a shot to the neck just before the Battle of Gettysburg, but he recovered to continue fighting in 1864 through the rest of the war.

Von Borcke

After being seriously wounded in battle while fighting at Stuart's side, von Borcke returned to Europe in December of 1864, and shortly after, began publishing his memoirs in *Blackwood's Magazine*; in 1866 he collected all his articles into *Memoirs of the Confederate Wars for Independence*. And in that von Borcke had no political agenda, was not a Southerner, and had no need to mythologize Stuart, this narrative is today viewed as one of the most objective accounts available of both Stuart and the war itself.

Echoing no Southern self-righteousness or support of the Confederacy's social or political grievances, *Memoirs* presents an insightful, humanized look into Stuart the man: a comrade; a friend; a dashing and daring cavalryman who "knew how to enjoy himself even in dangerous circumstances."[89] A man who, according to von Borcke, lacked any of the arrogance, mean-spirit, or self-centeredness associated with many of the Civil War's key figures, and who instilled lightheartedness in his men even in the most desperate of times.

As fate would have it, von Borcke died on May 10, 1895, 32 years to the day Stonewall Jackson died and nearly 31 years to the date of the Battle of Yellow Tavern, where Stuart was mortally wounded. Von Borcke died of complications from the grievous wound he suffered during the Battle of Middleburg in June 1863.

Similarly, in 1907, Union General Oliver O. Howard (who Stuart handily defeated at Chancellorsville) discussed Stuart in his autobiography, writing: "J. E. B. Stuart was cut out for a cavalry leader. In perfect health, but thirty-two years of age, full of vigor and enterprise, with the usual ideas imbibed in Virginia concerning State Supremacy, Christian in thought and temperate by habit, no man could ride faster, endure more hardships, make a livelier charge, or be more hearty and cheerful while so engaged. A touch of vanity, which invited the smiles and applause of the fair maidens of Virginia, but added to the zest and ardor of Stuart's parades and achievements. He commanded Lee's cavalry corps--a well-organized body, of which he was justly proud."[90]

Tribute

On May 30, 1907, a statue of "General J.E.B. Stuart" on horseback, sculpted by Frederick Moynihan, was dedicated on Richmond's famed Monument Avenue, at Stuart Circle. The fifteen foot statue has the horse's right foot raised and Stuart turned in his saddle facing east.

---

[89]   Escott, Paul D. "The Uses of Gallantry: Virginians and the Origins of J. E. B. Stuart's Historical Image." Page 1.
[90]   Howard, O. O. (Oliver Otis), *Autobiography of Oliver Otis Howard, Major General, United States Army.*

Stuart's Equestrian Statue in Richmond

In the 1940s, the U. S. Army named two World War II tanks, the M3 and M5, the "Stuart" tanks in his honor.

A high school in Falls Church, Virginia, is named the J.E.B. Stuart High School; the school's team nickname, "Raiders," honors his famous Civil War tactics.

In 1864, C. Nordendorf composed the song, "Southern Troopers Song," which is *Dedicated to Genl J. E. B. Stuart and his gallant Soldiers."* (Sheet music, Danville, Virginia.)

Chapter 36: Chamberlain's Legacy

"A seemingly ordinary man thrust into extraordinary circumstances" seems to best describe Chamberlain, the 33 year old professor of rhetoric and languages who, along with the 20th Maine, made a heroic stand at the Battle of Gettysburg. Wounded six times in battle, he not only proved his professional colleagues conclusively wrong -- that he *would never amount to much of a leader* -- his actions on the battlefield were so exemplary that he was awarded the Congressional Medal of Honor.

Though not an especially prominent or revered figure of the Civil War, Major General Lawrence (Joshua) Chamberlain fought in 24 battles while proving to be one of the bravest and most influential regimental commanders in the Union Army. While famous and well-respected in his native state of Maine, Chamberlain's reputation did not extend far beyond his native borders until early in the 20th century, when his books were published and his story was told. And it wouldn't be until the 1990s, after Sharaa's book and several television documentaries about the Civil War (and particularly the Battle of Gettysburg), that he was recognized as a significant war hero.

While many feel that the new focus Lawrence Chamberlain has received in recent decades-- particularly documentaries and renewed attention to the events at the Battle of Gettysburg that focus on Chamberlain's involvement--has brought the professor-turned-soldier due respect, many feel that he has today reached an undeserved lofty status. Many military historians point out that although he appears to have fought bravely at this decisive battle, his performance was equaled, if not exceeded, by many of his fellow regimental and brigade commanders.

Nevertheless, today his leadership at Gettysburg (though somewhat controversial in technical terms) is viewed as having played a major role in preventing the Confederates from turning the Union flank at Little Round Top -- and potentially winning the Battle. His unrelenting performance and display of bravery in the face of the enemy earned him direct promotion to brigadier general by General Ulysses S. Grant himself, and the privilege of receiving the formal surrender of Lee's infantry at Appomattox Court House.

Meade Bibliography

Catton, Bruce. *Grant Takes Command*. New York: Little, Brown and Company, 1968.
        This Hallowed Ground. Great Britain: Wordsworth, 1998.

Civil War Women website, "Margaretta Sergeant Meade" accessed via:
http://www.civilwarwomenblog.com/2009/06/margaretta-sergeant-meade.html 07.25.2012.

Davis, Kenneth C. *The Civil War: Everything You Need to Know About America's Greatest Conflict but Never Learned.* New York: William Morrow and Company, Inc., 1996.

Eicher, John H., and David J. Eicher. *Civil War High Commands.* Stanford, CA: Stanford University Press, 2001.

Gaffney, P., and D. Gaffney. *The Civil War: Exploring History One Week at a Time.* New York: Hyperion, 2011.

General Meade Society of Philadelphia website: http://www.civilwar.com/news/recent-postings/150484-the-general-meade-society-of-philadelphia.html accessed 07.20. 2012.

Historynet.com, "Day One at Chancellorsville" accessed via: http://www.historynet.com/day-one-at-chancellorsville-march-96-americas-civil-war-feature.htm 07.24.2012.

Lanning, Michael Lee. *The Civil War 100.* Illinois: Sourcebooks, Inc., 2006.

Meade George G. Jr. *The Life and Letters of George Gordon Meade.* 2 Vols. New York, 1913, accessed via: http://www.rocemabra.com/~roger/tagg/generals/general01.html 07.18.2012.

McPherson, James M. *Ordeal by Fire: The Civil War and Reconstruction.* New York: McGraw- Hill, 2001.

Porter, Horace. *Campaigning with Grant.* New York: Bonanza Books, 1961.

Sell, Bill. *Civil War Chronicles: Leaders of the North and South.* New York: MetroBooks, 1996.

Stevens, Joseph E. *1863: The Rebirth of a Nation.* New York: Bantam Books, 1999.

Hancock Bibliography

Catton, Bruce. *Grant Takes Command.* New York: Little, Brown and Company, 1968.

Davis, Kenneth C. *The Civil War: Everything You Need to Know About America's Greatest Conflict but Never Learned.* New York: William Morrow and Company, Inc., 1996.

Gaffney, P., and D. Gaffney. *The Civil War: Exploring History One Week at a Time.* New York: Hyperion, 2011.

Goodrich, Frederick Elizur. *Life of Winfield Scott Hancock, Major-General, U. S. A.* Boston:

B. B. Russell, 1886. Accessed via:
http://books.google.com/books?id=g1B9CIlrGbwC&pg=PA23&source=gbs_toc_r&cad=4#v=on
epage&q&f=false 07.13.2012.

Kopel, David, et al. "The Hero of Gettysburg: Winfield Scott Hancock's shot straight."
National Review Online, accessed via
http://old.nationalreview.com/comment/kopel200407020018.asp 07.15.2012.

Lanning, Michael Lee. *The Civil War 100*. Illinois: Sourcebooks, Inc., 2006.

McPherson, James M. *Ordeal by Fire: The Civil War and Reconstruction*. New York:
McGraw- Hill, 2001.

Porter, Horace. *Campaigning with Grant*. New York: Bonanza Books, 1961.

Tagg, Larry. *The Generals of Gettysburg*. Campbell, CA: Savas Publishing, 1998.

Tucker, Glenn. *Hancock the Superb*. Indianapolis: Bobbs-Merrill Co., 1960.

Chamberlain Bibliography

Bowdoin College Archives, accessed via: http://learn.bowdoin.edu/joshua-lawrence-
chamberlain/ 06.27.2012.

Davis, Kenneth C. *The Civil War: Everything You Need to Know About America's Greatest
Conflict but Never Learned*. New York: William Morrow and Company, Inc., 1996.

Desjardin, Thomas A. *Stand Firm Ye Boys from Maine: The 20th Maine and the Gettysburg
Campaign*. Thomas Publications, 1995.

"Why People Admire Joshua Lawrence Chamberlain." Accessed via
http://www.joshua.lurker00.com/jlcadmirers.htm 06.30.2012.

Gaffney, P., and D. Gaffney. *The Civil War: Exploring History One Week at a Time*. New
York: Hyperion, 2011.

Lanning, Michael Lee. *The Civil War 100*. Illinois: Sourcebooks, Inc., 2006.

Sell, Bill. *Civil War Chronicles: Leaders of the North and South*. New York: MetroBooks,
1996.

Wallace, Willard M. *Soul of the Lion: A Biography of General Joshua L. Chamberlain.* Gettysburg, PA: Stan Clark Military Books, 1991.

Lee Bibliography

Freeman, Douglas Southall. *R.E. Lee: A Biography*, 1934-5.

Blount, Jr., Roy. *Robert E. Lee.* New York: Penguin Books, 2003.

Connelly, Thomas L. *The Marble Man: Robert E. Lee and His Image in American Society.* New York: Alfred A. Knopf, 1977.

Dowdey, Clifford (editor). *The Wartime Papers of R. E. Lee.* New York: Bramhall House, 1961.

Fellman, Michael. *The Making of Robert E. Lee.* New York: Random House, 2000.

Flood, Charles. *Lee: The Last Years.* New York: Houghton, 1981.

Horn, Stanley F. (editor). *The Robert E. Lee Reader.* New York: Konecky & Konecky, 1949.

Nagel, Paul C. *The Lee's of Virginia.* New York: Oxford University Press, 1990.

Pryor, Elizabeth Brown (October 29, 2009). "Robert Edward Lee (ca. 1806-1870)," *Encyclopedia Virginia.* Retrieved March 11, 2012.

Thomas, Emory M. *Robert E. Lee: A Biography.* New York: W. W. Norton & Company, 1995.

Van Doren Stern, Philip. *Robert E. Lee: The Man and the Soldier.* New York: Bonanza Books, 1963.

Longstreet Bibliography

Alexander, Edward P. (Gary W. Gallagher, editor). *Fighting for the Confederacy: The Personal Recollections of General Edward Porter Alexander.* Chapel Hill: University of North Carolina Press, 1989.

Catton, Bruce. *This Hallowed Ground.* New York: Doubleday & Company, Inc., 1956.

Davis, Kenneth C. *The Civil War: Everything You Need to Know About America's Greatest Conflict but Never Learned.* New York: William Morrow and Company, Inc., 1996.

Dowdey, Clifford. *Lee's Last Campaign: The Story of Lee & His Men against Grant--1864.* Lincoln: University of Nebraska Press, 1988.

Gaffney, P., and D. Gaffney. *The Civil War: Exploring History One Week at a Time.* New York: Hyperion, 2011.

Garrison, Webb. *Civil War Curiosities.* Nashville: Rutledge Hill Press, 1994.

Lanning, Michael Lee. *The Civil War 100.* Illinois: Sourcebooks, Inc., 2006.

Neely, Mark E., Holzer, Harold & Boritt, Gabor S. *The Confederate Image.* Chapel Hill: The University of North Carolina Press, 1987.

Phillips, Kevin. *The Cousins' Wars.* New York: Basic Books, 1999.

Rhea, Gordon C. *The Battle of the Wilderness May 5–6, 1864.* Baton Rouge: Louisiana State University Press, 1994.

Sanger, Donald B., & Thomas Robson Hay. *James Longstreet, I: Soldier.* Baton Rouge: Louisiana State University Press, 1952.

Sell, Bill. *Civil War Chronicles: Leaders of the North and South.* New York: MetroBooks, 1996.

Stepp, John, W. and Hill, William I. (editors). *Mirror of War, The Washington Star Reports the Civil War.* The Evening Star Newspaper Co., 1961.

Tagg, Larry. *The Generals of Gettysburg.* CA: Savas Publishing, 1998.

Wert, Jeffry D. *General James Longstreet: The Confederacy's Most Controversial Soldier: A Biography.* New York: Simon & Schuster, 1993.

Stuart Bibliography

Catton, Bruce. *This Hallowed Ground: The Story of the Union Side of the Civil War.* New York: Doubleday & Company, 1955.

Davis, Burke. *Jeb Stuart: The Last Cavalier.* New York: Random House, 1957.

Eaton, Clement. *Jefferson Davis*. New York: The Free Press, 1977.

Eicher, John H. & David, J. *Civil War High Commands*. Stanford: Stanford University Press, 2001.

Escott, Paul D. "The Uses of Gallantry: Virginians and the Origins of J. E. B. Stuart's Historical Image," *The Virginia Magazine of History and Biography*, Vol 103, No 1, 1995. Accessed via Jstor: http://www.jstor.org/discover/10.2307/4249485?uid=3739600&uid=2&uid=4&uid=3739256&sid=21100770232471 05.05.2012.

Garrison, Webb. *Civil War Curiosities*. Nashville: Rutledge Hill Press, 1994.

Howard, O. O. (Oliver Otis), *Autobiography of Oliver Otis Howard, Major General, United States Army*. New York: The Baker & Taylor Company, 1907. Accessed via http://archive.org/details/autobiographyofo01howarich 05.07.2012.

Lanning, Michael Lee. *The Civil War 100*. Illinois: Sourcebooks, Inc., 2006.

Lee, Robert E., Jr. *Recollections and Letters of General Robert E. Lee by Captain E. Lee, His Son*. Retrieved via http://www.quillspirit.org/ebooks/Letters_of_General_R_E_Lee/6.php 05.06.2012.

Mosby, John Singleton. *The Memoirs of Colonel John S. Mosby*. Boston: Little, Brown, and Company, 1917. Accessed via http://docsouth.unc.edu/fpn/mosby/menu.html 05.05.2012.

Philips, David. *Crucial Land Battles*. New York: MetroBooks, 1996.

Sears, Stephen W. *Chancellorsville*. Boston: Houghton Mifflin, 1996.
   Gettysburg. Boston: Houghton Mifflin, 2003.

Sifakis, Stewart, "Who Was Who In The Civil War." Accessed via: http://www.civilwarhome.com/stuartbi.htm 05.07.2012.

Stuart Family Archives: http://archiver.rootsweb.ancestry.com/th/read/STUART/2006-04/1144035927 Accessed 05.04.2012.

Stepp, John W. & Hill, William I. (editors), *Mirror of War, the Washington Star Reports the Civil War*. The Evening Star Newspaper Company, 1961.

Thomas, Emory M. *Bold Dragoon: The Life of J.E.B. Stuart*. Norman: University of Oklahoma Press, 1986.

Wert, Jeffry D. *Cavalryman of the Lost Cause: A Biography of J.E.B. Stuart*. New York: Simon & Schuster, 2008.

Wright, C. M. "Flora Cooke Stuart (1836–1923)." Retrieved via Encyclopedia Virginia: http://www.EncyclopediaVirginia.org/Stuart_Flora_Cooke_1836-1923 on 05.06.2012.

Made in the USA
Coppell, TX
28 January 2022